Realms of Dragons

The Worlds of Weis and Hickman

Dragons at War PAUL JAQUAYS

Realms of Dragons

The Worlds of Weis and Hickman

MARGARET WEIS AND TRACY HICKMAN

HarperPrism
A Division of HarperCollins Publishers

HarperPrism

A Division of HarperCollins*Publishers*

10 East 53rd Street, New York, NY 10022-5299

HarperPrism books may be purchased for educational, business, or sales promotional use. For information, please write: Special Markets Department, HarperCollins Publishers, Inc., 10 East 53rd Street, New York, NY 10022-5299.

HarperCollins®, ®, and HarperPrism® are trademarks of HarperCollins Publishers Inc.

Library of Congress Cataloging-in-Publication Data

Realms of dragons: the world's of Weis and Hickman / edited by Denise
    Little.—1st U.S. ed.
      p.   cm
    ISBN 0–06–105239–6
     1. Weis, Margaret—Interviews. 2. Fantasy fiction, American-Concordances. 3. Fantasy fiction—Authorship.
     4. Hickman, Tracy-Interviews. 5. Krynn (Imaginary Places) 6. Dragons in literature.
    I. Little, Denise.
    PS3573.E396733 1999
    813'.0876609—dc21   99-12857

Visit HarperPrism on the World Wide Web at http://www.harpercollins.com

99 00 01 02 03 ❖ / RRD 10 9 8 7 6 5 4 3 2 1

To all the fans who made this possible

Contents

Introduction
By Denise Little

hen Margaret Weis and Tracy Hickman first started working together at TSR, neither of them would ever have predicted what lay ahead of them. Who could have guessed that they'd fuel the imaginations and fantasies of millions of readers, gamers, and collectors all over the planet? The universes they have created are as real to their readers as the one we live in—completely crafted right down to the last detail. And their message, one that emphasizes the importance of reaching out to each other to overcome our differences, no matter how overwhelming they seem, has never been more relevant than it is today.

The body of work that these two very creative people have assembled is remarkable for its diversity, for its ability to surprise and amaze even the most jaded of readers, and for its complexity. In this volume, we hope to give readers a window into the marvelous world of Margaret Weis and Tracy Hickman. With everything from in-depth, candid interviews with both authors, to a detailed overview of their books by their award-winning editor, to concordances for each of the series these authors have collaborated on, these pages are both a resource for, and a gift to, Margaret and Tracy's vast number of fans.

So open up this volume, browse through its pages, and enjoy. I can guarantee the author interviews will bring you closer than you ever thought you could get to Margaret Weis and Tracy Hickman. And I can also promise that flipping through the pages of the concordances will bring back fond memories of the first time you read one of their books. All of your favorite characters are here . . . and all the names of the ones you've forgotten. You'll probably find yourself wanting to go back and reread some of the stories—I know I did. And this time I had a guidebook, a treasure trove of knowledge in my hands. I stayed up all night, and by the time the sun came up, I'd finished the *Chronicles* and was halfway through the *Death Gate Cycle*, enjoying every word.

I only hope you have half as much fun as I did. Happy reading!

Realms of Dragons

The Worlds of Weis and Hickman

1 The Novels of Margaret Weis and Tracy Hickman: *An Overview and Title-by-Title Guide*

BY AMY STOUT

Dragon Knights LARRY ELMORE

From the moment Margaret Weis and Tracy Hickman first put their collaborative words to paper, it was clear they were destined to be one of the most powerful writing teams in fantasy. In a field of fiction that is as ancient as fairy tales but as recent as the masterpieces of J.R.R. Tolkien, Margaret Weis and Tracy Hickman have paid homage to those who have gone before them while producing work solely theirs.

Both authors are marvelous storytellers who have each written—and continue to write—outstanding fiction on their own; however, it is the uniquely compelling stories that result whenever the two writers join together that have captivated their legions of fans since the publication of the first *Dragonlance*® collaboration.

They used to answer the oft-asked question "How do you collaborate?" with this partially whimsical, partly serious response: "Margaret does the nouns and Tracy does the verbs." In observing some of their early drafts, one might almost have believed the statement, so seamless was the transition from one to the other as the first concentrated on plotting and characterization while the second focused on world-building. Their methods may well have changed over the years, but

there's no mistaking a Weis and Hickman novel. Each of their books, whether in collaboration or solo, bears their unmistakable stamp. While working with familiar icons, from dragons to dwarves, from time travel to faster-than-light travel, each and every story is set in a richly detailed universe and peopled with characters their readers come to know and love. Gracefully woven into the narrative are a variety of issues the authors care about, from concerns about our mistreatment of the environment to abuse of our fellow humans. Finally, uniting all these elements is an unerring sense of plotting that propels readers forward page after page. With such mastery, it's no surprise that Margaret Weis and Tracy Hickman have millions of fans around the world.

The Characters—A Few Good Men and Women

Like all good writers, Weis and Hickman use a range of characters. Among these, their main characters are often tortured people who are searching for their proper roles in the world.

Just as very little in the true world comes without a price, the central characters in these books—from Prince Joram in the *Darksword* series to Haplo the Patryn in the *Death Gate Cycle*—achieve peace of

1

mind only after great personal sacrifice. Male or female, mortal or immortal, human or elf, dwarf or djinn, all must learn the proper life lessons before they can triumph over their enemies.

The scholars, such as Saryon in the *Darksword* series or Alfred in the *Death Gate Cycle*, generally serve as advisors to the main characters. Often conflicted about the best course of action themselves, they are nonetheless able to pass along wisdom to their students in a manner that allows both tutor and pupil to ultimately come to understand and accept their destinies.

The collaborators also enjoy employing tricksters in their work. Two of the best loved of these are Simkin in the *Darksword* books and Raoul in Weis's *Star of the Guardians* and *Mag Force* series. In addition to adding humor, these characters frequently heighten suspense through their unpredictable behavior and mysterious access to essential information. Never altogether trustworthy, these jesters always add delightful spice whenever they appear.

World-building—Ingenuity on a Grand Scale

No novel is complete without a fully realized sense of place. The landscapes in Weis and Hickman's fiction are some of the most intricately detailed ever seen. Tracy Hickman's background as a game designer is evident here. Maps and charts, rules of magic and principles of political etiquette underlay every facet of each series. The handful of drawings included in the books represent only a fraction of the work done behind the scenes. But it is not just the extraordinary particulars which give readers the undeniable feeling that these settings are places they might well visit one day. It is the unerring knowledge of which fine points to include and which to exclude. Readers experience the story along with the characters, so that they are always aware that a wider universe exists without being subjected to lengthy passages of description weighing down the narrative.

Themes—Not Just Fun and Games

An exploration of the magic-science interface can be seen in all their works. In the now classic *Darksword* trilogy, magic is originally completely divorced from science, while in the more recently published *Star Shield* series, the two coexist as equals in a variable and unstable universe. In Margaret Weis's "galactic fantasy" series (as Tracy Hickman termed it), *Star of the Guardians*—about which the author herself has said, "I don't give a darn how the hyperdrive works!"—a dialogue between what is observable through the five senses and what is believed in the heart runs from beginning to end. Likewise, Hickman's solo science fiction novels, including his highly praised *The Immortals*, suggest that science doesn't replace the fantastical unknown so much as it exposes its murky depths for later study. In all their fiction, this interplay between magic and science leads the reader to wonder about the impact of the fantastic on the ordinary events in their own lives.

A second motif common to their novels is an ongoing discussion of the importance of striving to understand people different from ourselves. In the *Darksword* series, this is exhibited by bringing warring factions together to fight common enemies, who in turn eventually becomes allies—if not outright friends.

In the humorous *Rose of the Prophet* trilogy, worshippers of warring gods battle among themselves, mirroring their masters' hostilities. Eventually, both immortals and mortals learn to accept the existence of the disparate religious groups—though in keeping with the tone of the series, they don't exactly learn to live in harmony.

Much of the character growth in this series is facilitated through Mathew, a stranger who is very likely homosexual (though this is never explicitly stated in the text). Regardless of his preferences, Mathew's obvious differences make their own similarities plain to the other characters. In the end, they come to value both similarities and differences, in each other as well as in their foreign friend.

In the *Death Gate Cycle*, virtually all sentient beings are in conflict with each other. Some of the more powerful have already exterminated their weaker companions. The series consistently warns of the dangers of such discord and ultimately celebrates the spirit of harmony among diverse peoples. Similarly, the main characters in Margaret Weis and Don

Perrin's *Mag Force* novels personify cooperation. The main cast is an eclectic mix of human and alien, male and female, whose individual histories represent a wide range of what might be described as the human experience. Whatever scrapes the Mag Force gets into, there is never any doubt in the reader's mind that they will get out of it *together*. In Tracy Hickman's *The Immortals,* this issue above all others is the compelling reason he wrote the book. The novel is so well executed that no reader can come away from it unchanged.

A third theme their novels suggest is a general belief in the goodness of humanity. Though the consistent message is to counsel open-mindedness whenever cultures collide, their work demonstrates a fully-developed understanding of human nature. Evil does exist and is always punished by the series' conclusion; however, the overall tone of the books is upbeat and never preachy. Readers come back again and again to these novels in part because they know the good guys will ultimately win and in part to see if the bad guys might just have a rare change of heart.

Finally, in every Weis and Hickman novel the characters are aided and/or hindered by forces greater than themselves. The authors do not simply present a number of intelligent races and leave them to struggle on their own. Instead many of the main characters will find that both good and evil powers have influence in their lives. Priestly characters who have lost belief in their gods will find it again, while some who never had faith will discover it. Conversely, powerful but arrogant characters will receive their comeuppance at the hands of the powers they tried to ignore. Regardless of a person's place in a Weis and Hickman universe, one is never totally alone—but might well wish otherwise.

Plot—It Keeps Things Moving

While it's true that the authors have a number of commonalities among their novels, the best thing about their plots is the variety. Readers do *not* expect to find identical storylines from book to book—even after thirty novels. Instead, their audience has come to count on Weis and Hickman to do just the opposite. The authors keep their stories unpredictable and exciting by juggling plot twists

with the same inventiveness of the best magicians in this or any age.

A SERIES-BY-SERIES AND TITLE-BY-TITLE GUIDE

The *Darksword* Trilogy (1988)

The *Darksword* trilogy was Weis and Hickman's first departure from their bestselling *Dragonlance* series. Written within months of finishing the second *Dragonlance* trilogy, *Darksword* succeeded brilliantly in speaking to their established audience while attracting new readers unfamiliar with their previous fantasies.

> *There will be born to the Royal House one who is dead yet will live, who will die again and live again. And when he returns he will hold in his hand the destruction of the world.*

The *Darksword* series is set in Earth's far future. Long ago, magic users fled from persecution on Earth to the freedom of the uninhabited world of Thimhallan. To the refugees, magic is considered synonymous with life. They use no technology at all. From the shaping of buildings to conceiving children, all tasks are accomplished through the manipulation of magic. Any use of technology is heresy; its practitioners (referred to as "sorcerers") are sentenced to an eternal living death.

The trilogy follows a classic and powerful story. The kingdoms of Merilon and Sharakan are on the verge of war. Merilon's royal heir is born without magic. Rather than kill Prince Joram as tradition would dictate, he is reared unaware of his heritage. Nonetheless, the forces of fate govern the young man's life. He is predestined to rise to the throne through a long and arduous journey, a journey that irrevocably changes the world of Thimhallan and the lives of all its inhabitants.

Throughout the entire trilogy only the enigmatic Simkin appears to understand fully the stakes and the players, and he alone has connections in all camps. His magic and his knowledge are inexplicable. Though the reader suspects he's on the side of the protagonists, Simkin's unpredictable and unexplained behavior helps to keep the reader in suspense. In

Marquesta Kar-Thon, Warriors, Volume 2   JEFF EASLEY

addition, his scandalous demeanor gives the series some of its most outrageously wonderful moments. It's no surprise that Simkin is one of the fans' favorite characters.

A third important character in the *Darksword* trilogy is Father Saryon. The scholarly priest is a character type often seen in Weis and Hickman's novels—that of the man who is tormented by, but ultimately overcomes, a loss of faith. Father Saryon is a talented Catalyst—a magician who facilitates the flow of magical Life whenever any spell is performed. From the moment the priest first witnesses the testing of the newborn Prince Joram, he struggles to maintain his faith. When he is sent on a mission to observe the outlawed Technologists, a mission which ultimately brings him in contact with the now grown prince, it is only a matter of time before he joins with Joram. For all that he is troubled, Saryon is a good man whose intentions are pure. He advises the young man and aids him at the risk of his own body and soul.

Volume I, *Forging the Darksword*

Volume I, *Forging the Darksword,* opens with the fulfillment of an ancient prophecy. For generations, the clergy guarded against this dire threat. They approved the conception of every child and tested the magical abilities of every infant. But even these stringent measures do not prevent the birth of Prince Joram, who is born Dead—without magic. Rather than further the prophecy, the clergy proclaims Joram dead and secretly sends him to be raised in obscurity far from the capital. But there is no denying the power of destiny. Though Joram is the first newborn to fail the tests, he is not the last of the Dead children to be born in Thimhallan.

Volume One of the trilogy centers on the early years of Prince Joram as he comes to adulthood in outlying farmland. Anya, the only mother he ever knows, is a beautiful but bitter woman. He grows up believing his father was sentenced to the Turning—a hideous living death which converts its victims to breathing stone—in punishment for fathering an unsanctioned child. To protect Joram, Anya keeps the boy secluded from other children and teaches him sleight of hand to hide his lack of magic. Though

extraordinarily handsome himself, he is a dark and brooding child with few friends.

On the verge of manhood, Joram witnesses his mother's death. He kills her murderer in retaliation and flees to the Outland. Here Joram meets the Technologists, a community of renegades nearly as old as the capital itself. Joram finds himself an outcast even among outcasts. For though they practice the forbidden arts, he alone has no choice. Each of the Technologists possesses a small amount of magical ability. Joram has none whatsoever. Nonetheless, he lives among them for some while, ultimately befriending the enigmatic trickster, Simkin, and the scholarly priest, Saryon. It is these two who help him forge the Darksword, a forbidden sword made from the tabooed darkstone.

Volume II, *Doom of the Darksword*

Doom of the Darksword, the second volume, might be subtitled "Joram's Education." A bit faster paced than its predecessor, Joram learns painful lesson after painful lesson about what it means to accept who he is. After killing the powerful Blachloch in self-defense, Joram flees his home among the Technologists. On the run once more, Joram, Saryon, and Simkin are captured by Prince Garald of the neighboring kingdom of Sharakan. Simkin—known to many royals of both kingdoms and trusted by none, including Prince Garald—defuses a potentially deadly situation.

Garald befriends Joram. He teaches him the manners of court to prepare Joram to claim his rightful inheritance as a minor noble of Merilon. Though Saryon and Simkin know Joram is actually entitled to the royal throne, both keep this knowledge secret from everyone—including Joram himself.

The northern kingdom of Sharakan is preparing to go to war with Merilon. More lenient than the rulers of Merilon, Garald welcomes the Technologists and their particular talents. Thus the prince has learned the ancient skill of sword fighting, which he passes on to Joram.

Joram returns to Merilon, the city of his birth to claim what he thinks is his birthright. Here he meets the Lady Gwendolyn. It's love at first sight for both, but there are forces pulling the two apart.

The clergy's hierarchy knows Joram's true identity and has no intention of letting the prince sit on the throne. They trap Joram and sentence him to the Turning. Joram is helpless to claim his heritage or fight the judgment.

As the accused stands surrounded by his enemies on the edge of the Beyond—the realm of Death—Father Saryon steps in and disrupts the spell. The priest is inadvertently Turned while the others look on in horror. Joram seizes the moment to wield the Darksword to attack his adversaries and free himself. At the last instant the prince places the Darksword in the priest's hands. Saryon holding the Darksword is bound in stone to become a Watcher, while Prince Joram and Lady Gwendolyn disappear into the unknown mists across the Border.

Volume III, *Triumph of the Darksword*

Triumph of the Darksword, the third volume, opens to Merilon and Sharakan on the brink of war. Joram and Gwendolyn return from the land outside the magical realm of Thimhallan known as the Beyond. Aged unnaturally by their experiences, the two are barely recognizable from the young couple who disappeared a year ago. Whether or not he would have freely chosen it, Joram is now poised to fulfill—or deny—the prophecy.

Through the power of the Darksword, Joram accomplishes the impossible. He releases Father Saryon from his living death as a Watcher. Joram, Saryon, and Gwendolyn set off for Merilon.

The magical kingdoms of Sharakan and Merilon engage forces, but the battle takes an unexpected twist. An unknown, third army devastates both sides. Into the melee of certain massacre steps Joram. He has come to save his homeland from the Dead intruders, men from Earth who arrive in starships and use the forbidden arts of technology, men who don't quite believe that magic exists anywhere but in fairy tales.

With Joram's help, the kingdoms of Thimhallan unite and nearly subdue the Dead strangers. However, among the Dead invaders is an embittered magician who was exiled from Thimhallan. Joram strives to hold the alliance together, but enemies conspire against him. Though he saves the peo-ple of Thimhallan, he will long be considered the man who "held in his hand the destruction of his world."

Darksword (1988)

Darksword Adventures is the gaming manual and complete set for the role-playing game of Phantasia. The primary intention behind the publication was to be the first mass market role-playing game. The hope was that the much lower price associated with paperback books would allow *Darksword Adventures* to expand the already large audience of the bestselling role-playing games. Though it did sell very well in its own right, it unfortunately did not achieve the desired goal.

Nonetheless, with its myriad maps and illustrations, history and chronology, statistics and in-depth character descriptions, the book serves as an excellent reference for anyone interested in the background for the *Darksword* novels. *Darksword Adventures* is entertaining and intriguing reading for its own sake.

The Legacy of the Darksword (1997)

The authors stepped away from the world of Thimhallan for nearly a decade while they worked on other projects. However, as is often the case with their world-building, they did such a thorough job developing the universe that there were plenty of other stories to tell beyond those which initially saw print.

Every bit as enjoyable as the initial trilogy (and perhaps even more so), *Legacy of the Darksword* plunges the reader back into a familiar but now radically changed magical realm. Once again, this novel includes well-known science fiction notions (such as space travel and laser weapons) within the more traditional fantasy framework. The authors have also brought a new dimension to the *Darksword* series by adding other elements not in the earlier books. Dragons appear in this series for the first time, as well as time travel and parallel universes. They are all woven into *Legacy of the Darksword* to form a perfectly orchestrated and convincing whole. The result is a spellbinding journey that breathes fresh life into the classic *Darksword* series.

As with the previous books, Joram, Saryon, and Simkin play prominent roles. These three, along with Saryon's scribe, Reuven, and Joram's daughter Eliza, undertake a quest that is nothing less than saving the human race from extinction. Full of unexpected twists, *Legacy of the Darksword* once again proves the authors' storytelling prowess.

In this volume, at last all Simkin's fans learn the truth behind his wild antics. It's not terribly surprising to discover that he is a noble and heroic character worthy of his readers' admiration. However, to reveal more here would spoil both the surprises regarding the character as well as the ending of this novel.

The story begins a generation after the end of *Triumph of the Darksword*. Virtually all the former inhabitants of Thimhallan have been living on the mundane magic-free world of Earth. Father Saryon is among these. With Earth as well as the protectorate of Thimhallan under threat of imminent attack by the alien Hch'nyv, a handful of high-ranking officials have prevailed upon Saryon to travel to Thimhallan to retrieve the Darksword. The only inhabitants of this now desolate and stormy world are Prince Joram, Princess Gwendolyn, and their daughter, Eliza. Though Saryon does not trust the motives of the officials, he ultimately agrees to undertake the trip. Rather than asking for the sword, however, his primary concern is saving Joram and family from the alien attack.

Once Saryon reaches Thimhallan, nothing proceeds as he had hoped. Joram's peaceful homestead is attacked. Eliza flees with the Darksword in an attempt to protect her father. Joram is captured by power-hungry men interested in their sword only for personal gain. Princess Gwendolyn disappears in the melee. In what may be the most inventive plot to date, the story takes many twists as our heroes find themselves trying to rescue not only each other, but all of humanity.

The *Rose of the Prophet* Trilogy (1989)

Overall, the *Rose of the Prophet* might be considered a slightly lighter work. Rather than concentrating the humor around one character (such as Simkin in the *Darksword* books), the authors have spread it liberally throughout this trilogy in a number of

Dragon Duel JEFF EASLEY

laugh-out-loud scenes. However, as with all their works, a serious thread underpins the humor. In this case, Weis and Hickman explore one of their favorite themes—that of the need for different peoples to learn tolerance regarding each others' ways. From the warring Arabian tribes to their combative gods and djinn, to the natives' relationships with the character of the foreign-born Mathew, over and again this idea is examined.

In this trilogy, twenty gods wage war among themselves. Traditionally, each god has been content with his number of followers, but one of the gods has upset the balance. In a universe where more believers equals greater power, this unbalance has all the gods scrambling to retain the numbers they once held.

Akhran the Wanderer, like his nomadic believers, would just as soon be off about his business—whatever that might be. However, two of the twenty gods seem to have been murdered. And there's no doubt there will be more assassinations if the god Quar has his way. Therefore Akhran decrees the marriage of two warring clans—to unite and therefore strengthen his people against Quar's onslaught.

Quar's following reluctantly obey his will. Princess Zohra of the Hrana and Calif Khardan al Fakhar of the Akar are both strong of heart and strong willed. Neither will yield to the other in any respect. It seems certain one will murder the other before the marriage vows are consummated—and thereby doom both their peoples and their god.

Volume I: *The Will of the Wanderer*

The tribes of the Hrana and the Akar come together in uneasy peace through the marriage of the eldest daughter to the eldest son. Both tribes must camp at the foot of the Tel until the sacred flower, the Rose of the Prophet, blooms. During this time, each is forbidden to shed the blood of the other. All is so ordered by their god Akhran and proclaimed through his djinn.

Meanwhile, a group of foreign travelers is shipwrecked. The sole survivor is Mathew, who is mistaken for a woman and therefore kept to sell into the slave trade. Khardan happens upon Mathew on the slave block. Like the others, he assumes this exotic foreigner is a woman. Appalled at the practice of owning people, Khardan impulsively saves Mathew—only to find himself married to two wives with whom he can not consummate vows. The first, Zohra, refuses, and the second, Mathew, is a man.

Khardan, Zohra, and Mathew persevere as the book winds and turns with betrayals and double-dealings—some the result of evil-doing and some the outcome of good people forced to choose between difficult options. Mathew teaches Zohra the sorcery of his homeland and serves as mediator between the hot-headed couple.

This volume ends with the nomads in disgrace. Their people are captured by the zealous followers of Quar. Khardan is rumored to be seen running from battle dressed in woman's clothing. Very little is as it seems on the surface, however, for this is a world rife with magic. What magic doesn't conjure, simple human misunderstanding confuses.

Volume II: *The Paladin of the Night*

In the opening of the second volume, the two desert tribes have been overrun by the powerful army led by General Qannadi and are now held captive by the followers of Quar. Qannadi is a practical—rather than a religious—man and well suited to his role of military leader. He wisely recognizes the talent of Khardan's younger half-brother, Achmed. Overshadowed by Khardan's prowess within the tribe, Achmed is eager to receive the praise and attention of the strong general who has come to rule over the Akar people.

The rest of the nomads are demoralized to the point of apathy. The command to forsake their god Akhran in order to worship Quar weighs heavy on their hearts and minds. They are imprisoned within walls—a fate no desert wanderer can withstand for long. Worst of all, the unexplained disappearance of Khardan and Zohra inadvertently encourages the rumors of Khardan's humiliation—and therefore doubles his people's shame and increases the rift between the two tribes.

Meanwhile Khardan, Zohra, and Mathew have been kidnapped and drugged. They awake in the hands of the Black Paladin, who worships Zhakrin, God of Night and Evil. Struggling to survive a fate worse than captivity or death, while devising a plan to escape and rescue their people, consumes the three captives throughout this story. Only when they discover that the Black Paladin also holds the two gods who were presumed dead do they begin to have hope.

During the course of the book, Quar manipulates the prisoners by rumors, lies, and half-truths. Even the loyal djinn are tricked and betrayed by the djinn who serve Quar. By the end, the trust between brothers and long-time friends is tested and found lacking.

Volume III: *The Prophet of Akhran*

The theme in the third volume (and perhaps the entire trilogy) can be summed up in a conversation between Zohra and Khardan about Mathew, the man they've come to consider a friend.

"He is unhappy living among us."
"Whose fault is that? We looked down on

him and sneered at him and reviled him for his weakness ... But now we know what it is to be alone and afraid and helpless in a strange and alien place! Do we acquit ourselves any better? Did we even do as well?"

As the book opens, the "dead" gods have reappeared and accused Quar of trying to kill them. War erupts on the immortal plane. The djinn are recalled to assist their masters. Suddenly, the mortals are left alone to work out their problems.

Zohra, Khardan, and Mathew struggle to do the impossible. They must walk across the desert known as the Anvil of the Sun, a journey no one has ever survived.

When they finally arrive home, those of his tribe not imprisoned in the city try Khardan for the crime of abandoning his people. Khardan's only defense is to claim Zohra ensorcelled him, but he refuses to do so. While both still refuse to admit love for each other, neither will he blame her and have her killed to save himself. Eventually the truth prevails with such unlikely witnesses as Mathew and the Black Paladin.

The battle is joined once again on the mortal plane. Against all tradition, Mathew and Zohra are permitted to assist the armies with their powerful magic. When it seems certain that the nomads will defeat the city dwellers, the two desert tribes fall to fighting between themselves. Khardan and Zohra at last declare their love for one another with a kiss while their families feud all around them.

The balance has been restored in both the mortal and immortal realms, but many have suffered and a few have gained newfound respect for those beyond their own clans.

Death Gate Cycle (7 books 1990–1994)

The seven-volume *Death Gate Cycle* is an extraordinarily ambitious undertaking. Perhaps this is not obvious when so many fantasies run into multiple volumes. However, the *Death Gate Cycle* is the first fantasy series in which each of the four opening books is a stand-alone novel. The events in one are independent of those in the other three, though all are connected through the series' two continuing characters, Haplo the Patryn and Alfred the Sartan.

Each volume in this quartet constructs a different world. Each has its own political and social structure, as well as different planetary conditions. All are linked by their common past—though this is a closely guarded secret. Originally, the four worlds of sky, fire, stone, and sea were once all part of a single world. The Sartan used powerful magic to separate them in a cataclysmic event known as the Sundering. At the same time, they cast their mortal enemies, the Patryn, into a deadly prison realm known as the Labyrinth. Generations later, only a handful know about the Sundering and the Death's Gates, which allow travel between the worlds.

While there is some benefit in reading the opening four volumes in the conventional order, they are designed to be read in any order the reader might choose. The overarching conflict between Haplo the Patryn and Alfred the Sartan does progress in a linear fashion. However the plot for each book develops separately in the same way that the history of each world has advanced separately as subsequent generations have forgotten their mutual pasts. Characters from the various realms don't know of the existence of the other *worlds*, let alone of another world's most prominent (or obscure) citizens.

The structure of the final three novels more closely resembles that of what has come to be thought of as a traditional trilogy. The events of volume five, *The Hand of Chaos*, are a direct result of what has happened in the previous four books. *The Hand of Chaos* reintroduces characters seen before while at the same time involving these characters in the affairs of other realms for the first time. The centuries-old war between the Sartan and the Patryn escalates as the mensch—that is, the lesser races of humans, elves, and dwarves—come to discover how the mighty Sartan have been manipulating their peoples over the millennia.

The *Death Gate Cycle* also marks the first time Weis and Hickman include behind-the-scene bits of worldbuilding within the novels themselves (rather than in separate gaming companion volumes). Footnotes are scattered throughout the books. Appendices with material ranging from local songs to essays on the nature of magic in this universe give the reader a strong understanding of the worlds and their people—as well as leave open the doors for supplements to be enjoyed by their many role-playing and computer-gaming aficionados.

Volume I: *Dragon Wing*

Volume I, *Dragon Wing,* is set on Arianus, the world of sky. The world is divided into the Low Realm, the Mid Realm, and the High Realm. Dwarves live indoors on the stormswept Low Realm, where water is in plentiful supply. They trade this valuable commodity with elves and humans in the Mid Realm, but otherwise the races avoid each other and the human Mysteriarchs who live in the High Realm.

Dragon Wing introduces the series two main antagonists, Haplo the Patryn and Alfred the Sartan. Alfred has disguised himself as a bumbling, royal retainer. As the book begins, he is serving as the manservant to the royal prince, Bane.

The human assassin Hugh the Hand has been hired to eliminate the prince. Without revealing his extraordinary magical talent, Alfred does everything he can to protect the child—even though he knows the boy is evil and even though the child's unwilling foster parents lurk behind the murder plot. Bane is a changeling, whose true parents are Mysteriarchs.

Alfred, Bane, and the Hand find themselves in the Low Realm among the dwarves and the start of a revolution.

Meanwhile, Haplo the Patryn has been secretly sent to Arianus to learn all he can about the world, as well as to create dissension among the mensch. The revolution perfectly suits his mission. By the novel's end, the mensch are on the verge of war, and the evil changeling Bane still lives. Chaos in the world of sky appears certain.

However, in this book and throughout the series, nothing is quite as it seems. Haplo and Alfred are just two who conceal secrets. Bane, too, knows much more than he admits, as does Hugh the Hand. In fact, the Hand is such an intriguingly mysterious character that he proves to be one of the readers' favorites for the entire series.

Volume II: *Elven Star*

Volume II, *Elven Star,* is the most light-hearted of the novels in the cycle. The world of Pryan, world of fire, is a jungle world created by ever present sunlight and plentiful rain. As in *Dragon Wing,* the mensch races are extremely distrustful of each other. Elves live in the treetops, humans on the plains, and dwarves among the roots of the massive trees. The primary elven industry is weapons-dealing to both humans and dwarves. Not even the threat of annihilation of all three races is enough to halt the constant warfare and bring the groups together.

Mysterious tytans have suddenly begun to wreak havoc all across the realm. The giants repeatedly ask, "Where is the citadel? What must we do?" to no avail. None of the mensch know the answer. The tytans—strong both in magic and more mundane abilities—respond by destroying wantonly, killing everyone in their path.

The Patryn Haplo arrives on Pryan in the second leg of his duty to explore the four worlds. Eventually, he begins to understand the tytans' quest and travels to the source of this world's light: the citadel. Here he learns the people don't live on the outside of the world, but inside. Their artificial suns are ever blazing precisely because they are artificial—and because something went wrong with the mechanism which controlled them. Having learned all he can of this world and seeing no need to stir up further trouble among the mensch, Haplo departs Pryan to report back to the Patryns' leader.

But he leaves behind a handful of mensch who seem to have learned to overcome their differences, as well as a mysterious wizard named Zifnab and his dragon.

Volume III, *Fire Sea*

Volume III, *Fire Sea,* set in Abarrach, the world of stone is the grimmest book in the series. Abarrach is a world on the edge of doom. Generations of inhabitants abused the environment to the point that water is nearly gone and the planet barely sustains life. All the mensch died long ago. Only much weakened descendants of the Sartan still struggle to survive.

While searching for the child Bane (first seen in *Dragon Wing*), Alfred travels to Abarrach. He accidentally falls into Haplo's boat just as the Patryn is arriving on Abarrach through Death's Gate. As they pass through the Gate, it mysteriously recalls a brief memory for each from the other's life. From this moment forward, Alfred and Haplo have reached a new sympathy for each other. Though they will fight their growing kinship for the rest of the series, mutual understanding is ultimately inevitable. Here, surrounded by death, Alfred and Haplo discover a source for good far more powerful than any of their own people.

The two arrive on the shores of a terrible magma lake and soon discover the only native inhabitants, Sartan. But these Sartan have lost most of their original power. They are a hopeless people on the brink of death. Alfred and Haplo are equally horrified to learn that these once mighty Sartan have turned to the forbidden art of necromancy in their desperation. Phantasms of the dead perform many of the functions formerly carried out by the dwindling numbers of living—servants, laborers, advisors, soldiers. Still tied to their bodies against their will, they are becoming a resentful, angry lot.

As dismal as life has become on this planet, the Sartan still fight among themselves. Haplo and Alfred are drawn into the fray. But as the battle escalates, it is the dead who decide the fate of this world.

Volume IV: *Serpent Mage*

Volume IV, *Serpent Mage*, is set on Chelestra, the world of sea. Here the mensch have lived in peace for generations. Long ago, orbiting seasuns melted the frozen waters in the near vicinity of the seamoons—land surrounded by bubbles of air. Now the seasun's orbit is moving away from the moons. Though each race inhabits a separate seamoon, they have worked together to move all three groups to a large, recently thawed seamoon. The mensch have a more immediate threat, however, because the circuit of the seasun has also warmed the prison of the ancient and powerful dragon-snakes. The dragon-snakes massacre entire villages, feeding on fear and death.

Though Haplo was ordered to bring Alfred back to the Nexus, he let the Sartan escape Abarrach at the end of Volume III. Alfred awakes in the tombs of the Sartan on Chelestra. He finds the original Sartan who Sundered the worlds and magically revives them before he realizes they're not his own people on Arianus.

Xar knows Haplo let Alfred go. Attempting to cleanse the Patryn and prevent future displays of weakness, he separates Haplo from his dog—which Xar realizes is in truth Haplo's conscience. Haplo once again meets up with Alfred on the world of Chelestra. The Sartan too knows the dog's function and brings the animal back to Haplo. The two ultimately decide to trust one another as they recognize the dragon-snakes are much more dangerous to their respective races than they are to each other. There's no question that the two have a common enemy now.

As the dragon-snakes attack the mensch, Alfred discovers within himself the power of transforming into a dragon. He manages to defeat the creatures, but has no memory of his brave deed. Just as Haplo keeps his conscience separate from his conscious self, so too does Alfred purposely keep the knowledge of his own great power as a serpent mage from his conscious self. In Haplo's case, the self-deception helped him survive the deadly Labyrinth. In Alfred's, it allows him to ignore the guilt he feels over the millions who died in the Sundering—though he was not yet born at the time.

Alfred and Haplo both try to warn the Sartan about the dragon-snakes, but the Council of Seven casts Alfred into the Labyrinth for disputing their decision. War breaks out between Sartan and the mensch. Haplo is left to his own devices as enchanted Chelestran seas rise, nullifying Patryn and Sartan magic alike.

Volume V: *The Hand of Chaos*

In Volume V, *The Hand of Chaos*, the Sartan who first Sundered the world have opened the Death's Gate, thus allowing any who know of the gates to travel between worlds. This includes the dragon-snakes, who have escaped to spread suffering to the other six realms.

Haplo escapes to the Nexus, where he desperately tries to make Lord Xar understand the true danger the dragon-snakes represent. Since Haplo befriended the Sartan Alfred, Xar no longer trusts him. He accepts the creatures' claims that Haplo is a traitor and they are Xar's true servants.

Masters of deceit, the dragon-snakes are adept at

manipulating Patryn, Sartan, and mensch. Ambitious as well, they seek to dominate all the realms and gorge on their subjects' agony. The novel is a masterpiece of political maneuvering as the dragon-snakes scheme and set each faction against the others.

On Xar's instruction, Haplo returns to Arianus. The human child Bane, a native of Arianus who Haplo took back to Lord Xar (at the end of Volume I), travels with Haplo. The leader of the Patryns has ordered Bane to have Haplo killed, so the child hires the assassin Hugh the Hand.

Upon Haplo's arrival on Arianus, the dwarves are rebelling and Arianus is on the verge of all-out war. The giant Kicksey-winsey machine which serves as both home and livelihood to the dwarves has stopped. Against Xar's orders to create upheaval, Haplo works to do the opposite and helps the dwarves restart the Kicksey-winsey. For the first time in millennia, the machine is functioning as it was meant to do. It is realigning the islands of the higher realms to provide all of Arianus with water. In addition, it powers the citadels on the world of Pryan.

Meanwhile, Hugh the Hand now has three outstanding assassination contracts. He has yet to fulfill his contract with King Stephen to kill Bane. Prince Bane has in turn hired the Hand to kill King Stephen in addition to Haplo. In the end, Bane fails and receives his comeuppance.

While war is narrowly averted on Arianus, chaos reigns elsewhere. Samah, head of the Sartan, travels to Abarrach to learn the forbidden secret of necromancy. He hopes to form armies of the dead in his age-old battle with the Patryn.

Volume VI: *Into the Labyrinth*

In Volume VI, *Into the Labyrinth,* like Samah, Xar voyages to Abarrach to learn the arcane art of resurrecting the dead in order to build up his own troops. He captures Samah, head of the Sartan Council of Seven. At the last, Samah finally realizes the danger of the dragon-snakes and tries to warn Xar. Heedless, the Patryn allows the dragon-snakes to torture and kill Samah.

Eventually, he does gain the forbidden knowledge of necromancy. He also learns of the Seventh Gate—

the chamber from which the world was Sundered. Whoever controls this Gate, commands all realms. The Lord of the Patryns becomes obsessed with discovering the location of the Seventh Gate. His keys to this knowledge are Alfred and Haplo, who happened upon it unknowingly. He plots to capture the two, kill them, and force their reanimated corpses to reveal the Gate's position. Xar sends Haplo's one-time lover Marit to finish Bane's task.

Peaceful alliances among the mensch on Arianus are strengthening just as those between Patryn are weakening. Hugh the Hand still searches for a way to do in Haplo. Even though Bane is dead, the assassin is bound to the contract. He journeys to his guild's stronghold, where he acquires a magical, shapeshifting knife. He fights Haplo, but even his Sartan-forged weapon cannot overpower the Patryn. The Hand is killed and is resurrected: unbeknonst to the assassin, Alfred inscribed a rune on Hugh's chest, which makes it impossible for him to die. Haplo and Hugh agree to travel to the Labyrinth to find Alfred and remove the curse of eternal life.

In constant contact with Lord Xar, Marit tries to kill Haplo. Hugh's warning saves Haplo's life. When Hugh's magical knife attacks Marit, Haplo saves her life. By Patryn custom, she is now no longer bound to kill him, although she still plans to bring him back to Xar.

The dragon-snakes trick the Patryn leader into going to Pryan, in search of the Seventh Gate. Keeping him thus occupied frees them to attack the Labyrinth, where many Patryn—as well as some Sartan, including Alfred—are trapped.

In the Labyrinth Alfred learns that some Sartan and Patryn have long since joined together for their mutual survival. As the battle escalates, Alfred begins to come into his own as the Serpent Mage. He transforms into a powerful dragon to fight the dragon-snakes. He is injured and falls from the sky. Marit, who has come to agree with Haplo that the dragon-snakes are a greater threat than the Sartan, goes deeper into the deadly Labyrinth in search of Alfred.

Xar finds a gravely wounded Haplo on the battlefield and takes him back to Abarrach.

Brothers in Arms   DANIEL R. HORN

Volume VII: *The Seventh Gate*

In Volume VII, *The Seventh Gate,* the dragon-snakes wage the battle to close the Final Gate and trap the Patryn within the Labyrinth, thereby increasing their torture while making it all the easier to wreck havoc in the other realms.

Dragons created by the Labyrinth capture Alfred and torment him for sport while Marit and Hugh the Hand work to save him. Good dragons, who have remained in hiding on Abarrach, come to the rescue. They transport any who are willing to fight to the Final Gate. Here Patryn and Sartan wage war not just for their survival but for the existence of all the realms.

On Abarrach, Lord Xar lets Haplo die from his battle wounds. Though it genuinely grieves him to lose Haplo, he is intent on discovering the location of the Seventh Gate. When Xar attempts to resurrect Haplo, he finds he can't do it because Haplo isn't truly dead. The Patryn's soul, his essence of being, is settled within his dog. Haplo is therefore neither fully dead nor fully alive.

Marit and Alfred journey to Abarrach to rescue Haplo. Alfred confines Xar in a magical coffin and manages to grant Haplo a freedom of sorts. The lazar—resurrected dead whose souls are still attached and are therefore denied the peace of whatever awaits after true death—try to steal Alfred's ship. Likewise, those few remaining living Sartan seek to escape their wretched world by means of the same ship.

Haplo and Alfred decide the only way to gain peace for all the worlds is to close the door to the Seventh Gate. Together, Patryn and Sartan battle dragon-snakes, their leaders, and their own weaknesses. Only after Haplo the Patryn finally follows his own conscience (rather than the mistaken notions of the man who has treated him like a son) and Alfred the Sartan comes to accept the full responsibility of who he is and the powers he controls (regardless of the hideous past deeds committed by his people) can the door finally be shut.

The worlds now spin free of each other, although conduits stay open to stabilize them. Sartan and Patryn have learned they must work together, as well as the folly of their arrogance in assuming they are better than the mensch simply because they are more powerful. Now the mensch are free to live and grow without the intervention of either Sartan or Patryn. Balance has been restored to the universe.

Underlying the *Death Gate Cycle*'s complex plot is an equally intricately designed universe. This can be seen both in the marvelous appendices at the end of each volume as well as in the computer game. The game received high marks from the computer gaming trade and is still widely available.

Collaborations in Progress

Star Shield (1996–1998, 2 novels to date)

The first book in this impressive new series was published under the title of *Starshield: Sentinels* in hardcover and *The Mantle of Kendis-Dai, A Starshield Novel* in paperback. Though published under different titles, the two novels vary only slightly in the opening chapters. The second *Starshield* novel, *The Nightsword,* is the authors' most recently published collaboration at the time of the writing of this article. Starshield represents the duo's trademark world-building at its best. This is the captivating tale of a universe in which different laws of physics apply in different realms. In some places, magic functions; in others only the more mundane laws of our world hold true. Navigating travel across the quantum fronts is tricky indeed. Only those on a great quest to save their world are willing to take the risk.

Sovereign Stone

As this book goes to press, the irrepressible collaborators have also just finished the first manuscript in still another new series. *Sovereign Stone* returns to the classic fantasy storytelling of the *Darksword* trilogy and the *Death Gate Cycle* without covering old ground. Nothing is quite as simple as it seems in this adventure told from the point of view of a lifelong companion to a prince who murders his brother, the heir to the throne. Warring elves, dwarves, humans, and fantastical creatures abound in this wondrous tale of love, hate, and betrayal.

Notable Works Outside the Collaborations

Songs of the Stellar Wind: Requiem of Stars

Requiem of Stars marks Hickman's first solo venture as a novelist. Coming from one who is accustomed to working with a team—either in collaboration with Weis or with fellow game designers or artists—this book is noteworthy in part simply because it is a one-man effort. Space opera featuring the detailed universe-building Hickman is reknown for, *Requiem of Stars* is the rousing story of galactic privateers, the Pax Galicticus who rule the galaxy, and a mysterious armada large enough to threaten them all.

The Immortals

The Immortals is Tracy Hickman's second solo novel. It is an extraordinary, self-assured work, widely praised for its powerful vision. Unlike every other work he's been involved in, *The Immortals* was always envisioned as a stand-alone work. It is the thought-provoking and inspiring tale of Michael Barris, a powerful interactive-television executive who risks everything to challenge a repressive American government. Set just after the turn of the twenty-first century, when the country is ravaged by disease, the novel follows Barris on a search for his sick son. What Barris finds as he enters an internment camp is a carefully guarded nightmare—one that he helped to create.

The Immortals is almost certainly Hickman's most personal work. As he says in his afterword, it is not about AIDS—even though many characters in the story suffer from a particularly virulent form of the lethal disease. "It is a book about forgiveness and compassion." One should add "redemption" to that list, for as the reader experiences Barris's trials, we see him come to accept his part in aiding the evil the country is perpetrating on its weakest citizens and ultimately leading the fight against it. Not a particularly bad—or good—man at the start of the story, Barris grows into a genuine hero during the search for his son.

It is redemption which provides the strongest link between *The Immortals* and Hickman's other works. His readers always know that good will ultimately triumph and the dark forces will be pushed back.

Star of the Guardians (1990–1993)

Mag Force 7 (1996–1998)

Like Hickman, Margaret Weis is ever busy. She wrote the four *Star of the Guardians* books in between her work on the *Death Gate Cycle*. These novels were the first by either writer to come out as science fiction. Like that of their collaborative fantasies, the world and characters are fully realized. Hardly surprising in any event, but all the less so because Weis had put some ten years into the planning before *The Lost King*, the first book in the series, saw print.

Both the *Star of the Guardians* quartet and its spin-off series, *Mag Force 7*, written in collaboration with Don Perrin, have been compared to *Star Wars*. Rightly so. These are books about the broad sweep of galactic events: the overthrow of corrupt forces and the just return of the righteous to the throne. But these are also human stories: the tale of Prince Dion, who though unaware of his heritage at first must learn to accept his destiny and confront the usurpers; Maigrey, a female warrior long in hiding who must once again join the battle against evil and its primary focus—the man she has loved all her life; and Sagan, once a good man now corrupted, who struggles with his conscience as well as more ordinary lethal threats.

Set in the same universe as *Star of the Guardians*, though taking place after the events in the quartet, the *Mag Force* books have a delightful feel. Showcasing some of the characters from the original Guardians series—notably the human cyborg Xris, the assassin Adonian Loti Raoul, and his enigmatic, telepathic partner known only as The Little One—the books introduce an intriguing collection of new ones as well. The adventures follow a group of seven deadly mercenaries in the days before the rebellion. They're loyal to each other, their convictions, and cash credits in the bank.

Threaded throughout the books are such personal issues as Xris's coming to accept who and what he has become since the near fatal accident which left him a cyborg, as well as broader issues such as gender identification and sexual orientation. Endings are sometimes bittersweet, but the Mag Force always wins.

Not surprisingly, the Guardians universe is perfectly suited to game adaptation. With Don Perrin, Margaret Weis produced and distributed the Star of the Guardians™ collectible trading card game. Weis and Perrin approached the project with all the vitality of the original novels, employing rigorous play-testing. However, the myriad aspects of manufacture and distribution proved to be extremely time-consuming for the tiny Mag Force 7, Inc. Preferring to devote the time to writing, Weis ultimately set aside her foray into trading cards.

◆ ◆ ◆

Collaborators and friends for over fifteen years, with tens of millions of copies of their books sold worldwide in a dozen languages, there's no question that Margaret Weis and Tracy Hickman are still going strong in all quarters. Their work and their relationship will continue to evolve in the years to come, as is true of all good writers, and fans can look forward to many more exciting novels by this talented team.

2

An Interview with Margaret Weis and Tracy Hickman

BY JANET PACK

Robot Blues   STEVE YOULL

Solo: Margaret Weis

 he lives in a converted three-story stone-and-shake-shingle barn on a hill near Lake Geneva, Wisconsin, which she shares with husband/author/game designer Don Perrin, three dogs, and three cats. In summer she gardens roses, encouraging their delicate red faces to disguise the chain link backyard fences. Weather and health permitting, she walks the dogs daily. Her Jeep Cherokee truck license declares simply: "M Weis."

Margaret Weis's home is also her office. A nook in the third-level loft is where her Apple computer resides. The machine rests on a desk littered with memos on yellow sticky-backed paper, short story manuscripts from the most recent anthology she's editing, pens, faxed letters, a few trinkets given to her by her husband and friends, and the odd coffee cup. A shelf above the computer screen keeps reference books such as the *Oxford Book of Quotations* and the *Oxford English Dictionary* handy. Twin double-hung windows in the wall behind the screen look through crowding walnut trees toward Geneva Lake, which she can just glimpse during the winter. An antique writing desk willed to Margaret as part of her grandmother's estate fits in the space on the left toward the back of the room, between the printer

and another bookshelf. Through the plain square railing made from unfinished two-by-two wood planks on her right she can look down into her living room through the blades of the antique ceiling fan. This office is a small space, an intense space, obviously the work area of a creative, busy person.

Margaret writes here from 7 until 11:30 each morning, then eats lunch and goes out for exercise at a local spa. Afterward she completes necessary errands, then returns home to feed her menagerie of furry pets and check her e-mail. If she's on a deadline, she may work on a book until dinner. In the evening she listens to television while she beads, makes jewelry, or knits. Occasionally she goes out again to play games or party with friends at the Game Guild, a store in nearby Lake Geneva she co-owns with husband Don Perrin.

"The Barn" (the name she gave her house always makes Margaret smile) is the home she bought in 1978. It has become a mecca for friends from around the world, both because of her hospitality and for the games she and Don host on weekends. It is decorated throughout with original artwork by Keith Parkinson, Larry Elmore, Thomas Canty, and Steve Youll. "Raistlin and Crysania" by Larry Elmore, the cover of *Time of the Twins,* hangs on the living room's west wall, along with Youll's portrait of Xris from

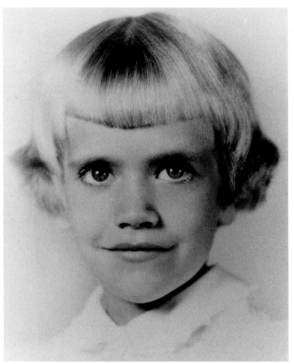

Margaret Weis, age five.

Knights of the Black Earth. Over the love seat in the conversation area is the original of Youll's confrontation between Lady Maigrey Morianna and Lord Derek Sagan painted for the cover of *Lost King.* Parkinson's large, dynamic *Fire Sea* painting from the third book of the *Death Gate Cycle* dominates the east wall over the couch, its dark red dragon glowering over our conversation.

JP: When did you decide to become an author?

MW: My English teacher, actually a graduate assistant, at the University of Missouri, Columbia, convinced me I was in the wrong major my freshman year. I took summer school during 1966. The graduate assistant kept me after class, really freaked me out—I thought I'd done something terrible. I'd had that in my mind all through school: if you were kept after hours, things were really bad. But she just wanted to talk to me. She said I had a real talent for writing. I was already disenchanted with the Art Department, although I was only a mediocre artist. Since I started in summer school they weren't giving a lot of the classes I needed for my degree. They just had general stuff.

[Margaret's smile turns into a laugh, which makes her face and her blue eyes glow.] I can almost point to

the place on the campus where my epiphanal moment occurred. It was almost a John Belushi-type thing that happened. On the way home from that meeting with the graduate assistant I stopped in my tracks, realizing she was right. The next day I changed majors. The university had just started a Creative Writing major, not much, really. I took thirteen hours of Creative Writing, and about forty hours of American Literature and English Literature, to get the degree.

JP: Why did you want to become an author? What finally stimulated you to go ahead and do it?

MW: It was just something I really liked doing, basically. I'd always been a storyteller, and I just enjoyed putting these stories in my head down on paper. It was intriguing.

JP: You were born March 16, 1948. Was there a particular element from your early years that influenced your career?

MW: Oh, yes. My mother always found time to read to my sister Terry and me. Especially mythology and the classics. I grew up with those great heroes and plots swimming around in my mind. That's probably why I was the only member of my kindergarten class elected by my peers to tell stories during rest period. Some I took from books, others came from television. For some I gleaned an element from this and another from that, and put it together on my own. The class seemed to like them. So did the teacher. It gave her a little extra time for paperwork and other things, but she often listened while she worked.

JP: With such encouragement from your mother, you probably started reading on your own at an early age.

MW: Very early. And as soon as I did, my mother and father got me my own library card. All of us went to the MidContinent Public Library every two weeks on Saturday. My sister and I were supposed to stay in the children's section. [She frowns, shakes her head.] There weren't many good children's books back then, the selection was very small and dismal. After the first couple of visits I'd read everything of interest, so I typically wound up in the adult racks. One day I found Ibsen's *A Doll's House,* and took it to the desk to check out. I was fascinated by the title. The librarian told me it wasn't about what

I thought it was, and wouldn't let me have the book. I got very angry.

JP: Did this happen often?

MW: Maybe not often, but a number of times. I always got mad. I couldn't understand why I wasn't allowed to check out any book I wanted, why I was confined to that dreadful children's section. So I went to my parents and begged them to check out books for me. Usually each of us checked out eight books, which was the limit. I could only have one or two titles on my parent's cards because they wanted their own choices. They were both voracious readers.

JP: What did they read?

MW: My mother, Frances, whom everybody including Terry and me called Tessie, read mostly modern fiction. I remember she hated Katherine Ann Porter's *Ship of Fools* after it came out. She said not even the dog had any redeeming characteristics. She liked Ayn Rand and mysteries. My younger sister Terry read books about horses, any book about horses. My father George liked mysteries, Louis Lamour, and he read all of Bruce Catton's Civil War books. He used to talk to us about them during dinner.

JP: What was your family life like?

MW: I had a strict German upbringing. My mother was German-English, my father all German. My father was an engineer at the American Oil Company refinery in Sugar Creek, Missouri, a little town between Independence and Kansas City. It used to be a little community wrapped around that refinery. When he retired, I think he was a vice president there. During World War II he was a bomber pilot in the European theater. My mother was a housewife who was very involved in her bridge games, PTA, and the like. We always had dinner at 5:00 or 5:30 every day when my dad came home from work. And we absolutely had to be in bed by 10:00. Other than going to the library every two weeks, we didn't do much. There were times I just shut myself in my room and read books for hours.

JP: Were the discussions about the Catton books with your father what sparked your fascination with Civil War history?

MW: Yes, part of the reason.

JP: What else about this period of history hooked you?

MW: I think the fact that the history was so immediate, particularly the connection with Frank and Jesse James. Growing up in Western Missouri, I heard a lot about Quantrill [former school teacher and Confederate Captain William C. Quantrill, head of Quantrill's Raiders, who rode into Lawrence, Kansas during August of 1863, killed 180 men, women, and children, then sacked and burned the town. Frank and Jesse James and Cole Younger were among the 450 men in the Raiders.—JP] and the James brothers. Tessie knew a woman who was related to somebody who had ridden with Quantrill, and who knew that Frank James was buried in this little cemetery across from where I used to go to grade school. Not many people knew because the gravestone is marked, I believe, with the name

Margaret Weis, Van Horn High School Senior, Independence, Missouri, 1966.

"Alexander F. James." The family was afraid of grave robbers digging around, looking for souvenirs or money stolen from banks. Just the idea of history being so close and so immediate, someone that everybody knew about, such as Frank and Jesse James, made it all the more real to me. I was very much interested in history anyway, so the two things came together and led me to do a lot of research on the James brothers and Quantrill. That's what led me to write my first book.

JP: So you were doing this research as early as grade school and high school?

MW: Yes, I'd always been interested in history, particularly in military history. I'd studied a lot on that. I read Winston Churchill's books on World War II, and I wrote a report on Rudolph Hess, things like that.

JP: Considering your father's interests, these sound like subjects you could talk to him about.

MW: We had relatives who had, well, not exactly fought in the Battle of Lexington, Missouri, which was a Civil War battle, but they were involved. My three great aunts carried water through Union lines to the Southern troops, and all that. And so I heard all about this from early childhood. My grandmother told a story about my great-grandmother standing by the stove as a young girl and being forced to make biscuits for hungry Union soldiers. She was always telling us about that.

JP: Did you and your sister read to each other?

MW: We read to each other while we did the dishes—one read, the other washed. Tessie complained about that because we often got so interested in the book it took us an hour to finish.

JP: It sounds like books were your close friends.

MW: They were. I was an unhappy child, very lonely. I didn't seem to fit in with my peers. We weren't on the same wavelength. Other kids always seemed more childish and didn't like to do the same things I did.

JP: What were the things you liked?

MW: Reading, obviously. And softball. At school, the teachers wouldn't let the girls play softball, especially not with the boys. It was undignified, not a girl's game. In seventh grade, several girls, including me, ganged up on the teachers and forced them to let the girls play with the boys. We had to wear skirts and petticoats. If we wore slacks, we had to put them on underneath our skirts. And they wouldn't let the girls have gloves. I think the school had a limited

number of gloves, and the boys had already spoken for all of them. So the girls had to learn to catch without gloves. I jammed my fingers many times before I learned how to catch. But I got pretty good at it.

JP: How did the boys feel about having you on their team?

MW: They really liked it. In fact, it was the boys that persuaded me to go to the teacher. Because I was the only girl in third grade that wanted to play softball, and I was pretty good, the boys wanted me on their team. They were a big help encouraging me to confront the teacher, and to try to persuade the other teachers that girls should be able to play softball.

JP: In that respect you were sort of a tomboy. Did this play true in other aspects of your life?

MW: Basically that was just about it. I mean, I liked to play with dolls, paper dolls especially. I liked to design dresses for them. So softball was really the only boy's sport I ever wanted to play, the only one I ever got into.

JP: What did your sister Terry think of your artistic/creative bent?

MW: She liked to draw horses. Terry was more the student than I. She was tested for IQ, and when they got back the results she'd scored really, really high. They put her in a special school for gifted children.

JP: Isn't there a famous person you're related to?

MW: [Grins.] Oh, yes. Attila the Hun. I had an aunt who decided we must be related to royalty when the genealogy craze first started. So she started tracing the family, even went to Europe to unearth our background. My grandparent's name was Etzold, which is very uncommon. We're somehow related to every Etzold we've run across so far. That made the name easy to trace. My aunt found no nobility in the line anywhere, and when she discovered that Atilla's family name was Etzold, she stopped in disgust. She came back home and refused to discuss our family background. Terry and I were told never to bring up the subject. But I think it's funny.

JP: How did you get started in art?

MW: I had always enjoyed drawing and working with watercolors, from the time I was a very little girl. My teachers encouraged me to continue this. And so I think that's how I got slanted more toward art than writing, because art was something that everybody could see but not everybody could do, and writing was something everybody just took for granted.

JP: When did you invent "Mice by Weis"?

MW: Oh. Oh, wow. Let's see, it was in high school. It was during an art project where I was doing kind of weird piglike creatures made of circles. Very odd, very stylized, made of nothing but circles and stuff like that. I did those on a piece of wood. People were always mispronouncing my name, with a long e instead of a long i, which is the German pronunciation. And I kept saying, "It's Weis; it rhymes with mice," which kind of gave me the idea to do Mice by Weis, which I drew on yearbooks when we had the big signing at the end of the year. [The Mice still appear occasionally on cards to friends, within the borders of plot notes Margaret scribbles to herself, or on autographs.—JP]

JP: You need to use Mice by Weis more often— people still mispronounce your name.

MW: Yes, I get a lot of that. Misspellings, too. "Weiss" is a more common spelling, so I get fan mail, letters from businesses, and other places addressed to "Margaret Weiss."

JP: Did your early storytelling talent weave through the rest of your school years?

MW: Yes. I had a teacher in grade school who was very interested in the class putting on plays. And somehow I wound up writing and directing those plays. We put one on several times a year. I had another teacher later who was interested in music and formed a choir. I sang soprano. We were good enough to do parts, can you believe that? The best singers were chosen to be in a special choir that included children from all over town. We performed during a choral program in Kansas City. That was a big thing.

I still like to sing, but I only do it in the kitchen, especially when other people are singing parts—it's the only place I can hear myself.

JP: Did your parents come to your performances?

MW: Always. They were always there.

JP: When did your interest in classical music start?

MW: Oh, from the beginning. I don't know if it was hearing so much of it while in the womb, or what. My mother always played classical music on the record player, especially her favorite operas: *La Traviata*, *Madame Butterfly*, *La Boheme*, *Faust*. Music just always interested me. I grew up knowing *Faust*. Tessie always told Terry and me the stories associated with the operas. I guess that was part of

Margaret Weis and the Laughing Headsman, Kansas City Renaissance Festival, 1977 or 1978.

the fascination about them. That, and I really liked the music. There was something magical and haunting in it. It was comfortable somehow, too.

JP: Did you ever go to operas when you were young?

MW: Not that I remember. The school at that time had cultural programs, though. We'd all get on buses three or four times a year and go to a play, or to hear the Kansas City Philharmonic Orchestra. I really liked that! Oh, and my family always went to hear musicals at the Starlight Theater every summer. [Starlight is a lovely open-air theater in Kansas City that produces live musicals throughout the warm months.—JP] I remember *Brigadoon, Carousel*, and *The King and I*. I saw Yul Brynner there live on-stage when I was five years old. He was riveting!

JP: Did your unhappiness start during middle and high school?

MW: Yes. We really didn't have a junior high. The Independence School District had just built Nowlin, and after sixth grade I went there for one year, then I went to Van Horn High School. It was horrible. The schools were crowded at that time with baby boomers. Often we had thirty-five children in a class. The teachers were mostly interested in normal students, ones who got their homework done and didn't disrupt class too much. I was stuck in the middle of a bunch who were only interested in marking time, throwing spitwads, and keeping up their grades just enough to graduate and get that diploma so they could do something else. They had no plans for continuing their education, and little interest beyond their next date.

JP: It sounds like most of your teachers didn't know what to do with you, either.

MW: That's true. But there was a man called D. R. Smith who taught English and ran the newspaper at Van Horn. [Her eyes begin to sparkle again.] What a character! He was the only one ever to tell me it was all right to be different, to walk another path from everyone else. He convinced me of this. It made me feel a little better about myself. He himself was always in trouble with the administration. Mr. Smith constantly encouraged us to publish things that were likely to get the newspaper in trouble. He also told me that I'd never be a journalist. So he was quite a rebel himself and was very unusual among the other teachers.

JP: Did he gravitate to other rebels?

MW: Yes, definitely. He loved music and literature. He really encouraged us to think for ourselves, not to stay in comfortable little molds, and to pursue the arts. He was very outspoken, kind of like Pat McGilligan in that aspect—he was never afraid to say just what he thought. [Patrick McGilligan is a freelance editor for TSR/WotC who lives in Milwaukee, also the author of several highly-acclaimed controversial books on actors and movie directors.—JP]

He had a dry, biting, sarcastic sense of humor. Our principal at the time just hated him.

JP: Who introduced you to the works of Charles Dickens, and when?

MW: We had to read *Great Expectations* in high school. That book really turned me off. But I'd read *Oliver Twist* before, possibly because the musical was just out, and enjoyed it. It wasn't until my friend Anne Nichols read *Bleak House* at the university and raved about it that I tried Dickens again. I was hooked from then on.

JP: Did Dickens change your outlook on how to write? How?

MW: Yes. Dickens especially helped me in characterization and in use of the language. I think that's what I really love about Dickens—he has the ability to bring his characters to life. And he has created characters that have lived for over a century, and that will probably continue to live. If you ran into Mr. Micawber on the street, you'd know him and could talk to him. That's what I really admire about Charles Dickens.

JP: When did you first start playing bridge, one of your abiding passions?

MW: Oh, that was after I started at the University of Missouri at Columbia. Tessie had always played bridge, and in fact had been several times at a gathering where Bess Truman was playing. I didn't get into bridge until the university. A bunch of us played every chance we got in the Student Commons. In fact, we played so much that a few of us almost flunked some classes. Bridge was our escape. The group that played was very diverse—I was in Creative Writing, we had a Vietnam vet, and a number of others. It was as if the game was always there, and we rotated in and out when we had time.

JP: I know you used to suffer from migraine headaches. When did those start, and how did they affect your life and work?

MW: Those were mainly during my twenties. My mother had suffered from migraines also. In her day they had no medication at all, so she would just deal with it. Often the pain was so bad Tessie couldn't sleep. She would literally sit up all night with the headache. She remembered the big flood of the early 1950s there in Kansas City. Tessie, my grandmother, and my aunt had been coming back from Liberal, and had stopped at my aunt's house, which was on the opposite side of the Missouri River there in Kansas. They were going to spend the night there and then come back across the bridge in the morning. Tessie had a terrible migraine that night. She spent the entire night sitting up with the headache and watching it rain. She realized that the storm was so bad that if she and my grandmother didn't get across the river soon, they might not make it. So she woke my grandmother up really early in the morning, as soon as there was the least bit of light, and hustled her into the car. They were one of the last cars to get across the bridge over the Missouri River before they closed it for safety reasons.

My migraines were very bad. I usually had to take to my bed with them. There was nothing else I could do—they were debilitating, made me physically ill and so dizzy I couldn't do anything else: I couldn't walk, I couldn't drive, nothing. My doctor actually put me on antidepressants for six months to break the cycle, because at that time I was getting one every two weeks. The only medicine available made me as sick as the migraines did. So it was a toss-up as to whether I suffered with the headaches, or I took the medicine to help the headaches and then got terribly ill from that. There wasn't anything they could do except to try and make them manageable. I didn't have the auras so much, I had the odd talking instead. My mother had the same thing: putting words in odd places, and you didn't know you were doing it until you'd said something and then realized it had come out completely garbled. Once a month I could cope with them. Twice was too much. Then the doctor told me about the food relationship, triggers actually, for migraines. I began to notice chocolate would bring them on. I've never really liked chocolate a whole lot since, even though I don't get the migraines anymore.

JP: What were your first strong memories of growing up during the 1950s?

MW: We lived in the Maywood subdivision of Independence until I was three, then we moved to 28th Street. That didn't make much of an impression, except I liked the house we moved into. We lived close to North Rock Creek School. After I was

old enough to be enrolled there, I walked to and from the school five days a week. After the Bobby Greenlease kidnapping and murder, though, I was always terrified of being kidnapped. Absolutely terrified. The reports on him ran for weeks in the local papers and on the Kansas City radio stations. I always thought someone was going to leap out of the bushes and carry me off. [She laughs.] I didn't realize my parents weren't wealthy enough to have that happen.

JP: Do these memories impact your writing?

MW: They might, but if so I'm not aware of it.

JP: What made you actually decide to become an author, over and above the graduate assistant your first summer at the university and the change she helped cause? Was there more impetus behind it than what you've already told?

MW: Well, of course what I took in college was mostly poetry, because that's pretty much all they taught. At the university, particularly at that time, they expected you—if you were majoring in writing—to go on and get a graduate degree and stay at the university. They never taught you anything about getting published or anything like that. After I graduated, my mother decided that with a worthless degree like Creative Writing I was going to starve to death, so she got me the job at Herald House. I started there as a proofreader. I think it was being involved with the industry that really set my thoughts to the fact that being published was something I'd like to do, and gave me the opportunity to learn how one went about doing it.

JP: So this was a much longer process than just deciding to major in Creative Writing and sitting down to write a book after graduation.

MW: Yes, definitely.

JP: Did you have any idea of what to do after graduation?

MW: Not really. I just knew I wanted to write and try and get my books published.

JP: How did your parents react when you decided to become an author?

MW: My mother reacted most, of course. Tessie was convinced I'd starve to death. So she scurried around and found a job for me—proofreading Bibles and other religious materials at Herald Publishing

Weis and Hickman Traveling Road Show Principals: GenCon 1986 (l. to r., back row) Gary Pack—Tanis, Tracy Hickman—Fizban, Janet Pack—Tasselhoff, (l. to r., front row) Terry Phillips—Rastlin, Doug Niles—Flint, Chris Niles—Silvara, Margaret Weis—Narrator.

House in Independence. They printed all the religious education materials for the Reorganized Church of Jesus Christ of Latter Day Saints, and sent it all over the world. [Margaret grins.] Not the Utah Mormons that Tracy Hickman belongs to; the smaller group headquartered in Independence. They're called the RLDS instead of the LDS because of the things that went on after their leader, Joseph Smith, Jr.'s, death. After I graduated, the interview with Gib Gordon, head of the press crew, was waiting for me; Tessie had already put in the application, done everything that needed to be done, except that.

JP: Why were you chosen for the job?

MW: [Shrugs.] I may have been the only person to apply. They needed someone who could read well, who could spell, knew some grammar, and catch mistakes. I got to learn that the guys setting type had a tendency to make the same mistake over and over, like spelling "church" as "chruch," so I learned what to look for. It's the same with typists who have computerized systems now. There are some patterns that will always show up because it's just easier to put in the "r" before the "u." So I always double-checked the word *church*, as well as a number of others.

JP: How were you treated there? You aren't a member of that church.

MW: They were very nice, but there was always that little difference because they were all so involved with their church, many of them with the church pol-

itics. I didn't have a religious affiliation, and there I was in the middle of all this stuff. I learned a lot. I got really interested in the history of the church. I found the background of the Mormons absolutely fascinating. Joseph Smith, Jr., the founder of the church, and what happened at Nauvoo, and the battles Brigham Young's group fought going out to Utah. I really enjoyed learning that. And I enjoyed picking up more biblical history. I had taken a Bible course in college, but hadn't really studied it all that much, so I loved learning more about that. And basically it was an interesting job, just sitting there reading.

It also set me in an excellent position to observe what went on in a church hierarchy, especially the controversies which consistently went back and forth between the RLDS and the [other] Mormons—which had the more accurate doctrine, which had the better succession of leaders, the theories on why the basic tenets were more right or more wrong than those of the other religion. Working there also showed me the controversies that go on within a church, especially around the times of the RLDS World Conference, held every two years. It taught me a lot. [Margaret pauses to sip bottled water and glance out the French doors to the deck, where the dogs are playing. Her free hand reaches out to stroke the blue cat Nickolai MouseSlayer, who's snoozing on the back of the couch.]

JP: When did you become head of the Independence Press imprint?

MW: It must have been about 1973. I was pregnant with Lizz at the time, and Herald House was just getting the idea that their own imprint could be a good thing. A couple of children's authors came to the publishing house, and they were the ones who really got us going on that—Rhoda Woolridge and Gertrude Bell. They suggested we start doing the Missouriana type of stories. I liked Gertrude Bell. She was sweet. She and Rhoda were juvenile writers, but they also wrote Missouri history. Rhoda's book, I think it was called *Hannah's House*, was fairly successful.

JP: When did you meet Pat O'Brian, your first coauthor?

MW: It was . . . oh, remember when Harry Truman died, and Herald House did that book about him? I think I met Pat working with something on the Truman Heritage Society, or something like that. I decided to work with him on the Jesse James book.

JP: How did that come up?

MW: I knew I wanted to do the book, and needed a person well founded in the history of the area. I was just starting to do in-depth research on it, and so I needed somebody to work with who I could ask things like, "Am I taking the right sort of slant on this aspect of history, or am I approaching it from the wrong direction?"

JP: So you began the collaboration. Did you send a proposal to Messner first?

MW: I sent it to Ray Puechner, my agent in Milwaukee, and he sent it to Messner. It was accepted. My first book was *Wanted: Frank and Jesse James, the Real Story*. It's been out of print for years, but a small publisher in Independence just wrote me for permission to reprint it. I think that's great!

JP: When that book was published, the Jackson County Historical Society and members of the Old Town Jail on Independence Square gave you a party.

MW: Yes, and an actor came in costume and played Frank James all evening. That was fun, as well as being a great launch for the book.

JP: And that volume began your foray into young adult literature.

MW: I guess I did eight or ten titles, including *Lost Childhood*, the one we wrote together. The subjects included everything from lasers to fortune-telling. Most of them were printed by Messner or Franklin-Watts, to be sold to schools. I think all of them are out of print now.

JP: When did your interest in games and gaming begin?

MW: We had always played games at home. I had a baby sitter once that taught Terry and me to play Sorry! We just loved it when she came over because she always played games, particularly that one. My family used to play Monopoly, and my mother was a good solitaire player, and of course a bridge player. George, Tessie, Terry, and I used to sit around and play poker. My dad taught us how to play that. I've always been very interested in games.

JP: So when you found out about Dungeons and Dragons, it seemed a natural thing for you to be curious about.

MW: I was really interested in that game when I heard about it, although I couldn't find anyone to lead one. Until John Lehman said he'd do it.

JP: So you'd been researching it?

MW: Yeah, I'd been looking at it. I even went so far as to read the *Dungeon Master's Guide* and the *Player's Handbook*, but it made no sense to me at all. And I realized that somebody was going to have to teach me how to do it.

JP: You and Lehman both belonged to a social group interested in Sherlock Holmes, correct?

MW: We were in the Baker Street Irregulars group known as the Great Alkalai Plainsmen. I joined them when I was fifteen, was one of the founding members. I read about it in the newspaper and wanted to join. They weren't certain at first they were going to allow women. They held a dinner, and I was invited. They had a quiz during the gathering, because every Holmes group always has a quiz. I won it. They told me afterward that they didn't feel like they could keep me out of the society since I was the one who had won the quiz. So the Great Alkalai Plainsmen was one of the first groups to admit women into their Sherlock Holmes society. We had a number of women join after I did. It was really fun.

JP: That got to be quite a large gathering, as I remember from the couple of meetings I attended.

MW: Yes, it did. I'd say we had twenty-five or thirty members at its height. I met John Lehman there. He was acquainted with the Dungeons and Dragons game and had actually played it. So I talked to him about being Dungeon Master for our party, and he was the one that led us in the game.

JP: That was some game, very intricate. Thirteen hours over two Saturdays. The players were you and Bob, my husband Gary and me, Margie and Steve. John Lehman really did some research into our characters and personalities before we played.

MW: John was very good. I thought the whole game was fun and very interesting. I really enjoyed it.

JP: You and I were the only two who survived.

MW: Yes. I think John felt bad about that. That's why he made the cleric's goddess resurrect Gary's character. That way half our party lived. I can't even remember the kind of being I played.

JP: *You were a short person who carried a mace—a footman, I think. Every time you had the chance, you yelled, "I'll hit it with my mace!" At one point you clobbered something floating overhead and got covered with smelly green goo. We made you march at the end of the line from then on.*

This game cemented your interest in TSR. When did you put in your application there?

MW: After my divorce, I felt like it was time to move on. I found an ad in *Publishers Weekly* for a game editor at TSR. And so I put in an application. That would have been 1982.

JP: *How soon did they contact you regarding that job?*

MW: It was pretty quick. They sent me this game editor's test I had to take. I filled it out and sent it back. Apparently, from what I've heard from people who worked with TSR at that time, I didn't pass it. Mainly because I didn't know anything about the game. So I got a "Thanks for applying, but . . ." letter from them. But Jean Black, who was head of TSR's book department, was looking for a book editor. Jean knew Ray Puechner, who was my agent then. Jean happened to talk to Ray and told him of the opening in the book department, saying that she needed someone right away. Ray told Jean he had a friend who'd put in an application for game editor. Jean went to the games department and pulled my application. After reading it, she invited me to come to Lake Geneva for an interview. It was all very serendipitous that we got together.

JP: *When and how did you meet Ray Puechner?*

MW: [Smiling fondly.] That's one of my favorite stories. It must have been around 1976 or 1977, when I was working with Independence Press at Herald House during the Bicentennial celebrations. Independence Press was starting to get story submissions from agents, not very many, but a few. I got this package one day from the Ray Peekner Literary Agency. I opened it up. Inside was a nice cover letter that said they were submitting a fantasy book every bit as great as *Lord of the Rings*. It was going to be

a wonderful story and I should read it. I thought, Well, I'll give it a chance, and so I looked at the title page. It was called *The Legend of Pug Wug Gee Land*. I thought it wasn't a great title, but as we know authors aren't always good at titling their works, so I started reading the manuscript. It was horrible. It was one of the worst things I've ever read. I was really furious with this Mr. Puechner for even daring to compare this story with *Lord of the Rings*. I called my secretary into my office, and I said "We're going to fix this Mr. Puechner." So I wrote him a letter, and I said, "Dear Mr. Puechner: This is awful. May an ork eat you for breakfast. Sincerely, Margaret Baldwin," and I sent the manuscript back.

I didn't think anything else about it. Then I got another letter from the Ray Peekner Literary Agency [Ray spelled the agency's name the way his name was pronounced.—JP] And I thought, Oh my God, they've blackballed me. That terrible manuscript sold to Harper's or somewhere for millions of dollars, and I'm just an idiot. I opened up this letter, and it said, "Dear Margaret: You are the only one who actually said what you thought about that submission." What had happened was this kid had sent his book about Pug Wug Gee Land to Ray, and Ray had rejected and returned it. The kid took Ray's stationery, copied the letterhead, and forged the letter he sent out with the manuscript over Ray's signature, which he also copied. He sent it to every publisher in the United States.

This nearly ruined Ray's reputation as a literary agent. But, and Ray always thought this was really funny, he got back all these letters from editors that were very polite. Things like, "This does not suit our needs at this time," you know, the standard polite editorial rejection. And so Ray was calling the editors up, and they all told him, "We'd thought you'd taken leave of your senses, or you were on drugs. The manuscript was dreadful, we couldn't figure out why you were sending this to us." I was the only editor who'd actually written an honest response about the manuscript.

That tickled Ray so much that he wrote me back. Not being one to pass up an opportunity, I wrote him again, saying, "Thank you very much, Mr.

Puechner. And would you be interested in looking at my work?" He said sure, he'd look at it. So I sent some stories I'd written, none of which he liked or could use, but he did like my writing style. He told me to keep working, and that he'd like to see anything else I did. In the meantime, we continued our correspondence and got to be really good friends. Ray's the one that got me the Jesse James book contract, and eventually got me writing the juvenile nonfiction for Franklin-Watts and Messner.

JP: What did you see in Ray Puechner as a friend, over and above your relationship with him as an agent?

MW: He was one of the best people I ever knew. Just genuinely good. He had a very dry, wicked, sense of humor.

Ray was just a wonderful person, very gentlemanly, gentle manner, gentle voice. Gary Paulsen always said he looked like one of those guys hanging on the wire at Auschwitz . . . he was very tall and exceptionally thin, very emaciated looking. He had glaucoma, had to put drops in his eyes. His eyesight was very bad, and he wore thick-lensed glasses in heavy black frames—they were the only ones he could find to support the weight of those lenses. He smoked constantly and drank quantities of Tab, both of which probably killed him. He was a porno writer, wrote Westerns; he would write anything that anybody gave him. He was a hack, yeah, and he didn't mind being a hack. Very honest about it.

JP: I remember him being so poor that several times you sent him stamps, or money for postage.

MW: All his clients did—that was one of the things we all did. We sent Ray money for postage. But his clients all loved him. And he represented a lot of people—romance writers, juvenile writers, anyone he thought was good enough to be published.

JP: You sponsored a writer's seminar with Ray as speaker at your house once.

MW: That was tied in with the University of Missouri at Warrensburg. That was when we had Gary Paulsen and a lot of the juvenile writers at a Children's Literature Festival. I had them all over to my house. Ray gave a lot of advice about writing.

JP: Ray died after a prolonged battle with cancer.

MW: That was in 1986 or around in there. After

I'd been at TSR for two or three years.

JP: Was your work with Pat O'Brien on the James brothers book where you began to hone your style of collaboration?

MW: It's been different with each coauthor. Gary [Pack] and I worked differently together than Pat [O'Brien] and I did, or than Tracy and I did, or Don [Perrin]. You just kind of learn to work with the other person.

JP: You've always seem to be very open to this, and very willing to put in your seventy-five percent as long as your collaborator was willing to contribute his fifty percent. And I think that's really what may have made a number of your coauthorships work: your determination, vision, and talent pushing things forward.

MW: I think so, I think that's right. And I value very much what the other person gives to the project.

JP: I know when you worked with Gary Pack on the juvenile scientific books about computer graphics and robotics, he sat behind your shoulder and said things, you percolated them through your mind, and typed in the information. Then the two of you did corrections together.

MW: With those books, we had to be *so* careful about what we said and how we said it because we had those concept readers who would come after us and rip us to shreds. [Laughs.]

JP: Do you enjoy collaboration? Why?

MW: Yeah, I do, I enjoy collaborating. I think it's always good to bring somebody else's ideas to the table. It gives you new ideas and kind of sparks your way of thinking, and puts in different voices. Of course, like with Don and his military background, he knows all sorts of stuff that I don't know and could never know unless I'd spent four years in the army. Now with Tracy, it's just his sheer creativity. Tracy thinks up things that nobody else would ever think of. It's just fun working with him. And it's nice, if you get stuck in a spot, to be able to call up somebody and say, "Hey, help me get out of this."

JP: I remember you saying that when you wrote yourself into a corner, you used to call Tracy and yell, "Help!"

MW: That's right. I'd get on the phone and say, "Tracy, if you don't do something quick, everybody's

The Knights of the Black Earth   STEVE YOULL

going to die, there's just no two ways around it."

JP: *So in that respect, working with a coauthor is much easier than it is working by yourself.*

MW: Oh, yes. If you're by yourself, even though you've got people to talk to, really it's all up to you. It's your world and your characters; you're the one that's got to figure out what to do with them.

JP: *Would you rather have a collaboration as opposed to doing a solo work?*

MW: Really, it's kind of a toss-up. I enjoyed doing the book about Raistlin I finished last year. And I really enjoyed the *Star of the Guardians* books, both projects which I did on my own.

JP: *The* Star of the Guardians *series you started when we lived in Independence. I remember you coming up with the idea. Their publication was the fruition of a project long in process.*

MW: I worked on those for years. But then there are other books I couldn't have done, like the *Mag Force 7* books, without Don's help. And *Dragonlance®* was Tracy from the beginning.

JP: *Your move from Independence to Wisconsin proved a really traumatic time for both you and your children.*

MW: It was right after my divorce.

JP: *True to form, you bottled everything up inside during these difficulties and dealt with it as best you could, seldom complaining, just going from one thing to another as necessary.*

MW: Yes. That's what happened. But I did actively look for a job. I think basically the idea of finding a different job, of moving anywhere, was very appealing. I think back to what one of my poetry teachers, Dr. Drummond, used to say, and that was that it's all nonsense about not being able to run away from a situation. He told us that there are times when it's a good idea to run away from the situation, and it can help you make a change in your life. So that was basically what I was doing when I moved to Wisconsin—I was running away.

JP: *When did you change your name back to Weis, and why?*

MW: It was after my divorce. I did it for professional reasons. I'd just always liked my maiden name better. I never was comfortable with Baldwin as a last name.

JP: *After TSR called and told you they were interested in interviewing you, how long did it take to get hired and everything coordinated so you could leave for Wisconsin?*

MW: It was pretty quick, because they wanted me up there within thirty days after Jean had grabbed my application away from the games department. They were desperate for another editor. I packed the kids and the three cats in my tiny little Toyota, and we left.

JP: *So you started the great pilgrimage north. Did TSR put you up in a hotel, as they did with other new recruits?*

MW: No, I'd come up a couple weeks ahead of time and found a house to rent, so we actually had someplace to go and settle into. It was in Fontana. So we got to the house and unpacked the kids, the cats, and the cars, but the movers were more than a week late getting there. I had no clothes. We had no money. My agent Ray came down from Milwaukee and bought me a dress for my first day at work. We lived off my daughter Lizz's birthday money. Poor Lizz, but at least we had a little money to buy food with. I paid her back as soon as I could.

JP: *Your first published piece after you went to work for TSR was what?*

MW: I wrote some Endless Quest books. I also wrote one of those *Dungeons and Dragons*™ cartoon books featuring Bobby the Barbarian that Roger Moore still likes to hold over my head to this day.

JP: *You wrote a book with Roger Moore under an assumed name, right?*

MW: That was after I'd been at TSR awhile. Somebody had defaulted on a deadline. The book was due at the printer within the next few days. We had to write the book, Roger and I, in three days. So we divided it up: he took half, and I took the other half of the path, and then made sure that everything coordinated, came together. But it was really terrible. Neither of us wanted to put our names on it. So we used the name Susan Lawson.

JP: *Was that your shortest deadline ever?*

MW: Yes, I think that was it, yeah; the shortest deadline I ever had was three days for half a book.

JP: *When did you join the committee dealing with* Dragonlance?

MW: Right after I started work there. One of the main reasons they hired me was to work on *Dragonlance*. They needed someone with experience in writing adult books. Everybody else there, Jean Black, Bill Larson, and Bev Charette, had backgrounds in children's books. I'd actually done some adult books while I was at Herald House. One of my first assignments was to work with the *Dragonlance* committee. They were already meeting; they had the games designed, [and] the first three books all plotted.

JP: How did you feel going into the project?

MW: It was very exciting. I really enjoyed it. And of course, there was Tracy and Mike Williams. It was just a really fun group to work with. Plus the fact that hardly anyone in the book department had ever worked with the game department. My first weeks there, I didn't get to know anyone in Games except Tracy. I would see them walking by my cubicle occasionally, or hear them play-testing, or hear their water-pistol fights, or whatever else they were doing. Books, Games, and Magazines were all segregated.

JP: Dragonlance filled a great part of your working life at TSR from almost the moment you started there. How did you feel about the project itself? What were your initial impressions of Tracy Hickman?

MW: I loved the project. We had a great time. I really enjoyed working on it. I thought Tracy was extremely creative, and fun to be with. From the beginning, he and I worked really well together. Despite the short deadlines and the time we had to put in on it, it never got old, never lost its spark. It was a delightful process.

JP: Essentially, you were joining a bunch of rebels. You finally found your niche.

MW: That's right. I joined a group that was very creative. Also, I'd gone from being one of the youngest people working on the staff at Herald House to being one of the oldest at TSR—I was all of thirty-two, thirty-three, something like that. Kim Mohan, Larry Elmore, Jean Black, Bill Larson, and I were, I think, the oldest people in the R&D division. That was kind of a new experience.

Solo: Tracy Hickman

He lives in a two-story house of cream stucco and tile nestled among a development of houses that are not unlike his own. He describes it as a "transitional" house—he, his wife, and their four children moved there to simplify their lives. Most mornings he hops into his Honda del Sol V-Tec and zips to work. He hasn't lived in Utah long enough to get personal plates, but he's previously owned ones that announce him as "Simkin" and "Fizban."

He labors in a standard two-story office building set around a courtyard. His sanctum he describes as "a hole in the wall," a space just large enough for a desk, a couch, and an overflowing bookcase, surrounded by the radio station he owns with his father. This office is a former audio recording studio, with one window that looks onto an interior hallway, the other into a second recording chamber. A mean place in which to stuff a business with the impressive title Omniverse Dream Systems, and its imaginative creator Tracy Hickman.

"Not particularly inspiring," Tracy chuckles, looking around. "But I hope to change this soon, since my oldest daughter is in college. I can convert a room at home to my office and work from there. I don't like commuting. It takes too much time."

The place appears to have suffered a whirlwind—the desk around the IBM computer and the couch are littered with reference books, notes, and various manuscripts, both partial and whole. Tracy describes the effect as an "explosion of paper." Part of the couch (seldom used for its intended purpose) is buried under a collection of *Star Trek* toys he neglected to put away, including a phaser. In his bookcase are autographed copies of Asimov's *Foundation Trilogy* and Bradbury's *Martian Chronicles*, as well as other inspirations to his imagination. Larry Elmore's original oil painting "The Companions," showing the *Dragonlance* heroes gathered around a campfire, dominates one wall. Models including a Saturn V rocket, the space shuttle, and the *Nostromo* from *Alien* are scattered about.

JP: You have such an inspiring office at the moment. What kind of state of mind does it take to get you writing? How do you get into that mindset? How do you keep from getting distracted?

TRH: [Leaning back in his gray high-backed office chair, he smiles, making his blue eyes twinkle, and raises his feet to his desk. He always does this when he's thinking.] I have a hard time working. I think some people have a skewed view of a writer's life. They wonder why I continually write books when I've already got several out on the market. The work part is writing ten to fifteen pages per day. Getting past distractions is also part of the work.

Writing is painful for me, always has been. I know where the plot needs to go, but the getting there is difficult. A few months ago I got some software for my computer that, when installed, allowed me to speak into it, to dictate my books. I found when I tried that, I couldn't write at all—for me, much of the process is tactile. The concept must go from my mind into my hands; I must type to get the book to go where it ought to go. So I took that software off my computer and went back to my keyboard. After pushing myself through the process of turning out my daily pages, I'm exhausted. I want to go home and do something else. Sometimes there are days when writing is like pulling teeth—and I'd rather pull the teeth. The determination to write despite such conditions is the difference, I believe, between a craftsman and an artist.

JP: *You used to be difficult to get hold of, at least by phone. Is it true you had a secret office you could slip away to within a dimensional time-space fold? Or did you just use a magical spell from Simkin or Fizban's bag of tricks and disappear?*

TRH: For many years I was a very private person, much more so than previously. I guess people gave up being able to get hold of me. Now I have two e-mail accounts, a home phone, an office phone, a cell phone, and a pager. I also have a website (http://www.trhickman.com) and host an online newsletter. I'm very accessible these days.

JP: *Several female authors took male names when they began being published in science fiction/fantasy: James Tiptree, Jr. and Andre Norton, for example. Other women use only their first initials, such as C.*

J. Cherryh. The name Tracy Raye Hickman gives no clue whether you're male or female; in fact, much of your fan mail is addressed to "Ms." and even "Mrs." Hickman. Are you named for someone in your family? How does it feel to be consigned to the wrong gender much of the time? How do you deal with the confusion of your fans?

TRH: My name constantly misleads people. That's something of a mystery, since my picture has been on a number of book jackets. You'd think people would see my beard and could tell. Even when I was a boy, my name wasn't terribly comfortable. "Tracy" may have come from Spenser Tracy. It became a girl's name as I was growing up. I think "Raye" came

Exploring New Worlds: Margaret Weis and Tracy Hickman on a book-signing tour of England during the Gulf War.

from my Dad having the middle initial R—it doesn't stand for anything, doesn't have a period after it, it's just there by itself. My parents gave me the middle name he never had.

As an author, my name is great for helping me to keep my head on straight. I've been invited to address women-only writers' conferences and had to decline. Wizards of the Coast, the company that now owns

TSR, has been sending me contracts addressed to Ms. Hickman. My wife, Laura, with whom I've coauthored games such as Ravenloft, and I have been referred to as the Hickman Sisters. I was the ugly one of the two.

JP: Do you consider yourself famous?

TRH: No, I'm not famous. We have many—perhaps millions—of readers around the world, but the fans and Margaret and I are all in this together, sort of a symbiotic relationship. Without our fans, the people who read our books, who get interested in our worlds to the point they come back to read about them time after time, we wouldn't be where we are.

JP: When and why did you decide to grow a beard—are you aspiring to a patriarchal appearance?

TRH: [Chuckling again, a very warm sound.] When I first came to work for TSR, Harold Johnson, my boss, took one look at me and said, "We were expecting someone with a neck." As my girth grew over the years, my lack of neck definition also increased. One year my family and I went on a houseboating excursion on Lake Powell for a week. I didn't take a razor. After we got home, I grew the beard for another week. I finally realized that I didn't know how to grow a beard—I looked like an Arab terrorist, and was about to cut it off when I figured out perhaps I should actually *trim* it. I got a picture of Riker from *Star Trek: The Next Generation*—the only reference at hand— followed the contour of his beard, and now mine looks great. I believe the beard defines and frames my face, and hides that lack of a true neck. My wife Laura likes it, insists I keep it.

JP: Who is your favorite author?

TRH: Stephen Leacock, a little-known turn-of-the-century Canadian author. He wrote brilliant satire. He wrote a book of short pieces called the *Nonsense Novels* that included, "Guido the Gimlet of Ghent," "Gertrude the Governess," and others. His "Sunshine Sketches of a Little Town" is great, too. Leacock's works are timeless, very much current despite being written nearly 100 years ago, and his usage of language is brilliant. He's difficult to find, even in Canada, but every once in a while Margaret or someone else discovers a volume and sends it to me.

JP: And there's no doubt who your least favorite author is.

TRH: Oh, no, that's obvious after my experiences with him at DragonCon. I like to tell people that I spent a year with Tom Clancy one week.

JP: You were born in Salt Lake City, Utah, November 26, 1955, the oldest of four children. What's your earliest recollection of your parents stimulating your imagination?

TH: My mother reading to me. She married early and was dedicated to taking care of her husband and family. She read to me a lot, mostly Dr. Seuss, who was new and very popular then, and Golden Books. Dr. Seuss's *Yertle the Turtle* was my favorite. She also read to Gerry after he came along two years later. We were always encouraged to read, and to use our creativity and imaginations by both parents.

JP: Were you fascinated by or repelled by your brother, Gerald Todd Hickman?

TRH: We had our ups and downs, as all brothers do, but I love him dearly. He was interesting. He, too, was highly imaginative. I remember him fighting battles with his extensive marble collection as combatants on the bedroom floor. He was always more interested in sports than I. I tended toward more reading, music, and performing though he was quite an actor in his own right.

JP: What about the rest of your family in general?

TRH: I come from a long line of highly-educated, creative people with roots in England, Wales, and South Africa. My grandfather on my father's side was a banker. One of my uncles went into that business, too, and then recently become a state senator. Gerry is now a successful lawyer. My father, Harold R Hickman, got his doctorate in Communication Broadcasting from Brigham Young University. My mother, Joan Parkinson Hickman, used to regret not having gone to college. I'm proud to say she did finally go to college after raising four children, and graduated with a degree two years ago. My brother Gerry and I are only two years apart in age. The girls Kim and Kari came along much later—I was fifteen when Kim was born.

JP: What are some of your earliest memories?

TRH: We moved a lot after my father graduated. I think we didn't stay in any one place for more than four years because of his succession of jobs. I don't recall much about the first place we lived in because I was too young. For a time we lived in the basement of a house belonging to my Aunt Roma, who lived in Salt Lake City. My father was starting a job managing an instructional television station in Ogden, Utah, and he had to commute every day. I do remember that every time we moved, it was to the edge of town where new homes were less expensive. I used to think my mom and dad liked the edges of towns, because that's always where we seemed to end up living.

I think it was while we lived in my aunt's basement that my parents began to worry about me. I'd sit in Aunt Roma's basement for hours with blocks and a few other toys for company, making up elaborate stories about them. I'd rather do this than play with my brother or other kids my age. Mom and Dad were sure something was wrong with me, viewed this as bizarre behavior.

JP: This behavior persisted how long?

TRH: Throughout my life. I had friends, just acquaintances really, not what I consider good friends, and played with them, but I also really liked to play alone. I was in fourth or fifth grade when we lived in Ogden, and our house had a playroom. My father got two barrels to keep toys in, but I wanted to play in the barrels themselves. I dumped out all the toys, took my crayons, and drew control panels for rockets on the inside, my knees doubled up to my chin. My parents lost me for hours. Then I got into reading and escaped into books instead of barrels.

JP: Where else did you live as a child?

TRH: Before living with my aunt, I do remember living in an apartment in "Hodsonville," named for the landord who owned the group of four-plex buildings in Salt Lake City just west of the university. That was the first home I remember. My father was in school then, finishing his degree. I used to tumble down a mammoth slope in front of that apartment, and enjoyed sliding down it every time it snowed in winter. Imagine my disappointment when I visited there years later and discovered that what I'd considered an enormous hillside was only two and a half feet tall.

The Bookmobile came to the corner opposite these apartments every week or so. That must have been in

1960–61. My mother introduced me to its wonders and got me a library card. Within I found lots of crummy books without pictures, and a few good ones that had pictures I could enjoy. So I checked out all I could, quickly becoming fascinated with what lay between the covers. As I learned to read better, I

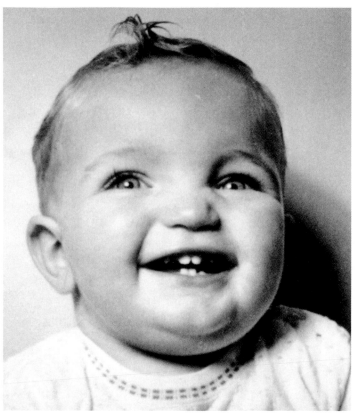

Tracy Hickman at age one. Impersonation of the Gerber baby.

came to appreciate the books that were mostly words. The arrival of the Bookmobile always excited me. Every time it appeared, I'd dash out to meet it so I could get more books.

Then we moved to a duplex in Bountiful, which was a closer commute to my father's work. I remember my family had good friends living in the house across the street. After that, we moved into Ogden into another duplex apartment, one across the street from a golf course. The year must have been around 1962, because I remember my parents talking about the Cuban Missile Crisis, bomb shelters, and the like.

JP: Your family sounds very supportive, very warm. Who meted out the punishments?

TRH: My dad when it was necessary. He never compromised—when he made the law, that was it.

No questions. Anything mandated by him must be obeyed.

JP: Is there another family member you particularly remember?

TRH: My grandfather on my father's side. I remember him as magic. He had a great silvery mane of hair brushed straight back from his forehead. He was a banker, a busy man, but he always had time, made time, for his children and grandchildren. I

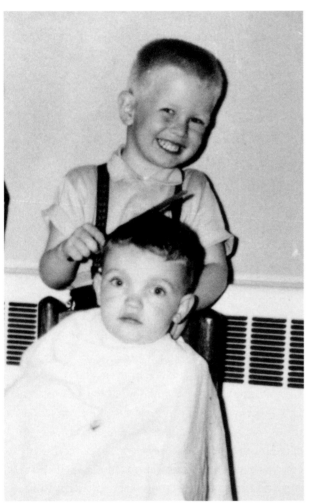

Styling as Always: Neighbor Barry Weed gives Tracy Hickman, age five, a haircut.

remember his laugh—it was so bright, so full of joy. I wish I had gotten to know my other grandfather better. He passed away when I was young. I remember him as an emotional and compassionate man.

JP: When did your interest in the space program start?

TRH: One of my most vivid early memories was of my father calling me over to the television one day because something important was about to happen. Glued to the set, I watched Alan Shepherd's launch into space. I also watched John Glenn's launch, and anything else that had to do with the space program. I started reading books about the solar system, space, anything like that I could find. The space program also began my fascination with science fiction.

I also remember watching the 1960 presidential election in that apartment. My dad managed to borrow two television sets from friends in addition to the one we owned, and we had a party. I don't remember this so much for seeing John F. Kennedy take the election, just the novel idea of having more than one television at the same time.

JP: How did you feel about those early space flights?

TRH: Oh, I identified with those space explorers greatly. That was the time of space exploration. I wasn't interested in sports. I mean, I knew who Arnold Palmer, Mickey Mantle, and a few other sports heroes were, but I just wasn't interested in them. The Mercury 7 astronauts were my heroes. Wernher von Braun was another. I clipped everything I could find out of newspapers and magazines and made a scrapbook about *Apollo 11* before and after that flight. I begged my father for odd jobs so I could earn money to buy model rockets and planes. I joined the AFJROTC [Air Force Junior Reserve Officer's Training Corps] in high school because the space program was mine, a very personal mania. I became a sail plane pilot because of the space program. I finally made it to Florida to see Cape Canaveral just after the *Challenger* explosion—I enjoyed seeing the launch site and all, but the loss of *Challenger* gave me nightmares for a long time after.

I'd really like to use the funds generated by the global *Starshield* project (if it ever goes global) to finance commercial orbital ships and the eventual colonization of Mars. I'd start with suborbital commercial transports flying the most lucrative runs, such as Los Angeles to Tokyo, or Los Angeles to London, then with the funds from that build commercial orbiters, part of which would be reserved for vacationers wanting to see the stars, the other part for shipbuilding, takeoff, and supply of the Martian colony. That's actually written into the proposal and the contracts.

JP: What was the first science fiction or fantasy book you remember reading?

TRH: That was probably *2001: A Space Odyssey* by Arthur C. Clarke. I read that mostly because of the movie. Before the movie came out, there was a big spread in a magazine about it and how it was made. My father pointed the article out to me. I held that magazine in my fists, staring at the pictures and reading the text until the print rubbed off on my hands. I remember my frustration with the article because the print came off, which made it harder to read. I read that again and again and again.

When we finally went to see the movie *2001*, my father said we could leave at half-past the hour. I remember sitting in front of the clock with five minutes to go and watching the second hand tick by each little second mark. I still think that thing slowed down just for my benefit. It seemed to take hours before we could leave. And when we finally got to the theater, I could hardly wait for the movie to start. I was awed by the really cool space stuff right there on the screen. It was a dream come true. After that, I read the book.

In my teens I became an avid reader of *Analog* magazine. I still recall many of the stories, such as "The Gold at Starbow's End," although I don't remember who wrote that one. The story detailed the first interstellar expedition from Earth. It had a really great twist. It made a big impression on me.

The first fantasy series I read was probably in the early seventies, Tolkien's *Lord of the Rings*. That was about the only fantasy book in town at that time except for C. S. Lewis's *Narnia* series. I still try to read *Lord of the Rings* once a year because it stimulates my imagination. I really love those books. In fact, it's about time to read them again. I'm looking forward to it.

JP: How about other books that influenced you?

TRH: I read Melville's *Moby Dick* when I was thirteen just because I was fascinated by the language the author used. When I started reading Isaac Asimov, I quickly became immersed in the stories because his characters seemed like real people and

his plots were so personal. I could identify with them.

JP: You started performing early in life.

TRH: Yes, that's one of the things the Mormon religious culture encourages. I've always belonged to the Church of Latter Day Saints, as do my parents, and I've performed all my life as most Mormons do. Kids are encouraged to give prewritten speeches, sort of small sermons, in front of the general gatherings in Sunday class. These can be about church history, historical figures, or something dealing with the subject that will be discussed later in smaller classes. Usually their parents write the speeches, and the youngsters practice until they get pretty good at reading them. It was different in my family. Both my parents encouraged me to write the speeches myself. I had fun listening to their suggestions, doing research, setting down the information, and practicing in front of them. They were a great audience, always giving me direction and suggestions rather than criticism.

Another thing I did regularly was plays with the ward. That's the Mormon equivalent for a parish or congregation. Someone would write a dramatic piece, and then we'd do a little road show, visiting other wards and performing the work. We had a great time.

My first shot on television came when I was on the *Romper Room* preschool show on KSL Channel 5 in Salt Lake City. I was five years old. My mother took me to the studio every morning and waited patiently with the other mothers while I sat under those hot, bright lights and tried my best to remain alert. Alas, stardom was fleeting—the gig was for only one week. I really enjoyed myself there. I was a spunky little kid. There was a wooden train set on the set, and each day a different child was designated to play with it. It was one of the most popular toys there. When it was my day to play with the train, people affiliated with the show asked me several times before we started where I wanted to go on that train. I told them one after the other that I wanted to go to Beaver, Utah. That's where my grandparents lived and where my parents are from. The show staff were assuring themselves I'd be familiar with the question when they asked it. But I didn't understand their reasoning. When we finally got down to the live performance, the hostess of the program finally asked me where I wanted to go in front of all the other kids. I shook my head and said, "I already told you several times. I want to go to Beaver, Utah!" I just couldn't understand why they didn't get it the first time they asked that question.

Our family was always doing productions, too. We had several large family gatherings during the year—Christmas, Thanksgiving, others. There was always something going on. One year my brother, cousins, and I produced and performed in a puppet version of "The Littlest Angel." The puppets had Play-Doh heads and cloth bodies. We found out during the play that the Play-Doh heads didn't stay on the bodies very well, and went rolling across the stage and sometimes into the audience. So that lent a comic tone to the whole thing.

My parents also urged me to sing hymns and anthems at the adult church meetings. I sang "The Holy City" innumerable times, as well as other pieces, accompanied by someone from the ward who played piano. I was a boy soprano with a pretty good ear. In elementary school I also performed solos; at Ruby Thomas Grade School I remember singing my rendition of "Love is Blue," and got smashing reviews. I was very popular as a singer.

I tried out for Menotti's "Amahl and the Night Visitors" when I was thirteen, a production at Brigham Young University. I didn't get the part. I was disappointed, but at the same time not really so disappointed—I didn't like hard work, and that seemed like very hard work. Learning to work was one of the hardest things I ever did.

JP: *When you did get a role in productions, what kind of parts were you cast in?*

TRH: Oh, never the lead. I always got the quirky supporting roles, ones where the character popped up and said something memorable or silly at the right time. Sidekick roles. But you can do a lot with those because some of those characters are interesting and pretty deep. A few are better than the lead himself, who is quite often fairly boring. Secondary parts allow the actor to work a broader background into the character. They're very human. Actors like Alan Hale, Jr. made a good living off those roles long before he became the Skipper in *Gilligan's Island*. I still play secondaries. They're fun. Look at Fizban.

JP: *How did you feel when your voice changed?*

TRH: [Chuckling, a warm sound that invites the listener to share his humor.] It was a relief—I didn't have to worry about hitting the high notes any longer.

JP: *But you kept performing. You didn't abandon vocal music like some adolescents do who can't get used to their voices, or who decide singing is for wimps.*

TRH: Oh, yes. It's in my blood. In my teens I was in a trio/quartet that sang folk music in restaurants, mainly Peter, Paul, and Mary tunes, Gordon Lightfoot, John Denver, and occasionally (very occasionally) an original piece. We sort of had a revolving membership—sometimes it was a trio, sometimes a quartet, depending on who was available. And I kept singing at church: solos, in choirs, and in small groups.

JP: *Choosing from musicals and operas, what part have you always wanted to play?*

TRH: [With a smile suffusing his face.] That's easy. Pseudolus from *A Funny Thing Happened on the Way to the Forum*. The part Zero Mostel played in the movie. I think I'd do rather well as Pseudolus.

JP: *Your musical tastes are eclectic. How did you become interested in music?*

TRH: Music has always been part of my life, both at church and at home. Mom and Dad played the radio and records when I was a kid, everything from classical to folk. The music was always there. Dad played piano by ear. I took piano lessons when I was old enough, but I wasn't much at discipline. I practiced, but not as much as I should have. We had a reel-to-reel tape machine, too, and a console stereo later. And we caught whatever musical specials were on TV.

Yes, I actually listen to some country and western music. I'd better—I co-own about a third of this radio station, and all they play is country. Mostly what I listen to is classical, rock, especially from the sixties, seventies, and eighties, and some New Age music.

Music is another way of expressing oneself, a window to the soul. It touches everyone differently. I like classical because it doesn't impose meaning on the listener except for a few pieces, such as *Peter and the*

Wolf. If I had the time, I'd love to develop enough dexterity to play an instrument really well.

I have recently turned out a couple of CDs with my old high school trio. It was fun working on them. I hope to do more.

JP: When did you start composing? What technique you use—do you hear the notes you want to use in your head or visualize them on a piano-type keyboard?

TRH: One summer years ago my dad taught school in Washington state, and my family went, too. On an outing one day, we went up on some mountaintop. I remember running back to the car after seeing the beauty of other mountains and valleys from that peak, clouds and rivers and trees, singing at the top of my lungs. I was making it up as I went. That was the first song I composed. It's a pity I don't remember it.

After my folks bought me a guitar in high school, I began making up my own songs as well as singing and playing anything and everything by Peter, Paul, and Mary. I wrote a song for Laura one Christmas.

We were newlyweds, very poor, and the song dealt with not being able to give her anything that Christmas but the song and my love. It's become a touchstone for us—I sing it every year, and it's grown with new verses as the years have gone along.

My heart sings all the time. The music bubbles up from that, and sometimes I can catch the tune and write it down.

JP: Are writing music and authoring books similar in your thinking?

TRH: Both writing and music are different disciplines—music is highly mathematical in discipline, very different from setting down words and plotting. They have different logics. Their macro rules are different, which means their symbology of expression are different. The ability to play an instrument with sufficient dexterity to accomplish presenting the piece well to an audience or pleasing oneself is similar to touch typing, but still not the same.

JP: When did your interest in games begin?

TRH: Very early. My family was very game-

Tracy Hickman (seated, far left) is a Doo-Bee during his appearance on *Romper Room* at age five on KSL-TV in Salt Lake City, Utah.

oriented: checkers, Monopoly, chess, Life. Games were also a part of family get-togethers. Both kids and grownups played. We loved them, and had good times.

JP: *What were your early years in school like?*

TRH: I started kindergarten at Marlon Hills Elementary, just up the street from our apartment in Ogden, Utah. It was a fairly new school, with modern architecture and the freshest ideas in teaching. Miss Reynolds and Mrs. Barr were the teachers I remember most vividly. Miss Reynolds was a kind, sweet person. Mrs. Barr had a reputation around the playground as the roughest, meanest third grade teacher in school. I remember thinking that if I got in her third grade class, I'd be dead by the end of that

Missing Front Tooth: Tracy Hickman at age six.

year and never see fourth grade. I was wrong: the woman was strict, but influential and generous. I was in her class when President Kennedy was shot. She sent us home that day.

I was a bored student even in grade school. The teachers just never talked about anything that inter-

ested me much. I understood what they wanted me to do, but I chose not to work with the system. I did enjoy AFJROTC in high school, but not history class, even though I was usually fascinated by that subject. Consider the fact my teachers were usually coaches and were plugged into those classes because they needed something else to do besides coach. Very dull. I became particularly interested in World War II and Nazi Germany during high school, did lots of research on it. Something urged me to try and discover why all that cruelty happened, as well as study the inroads people like Wernher von Braun made in rocketry. Getting interested in that period of history scared the beejeebers out of my parents, who didn't understand my motives.

There is an incident that hangs in my memory from grade school. Some of the kids were rocking a portable backstop on top of the hill just east of the school, lifting other children hanging onto the cross bar into the air. I ran to join in the fun, reached for the bar and missed, grabbing the twisted end wires of the chain-link fencing that formed the rest of the backstop instead of the cross bar. I tore open my left hand just below my index finger and ran back to the school to get it treated. A teacher stopped me in the hall and began lecturing me sternly about not being where I was supposed to be. I showed her my bloody hand. She blanched and hustled me to the school nurse. That wound was bad enough the scar from that incident still shows. I must have been in fourth or fifth grade when that happened.

JP: *You became a pugilist for a short while. When was that?*

TRH: Ah, yes. A very short while. My fourth grade year was quite memorable for a number of reasons. Even then I was something of a nerd. I carried a briefcase to school that held my books and pencils. Being picked on was therefore inevitable. My personal tormentor was a red-haired, freckle-faced terror named, believe it or not, Rusty. He used to push me around the playground and the parking lot when I was walking home from school. Rusty wasn't much for words, he mainly just pushed. When I complained about this at home, my dad decided to help. He wouldn't allow his oldest boy to be a wimp. He went out to the store and bought two pairs of boxing gloves, one for me, one for him. On his return, he laced them on my hands, then donned his own pair. "You're gonna have to fight him sometime," he said to me. "You might as well know how to do it." I wasn't so certain this was a good idea. Pain wasn't my strong point. "You won't feel a thing," Dad assured me. "Not while you're in the middle of the fight, anyway."

He showed me how to hold my hands to protect my face, told me to forget about receiving gut punches and concentrate on my opponent's face, and showed me proper fighting stance. I think he learned the majority of his technique from his older brothers, or from athletics when he was a boy. We sparred for several days. I learned the techniques, but still feared the coming event.

It wasn't long after that I ratted on Rusty to my teacher about some infraction or other. He caught up with me after school as I was walking with my friend Steve across the parking lot toward my church, which was practically adjacent to the school grounds. Rusty threatened me, calling me a snitch and a number of other names, then declared he was going to beat me up. Trembling, I handed my brief-case to Steve, turning to face my opponent with my guard up.

To my amazement, Rusty put both fists up on either side of his head, leaving his face completely exposed. His father hadn't taught him anything about boxing. I went for his nose with a seemingly endless series of right jabs, and threw in an occasional left uppercut to his chin just to keep him guessing. It wasn't long before the poor kid was staggering. By that time, a good church woman had noticed what was happening and recognized me. She ran over, waded between us, and stopped the fight. Rusty had a very bloody nose. He staggered off across the playground. The woman delivered me to my mother, who was then at church. Mom took me home. Emotionally spent, I wept like a baby even though I suffered no cuts, no bruises. At least none that I remember.

That was my first and last fight. No one ever bothered the kid with the briefcase again. I learned a lot from that episode, not the least of which was that my father had been right: in the midst of the fight, I never felt a single blow from Rusty.

JP: Wasn't this also the year you decided to write your first book?

TRH: Yes. I had this idea that the way to become a novelist was just to write page after page after page, and when I had enough pages, there would be the book all ready to be printed. I wrote it with pencil on ruled school paper. It's printed in its entirety on my Web page, bad spelling and all, should anyone want to read it. I called the book *The X-1*. I wrote two pages in pencil on ruled school paper, and got stuck so badly on the plot I had no idea how to continue. I did then what so many writers have done over the years—I just signed it "by Tracy Hickman" and let it end. The next time I looked at those pages, though, I knew I'd never be a writer.

Even though I misread my eventual vocation, I think my future was at least somewhat set from that time.

JP: You did better with some poetry than with your first book.

TRH: That's true. This one, written in elementary school, really shows that my interests were turning toward space and science fiction:

Thoughts
I think I'd like to live on Mars,
On any of the neighbor stars;
I'd look down on the earth and see
How very busy folks can be;
I'd watch them running round and round
Intent on looking at the ground.
If I could build a brand new sky
I would not make it half so high,
I'd hang it on the tops of trees
Where I could reach it at my ease,
I'd climb up through the evening bars
And see the wrong side of the stars.

I think it's clear that the same visions expressed in this poem still drive me today.

JP: Is it true your mother introduced you to the Star Trek *television show? How did that happen?*

TRH: It was when we lived in Ogden. I remember coming into the kitchen, and my Mom told me there was a program coming on the television featuring space ships. The beginning of that show with the *Enterprise* flashing across the screen was an amazing moment. I couldn't believe they were going to do a show every week.

JP: When did you move to Las Vegas?

TRH: That was while I was still in grade school, in 1966. My father had accepted a position with the Las Vegas School District. His job was to install an educational television station there. I thought the whole thing was pretty exciting—how many kids can say they're going to live in Vegas? Unfortunately, Dad had to start working almost as soon as he got the job and our house in Ogden had not been sold. Dad lived in a small apartment in Vegas while Mom stayed in Ogden with Gerry and me, trying to sell the house. It took awhile, but in time everything got straightened out. We took up residence on Geronimo Street just off Eastern Avenue in Las Vegas, once again on the edge of town. I liked it there.

The corruption of the Las Vegas School System worked against my father's ethics almost from the start, and he soon found his job impossible. Mom and Dad discussed it. He quit, and we packed up and returned to Utah, moved to the city of Provo, and settled into a split-level house. Dad went back to school to complete his doctorate in broadcast communication.

I finally figured out Dad's philosophy about property. He liked to buy into new tracts where prices were cheaper, and then let the neighborhood develop around him. Later he hoped to sell the house for its appreciated value and buy a bigger house in a location further out on the new edge of town. It was a trade-up philosophy that seemed to work.

JP: When did you become interested in girls?

TRH: Early on. I was actually rather romantically inclined from an early age. My first girlfriend was Lori Dean from my elementary school. She lived directly behind us in Ogden, Utah. Later in elementary school, about fifth or sixth grade, I paired up with Janet Ford. She lived across the golf course from us in Las Vegas. My years at Farrer Jr. High in Provo turned my interest to Joan Layton—I was terribly smitten with her, had a huge crush.

JP: When did you meet Laura Curtis?

TRH: It was during junior high. Laura Diane Cur-

tis. One day I wore a bright pink cardigan sweater to school. [Chuckling.] As I look back on that now, it seems a brave thing in and of itself. Laura took notice of my sweater—it was difficult to avoid its hue—and asked my cousin Heather who I was. She soon moved to Springville, a town several miles

Commanding Presence: Capt. Tracy Hickman in his AFJROTC dress uniform, 1973.

south of Provo, but the seeds of interest had been sewn. The first social event I attended that approximated an actual date was with Laura. It was a winter dance sponsored by the school. Her father drove her to my house to get me, and then to the homes of several of our friends, and delivered all of us to the dance. Laura was the first girl I ever dated, the first girl I ever kissed.

Our early relationship fell apart due primarily to my own stupidity. Over our high school years we dated off and on—mostly off—as our lives bounced through the tumult of teenage folly. I dated several girls during that time, but I was unhappy when Laura and I weren't together. By my senior year, however, I'd gotten myself together after a very difficult time. I found myself seriously pursuing Laura while she pursued me in return.

JP: You must have been about high school age when you moved back to Provo.

TRH: Yes. I attended Provo High School. I became a part of the AFJROTC, the Air Force Junior Reserve Officer Training Corps. I proudly wore my Air Force uniform every Thursday, and thought I looked pretty good in it. I was also in choir, directed by Mr. Barker, and in the Highbrows, an elite madrigal group. And, of course, dramatics. I graduated in 1974.

JP: When did you start your first job?

TRH: Oh, that was in junior high. I started, as so many youngsters do, as a paperboy. Not the most rewarding of endeavors. My first real job was as a stock boy at Allen's Supersave, a grocery store. I proved myself to be abysmal at anything I put my hand to in groceries. It lasted a very short time. This was the first job from which I was ever fired. I don't really blame them—I would have fired me, too. As I walked out of the grocery office with my pink slip, something inside my mind determined I shouldn't return home until I had another job. I went searching, and was hired as an usher at the Paramount Theater in downtown Provo that afternoon. Considering my proclivities for acting and music, that employment suited me far better than stock boy.

JP: What were the Thunderduds?

TRH: That was a bunch of friends who all became glider pilots one summer during the early 1970s. We christened ourselves the Thunderduds. The group included Lynn Alley, Harry Rising, and me. To celebrate this feat, Harry's mother knitted all of us incredibly long scarves. Mine remains a prized possession to this day.

Once a week we drove up Provo Canyon to the little mountain town of Heber, Utah. There our adventures began. Heber had a little airport, altitude 5240 MSL, next to the highway, which was the home of many gliders. It still is. It was also the domain of Dee Winterton, our awe-inspiring but easy-going instructor. He wore a flashy motorcycle helmet when cropdusting because his insurance agent insisted on it. Anyway, we got our training and began soaring.

Those were wonderful days. We sank every dime we could put together on flights, spurred on, no doubt, by that special rivalry that friendship often generates. None of us Thunderduds wanted to be left behind the others. We all started this thing together—it was a real pressure to determine which of us would solo first. Each one of us wanted that honor, and our jokes and digs at each other flew thick as the Saturday approached when every member of the Thunderduds would achieve enough course work and hours to solo. There was some question in our minds as to whether Mr. Winterton would let us go up on our own. Another question we didn't admit was whether any of us were actually ready to try such a stunt without someone experienced to rely on in the back seat of the glider. As it turned out, all three of us soloed the same day.

Two weeks after my solo flight, I drove up to the Heber airport to participate in their glider competition. This seemed the height of dumbness—I had taken only one additional solo flight since Mr. Winterton had decreed me ready and settled me into that glider alone. I can only say that I was young, and that certain aspects of intelligence had not yet dawned in me.

Glider competitions include many fascinating activities, from longest distance to fastest time over a fixed course to altitude contests. All of these were far beyond my capabilities. There was only one contest I could enter: the flour-bombing competition. This is a deceptively simple challenge where the pilot takes a paper sack containing dirt, rocks, and a good amount of flour, and has his passenger drop it out the open window of their sailplane over a designated target, usually on the downwind leg of the landing approach. The closest hit to the target wins.

When I arrived at the airport I wondered why all the experienced glider pilots were sitting around with their aircraft tied down. The winds were heavy, gusty. Older pilots knew better than to fly in such bad conditions. I didn't.

Since I had just soloed, I didn't yet have my "private ticket"—a private pilot's license—and therefore couldn't carry passengers. I took the glider up alone, the flour-bomb wedged between my legs and the rear window of the plane open. I still remember the worried face of Mr. Winterton through the canopy saying "Be careful . . . it's dangerous up there."

I soon figured out why all the smart pilots stayed grounded. The tow plane and my glider barely made headway against the wind as we lifted from the runway. Worse, the passenger window kept banging against the fuselage, and the wind whipped and howled in the cabin. I began singing to myself at the top of my lungs in an effort to calm down, but it didn't help much. Panic made more progress than my plane. I finally released, pulling up and away from the tow plane as the glider slowed. I turned, looking for the target, and felt my stomach flutter—I was flying sideways. The crosswind was pushing me to one side faster than I was flying straight ahead. Frantically I grabbed for the flour-bomb while fighting vertigo, dangerous stuff in a cockpit. I thought the glider had gone vertical. Quickly I sat up straight, let my eyes argue with my inner ear for a moment as I got my bearings, and dumped the flour-bomb out the window. I'd had enough. I no longer cared about the contest; all my concentration was fixed toward getting my plane back on the ground. Only dumb luck allowed that. And I won the contest.

I went on many other flights. I eventually took private lessons in power planes and soloed in single-engine planes, but I still maintain that nothing quite captures the freedom of flight like soaring does.

JP: Quite a few young Mormon men become missionaries, and you were no exception.

TRH: True, but I wasn't expecting the call when it came—it was an Epiphany. I had a good job, and good girlfriend, a good life. In fact, I hadn't planned on being a missionary at all. But it seemed that God wanted me elsewhere and was willing to go to extraordinary lengths to get me there.

I was working in a movie theater as a projectionist at that time. One night I was at work and began pondering what I should do with my life. God essentially tapped me on the shoulder and said, "You're going." I thought, "No." The message came again, much stronger. I couldn't deny it. That next day in November 1974 I submitted my name to become a missionary. It not only was a surprise to me, but also to my girlfriend Laura and to my family. The day after Christmas I got an acceptance letter from the church's President-Prophet Spenser W. Kimball. My

parents picked up the mail that day, saw the letter, and called several of my friends over to watch me open it. I had no idea why all those people were standing around when I got home until my parents handed me the letter with the official church seal. It told me I was to serve in the Singapore-Java Mission. No one at my house had any idea where that was. We had to get out a world atlas and look it up, found out it was most of the way around the world. That was a shock. But that day was a big day in my life.

JP: You had preparatory training for your mission?

TRH: Yes. I continued working my job and getting ready for my mission until March 1975, when I

Dating in the '70s: Tracy Hickman with his future wife Laura Diane Curtis at a high school dance.

became part of the Missionary Home in Salt Lake City. At that time, all missionaries sent into the field were put through a one-week intensive "boot camp" that gave us a basic understanding of what was expected of us. At the end of that week we were allowed to work in the Salt Lake Temple. I love that building. At the end of our session, the new recruits were escorted up to the Assembly Room where our questions were answered—at least those that could be answered were. It's an experience I've cherished since.

JP: Were you pleased at the prospect of going to Indonesia?

TRH: Yes, pleased and scared spitless at the same time. It was quite an adventure. I'd moved a lot as a child, but I'd never been beyond the limits of North America.

After that first week of initiation, the other new missionaries and I were driven to the airport for our departures. Laura was there to see me off, along with my folks, my brother Gerry, and my sister Kim. I was in a daze during that leave-taking. I noticed people around me, but didn't see what they were doing. Only later did I hear how my mother wept for several days after my plane took off. After a stopover in Los Angeles, where my Aunt Donna and cousin Becky took me and my companion Elder Bowers to lunch, we boarded a plane to Hawaii. My family members cried; I'm certain they thought we'd never come home again.

JP: Is this when you began language training?

TRH: Yes. In those days, all LDS missionaries learning Far Eastern languages were sent to Laie, Hawaii for language instruction. The BYU-Hawaii campus had a special dorm set aside for our housing and classrooms. My group included Douglas Middleton, Elder Bowers, Ronald (called Fu) Thompson, Elder Jensen, Elder Barlow, and another man whose name I can't recall. Soon after we got to Laie, it became evident that our mission wouldn't be a normal one. Indonesia—which is the most populous Islamic nation in the world—was notorious for not wanting Christian missionaries in their country. It's actually against the law for anyone to try and actively change anyone else's religion. We couldn't imagine being missionaries without converts. What

would we do when we got there if we strictly followed all the rules? Worse, what would happen to us if we didn't? Moreover, the government repeatedly delayed granting our visas. Without them, we couldn't enter the country.

The normal two-month language training extended to three. We were given temporary positions in the Hawaii mission just to keep us occupied. Eventually we were officially transferred to the Hawaii Mission because the Language Training Mission was moving to Provo, Utah. It was time we got to work.

Ronald "Fu" Thompson and I were assigned to a distant outpost on the island of Maui, a small town on the east shore named Hana. It was like heaven for us, just great. We got settled in and started our missionary duties there. Four weeks later, our visas for Indonesia came in. We scrambled to get ready for our flights, packed up, and were off again. I looked forward to the differences in culture, in people, and was very excited about the whole thing.

It normally takes missionaries two months to get into the country to which they're assigned. It was six months into my two-year stint when our visas finally came through. We took a 747 out of Honolulu as far as Guam, which has to be the mother of all red-eye flights. Then we were put on an old 707 to Singapore. It was very chilly on the plane—I got a head cold. When we were finally over the country, I looked down and was amazed that Singapore was actually beneath me. It was stunning. My world expanded greatly in that moment. We spent two weeks in Singapore trying to straighten our visas, then flew to Jakarta. The gap between my quick education in the language and what was practical there was shown when a person asked me for my ticket and I had no idea what he was saying. The people there are big on tickets. You need tickets for everything, so the word was one of the commonest in the country. Imagine: we didn't know it!

When we took our twenty-six-hour train ride to Surabaya, no one warned us that it would take that long. We were only told to get off the train when it would go no farther, and spend as little of the money given to us as possible. That was a long train ride made worse by hunger, thirst, and the tensions born of going into a situation we knew nothing about. But we had faith that everything would turn out all right. When we finally did disembark, a three-wheeled cab driven by a bicycle with one small man took us and all our luggage to where we were finally going. He complained all the way, trying to get more money out of us. I remember the scents there—spicy smells from cooking, the open sewers, and the redolent canals. There are few buildings over two or three stories tall, and no spaces between the buildings. It's very crowded.

I was in many different places with many different

Flying High: (l. to r.) Tracy's brother Gerry Hickman, Lynn Alley, Judy Rising, Harry Rising III (in cockpit), and Tracy Hickman on the day of Lynn, Harry, and Tracy soloing in sail planes.

people during my year-and-a-half stay in Java. It's a very old culture. The people there have interests and goals very different from people in the United States, but I found them to be consistently generous and warm. They're also very passionate about what they believe. Struggling with the influx of Western values isn't easy for them. I learned to look at my own people through another people's eyes while I was there. And that's a very special education.

I fear greatly for these people now. Their government has been based on the rule of one person for generations. Now he's been removed from office. If a war does come to pass, it will be a great tragedy.

JP: What about your girlfriend Laura during this time?

TRH: Well, we wrote to each other mostly throughout my stay there. Then late in my missionary stint I called home and found out that Laura was engaged to marry someone else. I spent $50 for long distance from Indonesia to the States to get my very own "Dear John" call. All I asked her was whether her fiancé was the best man for her. She burst into tears and we ended the conversation soon after that. When I returned to the United States a couple of months later, I wasn't even certain she'd be there to meet me when I landed in Los Angeles, which was where she'd moved with her invalid mother. But there she was at the gate, looking more beautiful than I remembered and no longer engaged.

My folks had moved to Flagstaff, Arizona, during my mission. I finally had my homecoming with them. Soon after that I was released honorably from my mission to Indonesia. All that training beforehand, as well as everything else that happened, made the brief release meeting finalized with a handshake seem anticlimactic.

I went back to southern California to see Laura before getting a job and registering for college in Utah. Laura didn't want to talk about our relationship because she'd just been through a difficult one that had caused her a lot of emotional pain. Within a week, however, the tune had become "If you ever ask me, it had better be at a romantic place."

It was before we left for a day at Disneyland that Laura's mother, who was bedridden, called me into her room. "Promise me something," she said. "Promise me you won't leave town until you ask my daughter to marry you." Of course I promised. Apparently all those letters I'd written Mother Curtis from Indonesia had done some good.

Mother Curtis then called Laura into her room and made her promise to say yes if I happened to ask her to marry me. We went to Disneyland and decided to have lunch at the Blue Bayou not knowing we had both been set up. I realized it was probably the most romantic place there. My mouth was dry as we ordered lunch. I leaned across the table, took her hand, and said, "Laura, I don't want to ruin your day or anything, but will you marry me?" She choked, pulled me farther across the table, and whispered, "Yes."

That happened, quite by accident, on April Fool's Day. We both laughingly refer to our marriage as an arranged marriage.

JP: When did you become involved with TSR?

TRH: I'd arrived home from my mission in March, got engaged in April, and we married in June. I enrolled at Brigham Young University in Provo, and moved there. My first job during that time was making double-paned windows. After that, I got short-term employment as the production assistant at BYU's motion picture production studio. Then I became a theater projectionist, as well as having a day job as a drill press operator and dark room technician for a genealogical house. Laura worked in the dark room, too. I was made the assistant theater manager, and I also drove a school bus. I had to quit school because we couldn't afford it. We moved to Logan, Utah, where I managed a theater in a mall there. I fell in with a ne'er-do-well partner, and soon found myself out of both a job and money. There was a recession on then, so work was hard to find. I drove a school bus for awhile again, but that didn't work out. Angel and Curtis, my oldest children who were both born while we lived in Utah, couldn't attend church that winter because we couldn't afford their shoes. The church was helping support us at that time. I was desperate.

Laura had introduced me to Dungeons and Dragons soon after we were married, in the fall of 1997. My fascination with that game was all her fault. When we lived in Provo, I rode a bike to work. Laura was supposed to pick me up one night, but she was late. So I biked to where her theater group was meeting, and she said she'd been playing this new game. It had no board and very flexible rules. I thought it sounded stupid. Laura bought me a basic D&D set for my birthday that year. I thought the rules were a mess, but managed to see through them to the heart. It excited me. I went out that night and bought graph paper upon which I designed my own module. Laura instantly regretted giving me that gift because she

became a widow for two months while I finished my first game design. I really wanted a *Monster Manual*, but we couldn't afford it. Laura told me that if I was going to spend that much time designing a game, I was going to have to find a way to make money at it. That's what spurred me to sell our first module.

JP: How did you approach TSR?

TRH: I sent the module to the company with a cover letter. Michael Gray, who worked at TSR, had picked it up from a retailer and was quite impressed. TSR's response to my query was that it would be easier for the company to buy my games if I worked for them. So I offered to go to Lake Geneva, Wisconsin, for an interview. I was picked up at the Milwaukee airport by Dave Sutherland, who I didn't know was head of Research and Development. We had a comfortable talk on the way from the airport, much more relaxed than a more formal office interview. The upshot was that my family and I moved to Lake Geneva in March of 1981, taking three days to drive from Utah to Wisconsin.

I was so excited to have work. And to finally have work I loved to do made it even better.

JP: When did you propose the Dragonlance *project?*

TRH: The original idea had been growing since very early in my experience with D&D. I did eventually buy the *Monster Manual* I wanted with a bit of money from my student loan. I actually created one of my first dungeons in the back row of Motivational Psychology class at BYU because I was extremely bored. You'd think a class with a name like Motivational Psychology would be interesting. I started a series we called "Night Venture" with Laura, selling the first installment under the name "Rahasia." While we were still in Provo I used to run dungeons, too. The original one was called Orthanc, after Tolkien's tower where Sauruman the White lives. I was working with a continent called Mnemen then (which anyone who's read the first *Starshield* book recognizes as the center of the Omnet). As I looked at it, I remembered McCaffrey's *Dragonriders of Pern*. There it was. I wanted to create a world where fighters on dragonback fought other fighters on dragonback.

Laura and I discussed what I could give to my new

work situation after I was hired by TSR. The notion of *Dragonlance* seemed natural. I rewrote our module for "Pharaoh" and came up with three new modules, as well as other role-playing games. All the while thoughts about *Dragonlance* were simmering, growing.

One day the TSR marketing department suggested that the company should do more with dragons. We had plenty of dungeons, they said, but very few dragons in the modules. I proposed a series of twelve game modules featuring dragons. I came up with the title, but I didn't want to do a "dragon of the month" type thing. I wanted a full-fledged world to work with. The difficulty was coming up with a story that covered the twelve modules. I had a meeting with Harold Johnson, and suggested we get additional support from other departments for the whole project. He agreed, and *Dragonlance* was launched. By this time, too, the story was overtaking everything.

We needed graphic assistance. Harold and I pitched the story to the TSR art staff one night in Larry Elmore's basement. They were instantly on our side. The rest of the project I sold very quietly, going from department head to department head and getting each one to agree to the project separately. We had a big meeting soon after this with a short presentation of contributions such as artwork and game design. The project generated lots of excitement.

Believe it or not, problems within the company almost killed *Dragonlance* several times. A number of people felt threatened by the project and tried to undermine it. Another time Harold Johnson came to the game designers and said, "I'm sorry, I have to fire one of you." Bruce Nesmith took Harold into the hall and offered his resignation. I found out later that the person who was supposed to be fired was me. If Bruce hadn't decided that he was the most readily employable of the game designers (he was a computer specialist) and been willing to leave the company, *Dragonlance* wouldn't have gotten as far as it did.

This was a labor of love that involved lots of resources on an unproven project. Its continuance was almost magical.

JP: You mentioned it was nearly killed several times.

TRH: Yes. Harold Johnson came to me one day and said the company was going to have to kill *Dragonlance* after it was established on the market. He claimed it wasn't selling as well as other products. I took a week away from my own duties as a game designer to dig up facts and figures in Accounting and distributed copies to the company. Those figures proved it was selling much better than other products. No one ever mentioned killing it again.

JP: What did you think of Margaret when she joined the project?

TRH: I'm trying to think back . . . it's a long way. Margaret now seems to have been part of my life forever. She was originally assigned as an editor of the books. After a little bit of getting to know her, I thought, "Here's someone like me." All the people who came to this place and this project bore scars from previous experiences and were looking for a home. She found one.

Going on a Mission: Tracy Hickman in his missionary passport photo, 1975

Duet: Margaret and Tracy

JP: *You and Tracy campaigned so hard for the* Dragonlance *project, and your bosses at TSR didn't want anyone within the company doing it. What were the steps you took to nail the contracts for yourselves?*

MW: There was another writer who'd been hired for the project, but he just wasn't working out at all. The whole idea started with Michael Gray, who was on the TSR staff at the time. We'd all get in the *Dragonlance* meetings, and Michael Gray was there too, and we'd get to talking about this other author and how his work wasn't up to what we thought the project deserved. Michael Gray would say, "I think Margaret and Tracy should write the books." He'd pop up and say that every once in awhile in the meetings or wherever: "Oh, I think you ought to let Margaret and Tracy write the books."

I had written a short story for *Dragon* magazine called "Test of the Twins." It was the first story about Raistlin. That got more fan mail than any other short story they'd ever run in the magazine. Everybody was really impressed about that. More than anyone else, Tracy and I realized what the author originally contracted for the books should be doing with the story, but he wasn't capable of writing it. So we took a weekend, and we did the prologue and the first five chapters of *Dragons of Autumn Twilight*. We submitted that to my boss Jean Black the next Monday, and told her we thought we should be the ones to write that book.

Jean sort of rolled her eyes and took the manuscript into her office, saying she'd get back to us. The deadline on this book was really tight—it was already May or June, and the publishing date was August, which meant it had to be ready by the end of July. So we really had to move quickly on this if we were to do anything.

Tracy and I sat in my little cubicle, which was across the aisle from Jean's office. We were both nervous wrecks. Pretty soon Jean's door opened. She stood in the doorway of my cube with the manuscript in her hand. She looked at us and said, "Wow!"

[Margaret laughs.] I still remember her saying,

"Wow. This is just what we were looking for!" Tracy and I said, "We know, we know!" And that very day she fired the other writer. I guess she talked it over with the Blume brothers [who owned TSR at that time—JP], but I'm not sure she did, because in those days the departments at TSR sort of ran themselves. No, I think she did, because they must have given permission to fire this other author and hire us to write the book. We still had to meet the same deadline, and he got to keep the advance. So we got no money for it initially. We had to write it in just a few months and work a full-time job at the same time. Both of us had families to support, so neither could quit to write this book. We did it at night and on the weekends.

TRH: It was wonderful working with Margaret. I told the story, and she typed it into the computer the way it ought to go. It seemed to grow like magic.

MW: And then Random House, TSR's book distributors, threw a fit: "Who are these people? We've never heard of Margaret Weis and Tracy Hickman!" By the time the book was published, Random House had TSR convinced it was going to be a flop. TSR only wanted to print 30,000 copies, but they had to settle for printing 50,000 because that was the lowest print run they could get. Then there was that snag with B. Dalton Bookseller.

The book went to Random House so they could distribute it. And it got out in the hobby stores, but not into the major bookstore chains. We were getting calls for it at TSR because it was generating a lot of interest, and the game had already come out. People were really intrigued with the game—the beautiful artwork, the two short stories about it. One was mine, the other was Roger Moore's story about Tasselhoff. And people just loved that first Tasselhoff story. Our audience knew it was out there somewhere, but nobody could find the book. No one goes to hobby stores looking for books—at least, nobody did in those days. Jean told me to investigate, try and figure out what was going on. So I called a B. Dalton store in Kansas City. And I asked them, just as if I was an interested customer, if they carried the new *Dragonlance* book. "Oh," the manager replied, "We've had so many requests for that. I don't know anything about it or who puts it out. But a lot of people are asking for it." I thanked her very much, and reported to Jean.

Directing Television: Tracy Hickman worked as an Instructional Television Production Assistant from 1977 through 1979.

She said, "This is ridiculous, because Random House is supposed to be telling B. Dalton and the rest of them that the book is available. Get the name of the book buyer at B. Dalton, and we'll send him a letter and a copy of the book." That was really supposed to be Random House's job, but we couldn't let that stand in the way.

I called B. Dalton and asked the operator for the name of the science fiction/fantasy book buyer. She put me on hold, and I thought she'd just come back and give me a name and address. All of a sudden, this guy is answering the phone, "Hello? Hello? This is so-and-so." It was the buyer himself.

I couldn't say, "I'm Margaret Weis and I've written this book." So I said, "Hi, this is Margaret Mnffff," and I garbled my last name. Then I said, "I'm from TSR, and I'm calling about the first *Dragonlance* book that we've published." And he said, "That's the

oddest thing. I just had a call from the head of one of our Kansas City stores, and she was wanting to know where that book is." That was after I called her. So I was just floored. "You know," he said, "I saw an ad for it in *Publishers Weekly*, but I don't know where to get it." And I said, "Oh, you can get it through Random House."

As it turned out, soon after I spoke with that book buyer, TSR got this call from Random House. Oh, they were so sorry, they apologized, the oversight was all a mistake, and they'd just neglected to mention the availability of *Dragonlance* to the chain bookstores. They didn't bother to tell anybody because they didn't think the book would do anything. So anyway, after it got into the chains, it hit the bestseller list soon afterward.

JP: When you finally finished the first book, how did you feel about it?

MW: Oh, we knew we had something good, something that people were going to like. We felt that way about the whole project. The book and the games and the artwork for the calendar had all come together so well that we were just really enthused about it.

TRH: It was a good project, a good world. The time was right for it.

JP: Tracy, your language training and learning to speak conversational Indonesian affected Dragonlance, *didn't it?*

TRH: Yes. I used many of the basics of Indonesian as the language of magic. It gave the books a richness they'd otherwise lack.

JP: The ignoring of Dragons of Autumn Twilight *by Random House was what inspired you to start the Weis and Hickman Traveling Road Show, right?*

MW: That was at the first GenCon I went to, the one in '83 held at the college in Kenosha. It was actually before the first book had come out when we first did the *Dragons of Autumn Twilight* show, the first *Dragonlance* Road Show, because we wanted to drum up enthusiasm for the book. And we certainly did! People were very interested in it after that. That GenCon and our promotion of the first book was another thing that helped launch it, helped get people interested in it.

TRH: You know, when I moved last year I found a whole bunch of the posters we signed and gave away after the play. Wish I'd kept one of the autographed ones.

JP: Whose idea was it to come up with the Weis and Hickman Traveling Road Show?

MW: I'm not sure whose idea it was. It might well have been Tracy's, because he was always very theatrical-minded, always involved in pageants and things like that for his church. It certainly might have been his idea. I know it was at the last minute, because we never did anything else other than things at the last minute.

TRH: I don't remember who came up with the Road Show idea though I did write the first one. I remember we talked about it. And it turned out that nearly everyone close to the project had some theatrical experience: Terry Phillips had been a musician and an actor. We'd gotten him involved with the play-testing, and he's the one who came up with Raistlin's whispery voice. Curtis Smith was our stage manager for a long time; he always got really tense before every show, but with him in the back we always knew lights, music, and everything would cue perfectly.

JP: Margaret called me asking if Gary (then my husband) and I could get involved, what, two weeks before? Three?

MW: It may not have been that much. It wasn't very long before we had to do it.

JP: Must have been at least two, because I arranged Tracy's "Goldmoon's Song" for harp that year and had Debbie Wells record it. Gary played the flute part onstage.

MW: Yeah, that's right.

TRH: We had that great little theater at the Kenosha university.

JP: I packed everything I had that might be appropriate for costumes and flew up about a week before to help coordinate things. I spent the day before we went to the convention making Tracy's costume on a sewing machine borrowed from Laura Hickman.

TRH: I was a little uneasy about you two, but Margaret kept assuring me everything would be all right.

MW: Gary flew up the day before the performance, and we handed him the script when he stepped off the plane. "Here, read this. You're Tanis." He skimmed it in the car on the way back to

my place in Lake Geneva. Good thing he was such an excellent cold reader. We went to the convention with Lizz, David, Gary, Janet, and me packed in my little Toyota.

JP: That was pretty strange, doing all that on such short notice. But somehow we managed. How did you come up with the idea of putting this group together? Who struck you as appropriate for which part?

Spreading the Word: Elder Tracy Hickman in a Morman Missionary in Bandung, Java, 1977.

MW: We just grabbed whoever we could get. We knew from the beginning that Doug Niles would be Flint, there was no doubt in my mind. Some of the people came from the role-playing game because we tended to fall into role-playing mode even when discussing the book. So I knew that Doug would be an excellent Flint. Tracy, of course, was Fizban, there was just no two ways about it. We cobbled together anybody else we could find, of course that's how we

Going Where Other Beards Have Gone Before: Tracy Hickman at the GenCon gaming convention in 1995 demonstrating just where he got the idea for facial hair.

got Harold Johnson involved as Sturm that first year. We pretty well had to use the people we had available to fill all the parts.

It came to the point that we needed two more people to play Tanis and Tasselhoff. And I told Tracy that I knew someone who could do that, and the same with Tass. I said, "I know Janet's a woman, but I think she'll make a really good Tasselhoff. She's got the long hair, she's small, and has an energetic personality." There was just nobody else at TSR. That's why I called you. Roger Moore might have been able to play Tasselhoff, but he was always so involved with *Dragon* magazine and everything else at the convention, we couldn't get him.

JP: Some of us doubled up on roles that year: I played Goldmoon in addition to Tass.

TRH: And I played Caramon and Fizban. Despite only getting one time to run through the whole thing, it worked out very well.

JP: Our infamous "hersels," because we never get to the "re" of rehersals.

MW: Most of us doubled parts out of necessity. And yes, it worked out beautifully.

JP: I remember the audience just stuffed that foyer of the theater afterward, asking us about the book, when it would be out, and where they could get it. The play idea really was a great thing and a lot of fun, even though most of us didn't have much of an idea what we were doing.

After that launch, after the book hit the stores, you immediately started writing the second one, correct?

MW: Not immediately. TSR had no plans to publish *Dragons of Winter Night* until after the first book started selling really well. But when volume one did well, and especially after it hit the *New York Times* bestseller list, of course TSR had to have the next book. We had volumes two and three all plotted out—we knew the plot and knew where it was going—it was just a matter of sitting down and writing it.

JP: How long did you have to write Dragons of Winter Night?

MW: Not very. They wanted to get it out right away, strike while the iron was hot. So I think we had another three months or so to put that one together. But because it was all plotted out, and I mean almost chapter by chapter, that was pretty easy to do because we knew right where we were going. Other than me leaving Elistan out of the first several chapters.

JP: You never liked Elistan. Did you do that on purpose?

MW: I think so, probably because I thought he was so incredibly boring.

TRH: I made her put him back in.

MW: So we had to get that book written and out really quick because people wanted more after reading the first one. It was much the same with volume three, *Dragons of Spring Dawning.*

JP: Meanwhile, the game was selling well?

MW: Yes, it was selling very well. And so was the calendar.

TRH: I was more surprised the second book did better than the first.

JP: *And that meant TSR was starting to make money again at that point. That must have felt like a landslide. You hit the market at exactly the right time, when readers were looking for a Tolkienesque fantasy series—they wanted the depth, the breadth, this totality of world you provided.*

MW: Yeah. Also, Dungeons and Dragons was very hot, too. There was a very strong role-playing market then. Everything we put out upheld the other products, and vice versa.

TRH: It was a good synthesis of products.

JP: *What did the public response do to you, how did it change you?*

MW: It was very overwhelming. We *knew* we had a good product, but we didn't know it would be as successful as it was. And that took a little getting used to.

TRH: I felt like a frog in hot water. Actually, it was a gradual thing with me. I'm still not certain I understand the global scope *Dragonlance* has attained. I try to keep the perspective on everything, however. Michael Crichton's *Jurassic Park* was the biggest runaway bestseller in recent memory, and it only impacted two percent of the market. *Dragonlance* hasn't hit anywhere near that. Although many readers are affected by *Dragonlance* and tell us they're moved by the story, the success came on fairly gradually. I never really felt it. Even now, I'm not sure I understand its scope.

JP: *How did you manage to get used to it? Did you work on changing your mindset in any way, or did you have to sit down and say to yourself, "Okay, this is where it's going"?*

MW: Yeah, I think it was more the latter because getting a book on the *New York Times* bestseller list is something you think might happen after you've been writing for twenty or thirty years. And for it to happen all of a sudden was amazing and more than a little daunting. It's as though just all of a sudden something you aim for, a goal you set for yourself ten or twenty years

down the road, is abruptly there and you've done it. And you think, "Well, what do I do next?" Then it's like, "If the next book I write doesn't make the bestseller list, have I failed?" So it's pretty scary in a way, and it's something you have to live up to, or feel like you have to live up to continually. It really puts pressure on you, much more pressure on you that you don't have when you're writing a book that you hope will sell 15,000 copies. [Laughs, somewhat self-consciously.]

TRH: It was definitely our fans who put us there. We couldn't have done it by ourselves.

JP: *How soon did TSR have to go back to press on* Dragons of Autumn Twilight?

MW: Once the book got out there, people passed around its availability by word-of-mouth. It was a matter of months.

JP: *Were you surprised that* Dragons of Winter Night *did as well or better than book one?*

MW: No, because we knew by then that the audi-

Launching a Legend: Group photo from the first *Dragonlance* reading just prior to the first book's release (l. to r.) Liz Baldwin, Gary Pack, Harold Johnson, David Baldwin, Doug Niles, Terry Phillips (hooded), Tracy Hickman, Janet Pack, Laura Hickman, and Margaret Weis. Taken at the University of Wisconsin, Parkside, 1984.

"Yup, he's dead." Weis and Hickman Traveling Road Show, Dragoncon, Atlanta, 1986 or 1987, (l. to. r.) Gary Pack—Cleric, Janet Pack—Tasselhoff, Tracy Hickman—Fizban, Nicole Harsh—Kitiara, Mike Sakuta—Slain Warrior.

ence was strong and was growing. We were getting letters about the books, about the other products. The following GenCon in 1984 was when the second book came out. And so we got to see a good reaction—everybody that had read the first book that came out after the 1983 GenCon seemed to be at the 1984 GenCon in Milwaukee at the Mecca Convention Hall. We had such a great response that we figured the second book would do at least as well.

JP: And of course that GenCon was the occasion of the second play, with much the same cast as the first year.

MW: Yes. And we'd printed up flyers and sent Lizz around the Dealer's Room handing them out. Again, the Traveling Road Show went over very well.

JP: Dragons of Winter Night was another runaway bestseller, and book three, Dragons of Spring Dawning, certainly held its own against the first two. What catapaulted you into doing the Legends trilogy?

MW: Again, TSR wanted more books, everybody buying Dragonlance wanted more books. Tracy and I had known early on that the story, particularly of Caramon and Raistlin, would continue to go on, that it just wouldn't end with the third book of the first trilogy. And so it was even before we finished writing Dragons of Spring Dawning that we'd suggested the

idea for the next three, the Legends, which they were eager to have. And so we started those.

TRH: We had such a wonderful time writing the Chronicles, the Legends were a natural followup. I knew the story was there. And sales on the first trilogy were such that TSR accepted our proposal.

JP: On much more lenient deadlines, I hope.

MW: No, not really.

JP: So you were writing 400–500 page books every three to four months and holding down a full-time job at the same time?

MW: Yeah. Until . . . I guess about the second book of Legends was when I quit and went freelance. Yes, it was just about at that point. I remember writing the third book at home.

TRH: We both quit at the same time.

JP: Hadn't TSR already given you and Tracy some guff about being prima donnas and all that—they were trying to control you at this point, declaring what you could and could not do?

MW: Uh-huh. They were even talking about refusing to let us work through an agent. Another of their bright ideas was that TSR would become our agent—that any books we wanted to write for anybody else would have to be approved by TSR. That was completely unacceptable. I'd had Ray Puechner as my agent long before I ever went to work for TSR, and I wasn't about to stop that relationship. Tracy and I weren't the only ones having problems with this; the artists were, too. Larry Elmore, Keith Parkinson, and Clyde Caldwell had become well-known enough that they wanted to break out, wanted the freedom to do work for other companies. In fact, it was Larry doing the cover for Bantam for the first Darksword book that got him called on the carpet. TSR upper management told him in no uncertain terms that he would not work for anyone else, or if he did, he wouldn't have a job any longer at TSR. And he said, "Well, fine, I quit." And Keith quit not long after that.

TRH: TSR just couldn't handle what was happening. What they should have espoused to become is a talent farm giving new talent a venue in which to create. Both of us felt like TSR was missing the point—we were of tremendous value by that time, and the company treated us as though we were still $18,000 per year employees without sellable names. It was frustrating. It wasn't as though we were demanding New York wages or royalties. We weren't.

JP: So TSR lost some of their best creative people during 1986, correct?

MW: Yes. Their attitude was—if you don't do what we want, you can leave, and we go can find somebody off the sidewalk that can do every bit as well. Instead of capitalizing on the names that they had and promoting them, they tried to get rid of anyone who made a reputation. They tried to replace you, because they didn't want anybody to be indispensable. And so instead of boosting people's reputations, encouraging them to do creative things and playing that to their own advantage, they kept slamming you down.

JP: How did the concept for Darksword start?

MW: Tracy and I were talking about other ideas for other books. In Dragonlance, Raistlin's story in particular had been about a man who began in light and goes toward the darkness. And so we thought it would be neat if we told the story of Joram, a man who's in darkness and goes toward the light. Tracy came up with the idea for a world where magic was the standard of life, the accepted norm, and technology or not having magic was outside the norm and something to be feared. It was a fun world to work in. The story was darker than Dragonlance.

JP: Did this cause you some concern about how your fans would accept it?

MW: Not me, but that's one reason TSR rejected it. They thought it too dark. So that made it easy to take the idea to Bantam Books.

TRH: It was a great story, one that just grew naturally between us. I thought it could do well.

JP: Was sending the manuscript to Bantam your idea, or your agent Ray Puechner's?

MW: It was Ray's. Ray didn't know any editors in the fantasy and science fiction industry. But he did know the Western editor at Bantam. So Ray sent the

Darksword proposal to the Western editor, and asked him to walk it down the hall to whoever it went to. So this guy walked it down to Lou Aronica, who at that time was head of the Bantam science fiction and fantasy department. The Western editor put it on Lou's desk. Aronica knew our names from the bestseller list, and had been thinking these would be good writers to get for the Bantam line. And so he had the manuscript on his desk for twenty minutes before he called Ray and told him Bantam wanted the project.

JP: Serendipitous.

MW: Yeah. But even then, people in the publishing industry hadn't heard of us. Lou Aronica took the book into a committee meeting and announced, "We've got Margaret Weis and Tracy Hickman!" and everybody else said, "Who? Is this a good thing?"

I really think the sale of this contract was what proved to me we were getting successful.

JP: Dragonlance was particularly about dragons, as well as elves, humans, monsters, and other races, and how they did, or didn't, get along. Before that time, dragons had previously been mainly evil characters until Anne McCaffery wrote The Dragon Riders of Pern series. Your dragons are both good and bad. What inspired this?

MW: The Dungeons and Dragons system. Well, in D&D I remember there was always an evil dragon, but I'm not certain there were good ones. That was Tracy's main emphasis on the whole plot—that there would be a war between dragons and a world where this war was going on, and the races on that world were just sort of caught in the middle. It was his idea for the three-part good, neutral, and evil-influenced dragons. There are neutral dragons, too.

JP: I've just heard that there's a new Dragonlance project in the works. Care to divulge?

TRH: We've been in and out of the project over the intervening years since we told the original stories, usually out. Dragonlance suffered during TSR's troubles, particularly the recent ones. [TSR's debt became so large that they were unable to pay their freelance artists and authors during part of 1996 and half of 1997. The company was bought out in June 1998 by Wizards of the Coast and moved to Renton, Washington—JP.] The direction of our book *Dragons of Summer Flame* was misunderstood. With the demise of the old TSR and its sale to Wizards of the Coast, we see an opportunity to heal these wounds without using cheap devices. *Dragonlance* is currently in a place we're not comfortable with. There is an opening to do something extraordinary. I recently told a meeting of the *Dragonlance* committee at the headquarters of Wizards of the Coast that Margaret and I should come back to the project, that we should be hired as consultants for the project. There was quite a struggle coming to an understanding of relationships in this new creation. I detailed what Margaret and I could do for the company, but everyone was apprehensive at first. Their fears vanished during the last hours of the meeting. I finally said, "Let me tell you a story," and I related what had actually happened to Krynn as opposed to what everyone thought had happened. Margaret's eyes were shining when I was done. Peter [Adkison, president of WotC] was practically bouncing in his chair.

We proposed a new trilogy, and figured out in the next two days of further meetings how all the product could come together again. The excitement and enthusiasm reminded me of the early days of *Dragonlance*. It recaptured much of the same spirit the project had so long ago when we began it.

MW: I think it's going to be a lot of fun. Tracy just came up with a stunning idea about the world of Krynn, and it's going to be really cool to watch it unfold.

JP: Can you tell us a little more about it?

MW: We're returning to the *Dragonlance* world in a new trilogy called *War of Souls*. Krynn has entered the Fifth Age, the Age of Mortals. Forty years have passed since the Chaos War, when the gods departed. Cruel and powerful dragons have seized control of Ansalon, dividing up the continent among them and demanding tribute of the people they have enslaved. Heroes of the past age have gone to their well deserved rest. New heroes have taken their place to continue the battle against the dragons and other forces of evil. But the battle is faltering. It seems that evil must prevail.

In the first book, *Dragons of a Fallen Sun*, change—for good or for ill—comes to the world. A

violent, magical storm sweeps over Ansalon, bringing flood and fire, death and destruction to all parts of the continent. Out of the tumult rises a young woman who will have a profound effect on the future of Krynn, a future that is strangely and inextricably bound to a terrifying mystery in Krynn's past.

We think it's a great story and we're really excited about it.

JP: The sale of the seven-volume Death Gate Cycle *was what made you both convinced of your success, correct?*

MW: For me, it was the signing of the *Darksword* contract with Bantam that spelled success. It meant that a major publishing house was interested in our work.

JP: People always want to know how you two work together.

TRH: I usually tell fans that I do the adjectives, Margaret does the nouns, and we vote on the verbs.

MW: It used to be Tracy created most of the world and told me the story, and I'd take notes and go to my computer and write it. If I had questions, I'd contact him.

TRH: But things change, especially since we've been writing together now for well over a decade. That's why her name always appears on the books first. She was the one hoping for a writing career. I hoped to be a game designer for the rest of my life. We still occasionally write the way we used to: basically it's talking through the plot, then I spin stories. Then we talk through the stories, and Margaret takes notes. I'd do maps, geography, history, social structures, etc., while Margaret got started on the book. I fed the background material to her as soon as I could. When she finished a manuscript, she'd pass it to me for a read-through, and I'd fill in the holes she'd left marked with "Describe this" or "Explain this." Margaret did the final pass through the book before we submitted it to the editor. And by the way, much to Margaret's credit and her own experience as an editor, our editors have commented many times on how clean our manuscripts are when they come in, how little they have to change.

As our lives evolved, the circumstances have

changed—Margaret now has more story duties, and I do more writing. I worked on the second book of the *Starshield* series at the same time she worked on the first book of our new project with artist Larry Elmore, *Sovereign Stone*.

[Chuckling.] You know, I still really like surprising Margaret with how the story twists.

JP: Margaret has a new coauthor in her husband Don Perrin. Tracy, how did you have to adjust to him?

TRH: I had to come to terms with another man, another coauthor, in Margaret's life. We've been the dearest and closest of friends as well as workmates for a long time. To a limited extent, we lived each other's lives. Margaret's life has not been easy; she had to overcome many personal trials. I felt from the time I met her and we began working together that I'd be there for her through good and bad. We were never more than friends, of course. I was, however, quite torn when she started seeing Don Perrin. My main concern was that I didn't want her to be hurt, especially after all the trials she'd already been through.

I was greatly honored to preside at Margaret's marriage to Don in August of 1997, but I hurt also because there would be another man in her life on a professional basis. It was a bittersweet experience. Some fans have even told me that they thought we'd split up, that we aren't working together anymore because they'd seen Don's name associated with Margaret's. That's not true. Margaret and I maintain a professional coauthorship, and Don and Margaret main their professional coauthorship. It's something Margaret wanted very much because Don can contribute his military experience to their books different from the situations in ours.

Sometimes I think we're still trying to work out a new relationship, a change of dynamics. Nothing like this is black and white, so it will take a while. But I'm confident things will work out.

JP: Margaret, you were diagnosed with breast cancer in 1993. How did you continue to write under that terrible shadow of disease?

MW: Basically the work was really good for me. It kept my mind off worrying about my condition. The chemotherapy wasn't really too bad—they've got the

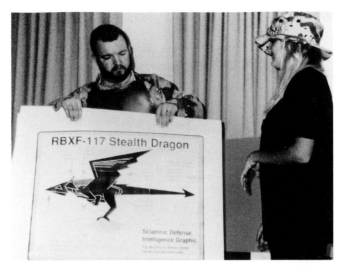

Tracy Hickman, Elizabeth (Lizz) Baldwin (Margaret's daughter), GenCon 1991, Milwaukee, Wisconsin.

medicines now that help you get over the illness that used to be associated with chemotherapy. I was only really sick once during the entire time I was on chemo. I'd be nauseated for a couple of days after the treatments, but once I got over that, I really didn't feel too badly. The only thing was that I lost all my hair—my eyebrows and everything. But I kept myself entertained with a series of hats while it grew out again. That was manageable. And I found out I really like it short, so I keep it this way now. I exercised regularly, and I kept working. I don't know that the work I did during that time was particularly good, but it kept me going. I was working on the last book of the *Death Gate* series.

JP: For the last few years, your doctors have given you a clean bill of health. To what do you attribute your optimistic attitude during your bout with cancer?

MW: I had very good doctors, in whom I have the utmost confidence. I have a lot of faith in their recommendations for treatment, which have since, according to the studies I've read, been proven out. The combination chemotherapy-radiation, the use of the radical chemotherapy as opposed to just mild chemotherapy, all of that, at least in my case, seemed to have worked.

JP: Tracy, what was your reaction to hearing your coauthor had cancer?

TRH: I was devastated. Also very concerned about Margaret. Lots of things ran through my head at that time, such as her cancer having put a gun to the head

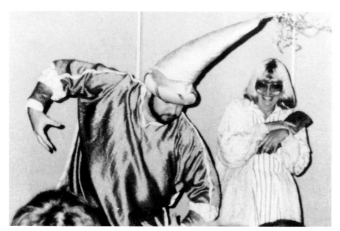

Margaret Weis and Tracy Hickman as "Fizban," GenCon 1991, Wilwaukee, Wisconsin.

of my career. I began wondering how I'd provide for my family, as well as how Margaret was going to take care of her own situation. There I was out in the western part of the United States in Flagstaff, Arizona—there wasn't much I could do except offer consistent moral and emotional support, and pray for my friend. This wasn't something she could solve in a weekend; it would take much longer. I like to charge in and fix things, but there are times when charging in gets in the way. I knew this was one of those times.

I'm greatly relieved that Margaret's doctors have said she's cancer-free over the intervening years, but having gone through that agony once, I understand that for her the specter of that disease is always there. The shadow always follows her. I think about that and worry about her from time to time. Margaret is a very strong lady, like fine steel that's been tempered in the crucible of the situations she's been through. She'll make the best of whatever comes along.

JP: If you had to name your most favorite character in any of your many books, who would it be?

MW: Lady Maigrey from *Star of the Guardians*. I think because she's who I'd like to be, a very courageous woman. I really hesitate to name my favorite character—Raistlin's also one of my favorites. Saying this one or that one is my favorite is very much like forcing a parent to name his or her favorite child. They're all different and have their own elegance or clumsiness, their own faults, their peculiar quirks. They're all individuals who tell their own stories in their own ways.

TRH: Fizban has been with us in nearly all our books. He's a touchstone for us. That character has depth that no one understands, there's always a side of him that no one sees. Just like me. People often look at me and see a prima donna author, or a ruthless businessman. Others see a wizard. There must be some of all of those elements in me, but no one completely knows me. And thus Fizban, Zifnab, or whatever his name is, will continue revealing himself to our readers in future novels.

JP: What's the most recurrent theme in your books?

MW: Probably that people are responsible for their own actions. You might blame it on fate or the gods or something else, but ultimately you are the one responsible for all your actions. This is part of a deep philosophy that runs throughout all our plots. It ties the characters to the reality of their situations.

TRH: You know, sometimes I worry about our books sounding the same because they all have the same theme. In *Dragonlance*, good redeems its own. Evil feeds on itself. Not to say that it always loses; it doesn't. Evil is an entropic, chaotic thing. Then there's order, a dynamic motion between forces that gives movement to the universe. Our books always contain these themes.

JP: Tracy, how does your religion impact your writing and your life?

TRH: Everything I do is my religion. There is no part of my religion that is not my life, and no part of my life that is not my religion. I live what I believe, and write what I believe. Otherwise I'd be a hypocrite. This doesn't mean I'm the best at living it because I'm always learning lessons in humility.

JP: Margaret, do you think Tracy's strong religious background makes your books better, or just different?

MW: I think it helps with the worlds we're writing, We're always interested in the interplay between man and the gods, the universe, or whatever. It makes for a deeper story, one that seems more real to the readers.

JP: You've both stretched into some different business ventures lately: Margaret, you co-own The Game Guild in Lake Geneva. Tracy, you've become involved in co-owning a radio station with your father as well as other things. Anything else expected in the near future?

MW: [Laughing.] I'm helping with *Sovereign Stone RPG.* That's lots of fun.

TRH: Business is not what I want to be in. I don't like warehousing, inventories, or accounting beyond the figures in my own checkbook. I'm not an enterpreneur. I like making cool stuff. Currently, I'm getting out of the businessess I have no business being in. The radio station is a family business, so I'll keep that. And the *StarShield* project will continue. I want to be in the middle of developing new things I'm excited about, things that are creative.

JP: One of the things about your writing is that after you've finished one book, you seem to only let slip a matter of hours before picking up the next one. And you go from the former world to the newer one apparently without difficulty. How do you make the switch?

MW: Actually, I usually give myself a couple of days to switch worlds, and also to clean up. Usually during one book my desk gets really cluttered with stuff, with notes that I keep. I hate to clean up in the middle of a book because I end up throwing away important notes about plot and characters and such. So I take a couple of days to get over one world, to get out of one world, and catch up on all the stuff I've needed to do before I start another one. And I think that just the fact that the worlds become very real to me helps. So it's like leaving New York and arriving in Kansas City—when you're in Kansas City, you don't feel like you're in New York anymore.

TRH: For me, it's not so much a question of time as effort. I can change the world I'm currently working in for another on a moment's notice, but I prefer the notice. I like to work on one thing per day: if that thing has to change, often what I've been working on blows up.

JP: Margaret, what do you think of the new Sovereign Stone trilogy?

MW: [Her voice warms.] Oh, I think it's a really neat project. I'm excited to be working with both Tracy and artist Larry Elmore. We're viewing typical fantasy races such as orks, elves, humans, and dwarves in unique ways.

A couple of years ago, Larry Elmore (well-known fantasy artist and a friend) sat down one night at dinner and told Tracy, me, and my husband Don Perrin a story. The story was of a fantasy world where powerful knights in magical armor battled knights who were living yet dead, brought back to life by an evil artifact and a man who proclaimed himself Lord of the Void.

The world Larry described is a world of elves, humans, dwarves, and orks. The elves are highly disciplined, with strict codes of honor and sworn loyalty to family and their ruler, the Divine. The dwarves are pony-riding nomads, who never spend more than two sunsets in the same place and who believe that the gods have promised that all the world will someday be theirs. The orks are seafarers, traders, and pirates. They are the engineers of the world. The humans are the most diversified of the races, with tribes of barbarians in the north and centers of culture and civilization in the south.

Weis and Hickman Traveling Road Show Principals: GenCon 1991, Milwaukee, Wisconsin (l. to r.) Janet Pack—Tasselhoff, Mike Sakuta—Lord Soth, Nicole Harsch—Kitiara, Margaret Weis—Narrator, Gary Pack—Tanis, Tracy Hickman—Fizban.

Into this world comes the magical Sovereign Stone. Given to the races by the gods, the Stone allows for the creation of Dominion Lords, knights who will help keep the peace among the united races. But mistrust and suspicion run deep, fomented by the Lord of the Void and his army of undead Vrykyl. Now the human portion of the Sovereign Stone is missing and the Lord of the Void has returned from the dead to find it.

The first book in the Sovereign Stone series, *Water from the Well of Darkness,* details the life of Prince

Dagnarus, his quest for power and his ultimate plunge into the dark well of the Void.

JP: If you were both writing your autobiographies at this moment, what would you call them?

TRH: I'd call mine *A Work in Progress*. It's up to me to better myself as well as those around me. I believe strongly in the immortality of the soul. I'm very grateful for that immortality. I'd love to compose symphonies, be an accomplished musician, study history in all its diversity, study mathematics and physics. Given enough time, a person can do all that. With eternity before me, I'm certain I'll achieve many of the things I haven't yet had time to study.

MW: Mine would be called *The Game is Afoot!* Hearkening back to my interest in Sherlock Holmes, obviously.

JP: Everybody always asks this in fan letters and at conventions: What's the best advice you give to a neophyte writer?

MW: Be patient. The advice Ray Puechner used to give, which is the best advice I've heard, is that it takes ten years to break into whatever market you want to write in. That's ten years from when you first seriously start writing until you're finally published. You've got to give yourself that time. You can't be downcast over a single rejection, you've got to keep going on, keep writing, keep sending your work to editors, even though you're going to get lots of reje-

Don Perrin, Margaret Weis, Tracy Hickman, Margaret and Don's wedding, August 5, 1997.

tions. You've just got to give yourself the time. And, like Gary Paulsen used to say, don't quit your day job.

TRH: Read everything you can get your hands on. Read for style, content, plot, characterization. And write every day, whether you feel like it or not. Type out your words, get them on paper. Come to terms with the necessary discipline and keep trying no matter what.

3 Characters, Places, and Things in the *Death Gate Cycle*

by Margaret Weis and Tracy Hickman

A CONCORDANCE BY JEAN RABE

Into the Labyrinth, Volume VI   STEVE YOULL

 ach entry in the concordance is followed by an abbreviation that indicates the novel in which it appears:

DW: *Dragon Wing*, Bantam hardcover, February 1990; Bantam paperback, November 1990
ES: *Elven Star*, Bantam hardcover, November 1990; Bantam paperback, August 1991
FS: *Fire Sea*, Bantam hardcover, August 1991; Bantam paperback, March 1992
SM: *Serpent Mage*, Bantam hardcover, April 1992; Bantam paperback, April 1993
HC: *The Hand of Chaos*, Bantam hardcover, April 1993; Bantam paperback, December 1993
IL: *Into the Labyrinth*, Bantam hardcover, December 1993, Bantam paperback, July 1994
SG: *The Seventh Gate*, Bantam hardcover, September 1994; Bantam paperback, October 1995

Characters who go by only their first names are listed alphabetically under their first names. Characters who have last names are listed by their last names first, such as: Blackthorn, Hugh.

Abarrach

The World of Stone, Abarrach includes the realms of Kairn Necros, Kairn Telest, the Underworld, and the Celestial Sea. When the Patryn Haplo journeys to Abarrach, he observes that the world is like a piece of cheese populated by mice. "It's filled with caverns like this one in which we're standing. These caverns are enormous. One single cave could easily hold the entire elven nation of Tribus. Tunnels and caves run all through the stone world, crisscrossing each other, delving down, spiraling up." The dead outnumber the living in Abarrach. Necromancers bring the deceased back to some semblance of life so they can serve as soldiers and laborers. Eventually, the dead rebel to conquer the living. Then the dead seek to leave the world to slay the living elsewhere. (FS, IL, SG)

Accursed Blade

The Sartan-designed weapon is intended for use by humans, elves, and dwarves against Patryns. Hugh the Hand is given such a blade to use; it was stored in the Brotherhood of the Hand's weapons vault. The blade blocks an opponent's ability to detect danger, and it eliminates an enemy's chance to retaliate against it. Finally, the blade studies an opponent's strengths and weaknesses, and takes on a life of its own when it attacks. The weapon can be controlled by outside forces, such as by the evil dragon-snakes. The Sartan Alfred believes more than one of these weapons was forged.

One account of the Accursed Blade reads: "The knife felt strange in my hand. It quivered, as if it were a live thing. And suddenly, when I started to thrust it playfully at my brother, the knife squirmed like a snake and I held—not a knife, but a sword. And before I knew what was happening, the sword's blade had passed clean through my brother's body. It pierced his heart."

When Alfred is captured by a red dragon in the Labyrinth, Hugh the Hand effects a rescue by hurling the blade at the dragon. The Accursed Blade turns itself into a wingless, sparkling blue-green dragon. Hugh, Alfred, and Marit run from the cave, not wanting to wait for outcome of the dragon fight. The blade appears minutes later on Hugh's belt. See "Blackthorn, Hugh" for more information. (IL, SG)

Agah'ran

The two-hundred-year-old emperor of the elves is doted on by slaves and advisors. Called Exalted One, Your Radiance, and His Imperial Majesty, he is an "extraordinarily handsome elf" who hides his features beneath thick makeup. Though he is brilliant and cunning, he plays a fop who must be constantly waited on and carried about his palace. When Bane is brought before Emperor Agah'ran, the pair begins scheming to eliminate King Stephen and Queen Anne, Bane's "parents." The assassinations would allow Bane to inherit Volkaran and Ulyndia in the world of Arianus. The emperor's advisor believes Bane would hand Volkaran to the elves as payment for their involvement. See "Bane" for more information. (HC)

Alake

This human girl is a sorceress of the Third House and the daughter of the chieftain of Phondra. She counts the dwarf Grundle and the elf Sabia as her best friends. Alake is tall, with ebony skin and black hair braided with beads that clack together musically. When the dragon-snakes demand the eldest daughters of Chelestra's rulers, Alake and Grundle sneak away on a ship to give themselves up—confident that they will be saving their people. Devon accompanies them, disguised as his betrothed, Sabia. When Alake attempts to summon dolphins to chat with during their sea voyage, she instead discovers Haplo, with whom she is instantly smitten. Alake is slain by the dragon-snakes when she and her friends follow Haplo. See "Sabia," "Heavybeard, Grundle," "Devon," and "Haplo" for more information. (SM)

Ander'el

The Tribus elf captain met an untimely death by getting drunk and wandering off into a harsh storm. However, some of his men question his passing, knowing that the captain could always hold his liquor, and wondering if his replacement, Captain Sang-drax, somehow engineered the death. (HC)

Ancient

On the island of Skurvash, an old man called the Ancient admits Hugh Blackthorn and Iridal to the Brotherhood's castle. The Ancient claimed to know Hugh for twenty years and said he taught Hugh how to kill with a knife. (HC, IL)

Andor

The dark-skinned SeaKing is introduced trussed up against a tree with the smuggler Roland Redleaf. Andor is the sole survivor of a caravan that had been attacked by forest giants, or tytans. Answering a "call of nature" when the attack occurred, he was spared—but subsequently captured by the giants and questioned about a mysterious citadel. He is slain when one of the tytans, without warning or provocation, slams a tree branch into his head, splitting his skull. (ES)

Anna

She appears corpselike in a crystal cocoon. Alfred the Sartan loved the woman. When Alfred and Haplo pass through the gate to Abarrach, the World of Stone, the pair trade memories. Haplo, as if he were Alfred, reaches out and rests his hand on Anna's cocoon, tracing the outline of her face. (FS)

Anne of Winsher

Together with her husband, Stephen of Pitrin, she formed an army that overthrew the elves and literally hurled them off Volkaran and Uylandia. She and Stephen proclaimed themselves queen and king of the Volkaran Isles and the Uylandia Cluster in the world of Arianus. About a year after Hugh the Hand takes Bane away, and the boy is believed dead, she and Stephen have a daughter. (DW, HC)

Antius

In the Labyrinth, the Runner Haplo is pointed to Antius, a young Squatter. Haplo is told Antius spent the night with Marit, a woman the Runner was fond of and was searching for. Haplo immediately gives up his search for the woman and does not question Antius. Haplo had held hands with Antius as part of the audience in what passed for a wedding ceremony in the Squatter community. See "Squatters" and "Runners" for more information. (ES)

Argana

Argana was a powerful sorceress, a village shamus, and a member of the Council of Magi on Chelestra. She was among one hundred and twenty villagers who were killed by dragon-snakes. Despite her magical skills, she could not stop the attack on her village. "Around her dismembered corpse lay the tools of her magic, spread about her as if in mockery," says Delu, wife of the Phondra chieftain. (SM)

Arianus

The World of Air was created when the Sartans split the universe. Arianus is made up of three levels of floating continents. The Low Realm belongs to the dwarves, called Gegs, who serve and operate a great machine named the Kicksey-winsey. The Mid Realm belongs to humans and elves, with the latter controlling the water supply that comes from the Kicksey-winsey. The High Realm was ruled by a powerful wizard who was plotting to take over the Mid Realm. However, the wizard is slain by the assassin Hugh the Hand. The lands of Arianus include Geg's Hope, Drevlin, Terrel Fen, the Maelstrom, Arista-gon, Uylandia, the Volkaran, Hesthea, Sharthea and Shegra. See "Kicksey-winsey" for more information. (DW, ES, FS, HC)

Baltazar

The necromancer serves Kairn Telest's king. His skin is "dead white," almost translucent from spending all of his time inside studying. His jet-black hair is considered rare among his people, who have white hair with brown ends. Baltazar explains to the king and council of Kairn Telest that their realm is dying and they must seek the safety of another realm—Kairn Necros. They eventually heed his words and strike off toward Necropolis in Karin Necros, the largest city in Abarrach. When the dead overrun the city and slay Kairn Telest's refugees, Baltazar is one of the last of his people left alive. He attempts to flee the realm with Haplo. However, the Patryn refuses to take the necromancer on board his dragonship and leaves him stranded on the dying world. (FS, SG)

Balthazar

An elderly mysteriarch in New Hope, the capital of the High Realm, Balthazar was one of the council members who voted the evil wizard Sinistrad their leader. (DW)

Bane

Prince of the Volkaran Isles and the Uylandia Cluster, Bane is ten years old when the saga begins. He is described as "small for his age, with large pale blue eyes; a sweetly curved mouth; and the porcelain-white complexion of one who is kept protectively within doors." Bane was switched with Queen Anne's real son the day after she gave birth, and neither Anne nor Stephen feel comfortable in the boy's presence. King Stephen directs the assassin Hugh the Hand to take Bane far away and kill him. However, Bane later turns the tables and tries, unsuccessfully, to kill Hugh. Bane's real father, Sinistrad, summons the child to his High Realm home. There, Bane discovers just how evil his father is and attempts, again unsuccessfully, to kill him.

Haplo takes Bane to Nexus and presents him to Xar. There, Bane and Xar study the Kicksey-winsey, and Bane begins to think of the Lord of the Nexus as his grandfather. He attempts to get Xar to distrust Haplo. Xar eventually directs Bane to return to Arianus and take control of the Kicksey-winsey. However, during the journey, Bane is taken by the elves. When Bane is brought before the elven emperor, the pair begins scheming to eliminate King Stephen and Queen Anne. That act would allow Bane to claim Volkaran and Ulyndia. The emperor's advisor believes Bane would hand the elves Volkaran as payment for their involvement.

Bane travels to King Stephen's castle and there attempts to kill the man so he can inherit the realm. Though he wounds Stephen, Bane is killed by Iridal, his real mother, and Stephen recovers. See "Iridal" and "Xar" for more information. (DW, HC)

Ban'glor

The Tribus elf lieutenant serves Captain Sang-drax. Ban'glor, Sang-drax, and a contingent of Tribus elves descend on Drevlin in the Low Realm of Arianus. The elves want desperately to gain the secret of the Kicksey-winsey. See "Kicksey-winsey" for more information. (HC)

Barkwarm

Humans and dwarves consider the hot drink restful, but elves regard it as a mild narcotic and a sedative. Barkwarm is concocted by boiling the bark of a ferben bush. (DW)

Bethel

The duke of Necropolis explains that Bethel was a sorceress who claimed to know a way off Abarrach. The world had begun to wither, and she volunteered to take those with her who wanted to escape. Kleitus VII would not allow Bethel and her followers to abandon the world. However, she defied him and led her people across the Fire Sea, preparing to leave anyway. She was betrayed and captured. Bethel managed to escape and flung herself into the magma to prevent her body from being brought back to some semblance of life. (FS)

Black Coffer

Inside the stronghold of the Brotherhood of the Hand is a vault called the Black Coffer. It is filled with special weapons, including enchanted ones. Hugh the Hand is shown to the vault and given a magical dagger called the Accursed Blade that could help him kill Haplo. The assassin had prided himself on never needing a magical weapon before. (IL)

Blackbeard

The dwarf, Drugar, also goes by the nickname Blackbeard. See "Drugar" for more information. (ES)

Blackthorn, Hugh

An assassin, Hugh the Hand is introduced as a prisoner tied to a cart pulled by an enormous bird. "The man's appearance alone was striking enough to arrest the eye and send a shiver over the skin. His age was indeterminate, for he was one of those men whom life has aged beyond cycles. His hair was black without a touch of gray . . . A jutting nose, like the beak of a hawk, thrust forward from between dark and overhanging brows." Hugh was raised by Kir monks after his mother died. He ran away from the monastery when he was sixteen. The first man Hugh killed was his own father. "I spoke my mother's name, told him where she was buried, and stuck the blade in his gut."

Hugh was accused of killing Rogar, Lord of Ke'lith on Arianus, and is rescued from the executioner's block by a messenger of King Stephen. The king offers Hugh his life in exchange for one task: killing Prince Bane. Hugh is directed to take the child far away and then perform the deed. During the course of the journey, Prince Bane tries unsuccessfully to kill Hugh. Later, when Bane's attempt to kill his real father, Sinistrad, fails, Hugh fights the wizard and eventually kills him—though he appears to also die. Alfred the Sartan manages to revive Hugh with a necromantic spell—turning him into a man who cannot die and who cannot kill.

Haunted, Hugh returns to the Kir Monastery, where he attempts to shut himself away from all people. His self-imposed exile is not long-lasting. Iridal, the true mother of Bane, arrives and seeks his help in finding her son. After Bane is found, Hugh makes an offhanded promise to the boy that he will assassinate Haplo. The keepers of the Citadel of the Albedo in the Mid Realm argue that Hugh must enforce this contract. Hugh is given a magical weapon by the Brotherhood to aid in his endeavor. However, he is not able to fulfill the contract, as he can kill no one.

Hugh is allowed to die when his companions reach the Seventh Gate. He falls helping defend Patryns in the Labyrinth from the chaodyn. See "Iridal," "Haplo," "Citadel of the Albedo," and "Brotherhood of the Hand" for more information. (DW, HC, IL, SG)

Blackthorn, Perceval

According to records in the Kir Monastery, Sir Perceval Blackthorn of Blackthorn Hall was Hugh the Hand's father. Perceval refused to acknowledge the boy and never married Hugh's mother. Hugh killed him shortly after he ran away from the monastery. (DW)

Bolttightner, Limbeck

A Geg, or dwarf, Limbeck is marked for execution at the same time Hugh the Hand is scheduled for beheading. Limbeck is the leader of WUPP—Worshipers United for Progress and Prosperity. He escapes his fate with the aid of a "bird contraption" that does not fly properly. Shortly after Limbeck lands, he discovers and rescues Haplo and his dog. Limbeck accompanies Haplo, Hugh, Alfred, and Bane to the High Realm. And when he returns home he is named High Froman of Drevlin—the leader of the dwarves of Arianus. (DW, HC)

Bond, James

The wizard Zifnab often forgets who he is. On Pryan, he thinks himself James Bond, and believes he must watch out for his enemies Goldfinger and Dr. No. Zifnab's dragon ally agrees that the wizard can be Bond this day. When Zifnab travels to Chelestra, he alters his appearance and introduces himself as James to Ramu, leader of the Council of Seven—and baits Ramu to go to the Labyrinth. See "Zifnab" and "Council of Seven" for more information. (SG)

Brotherhood of the Hand

The Assassins' Guild called the Brotherhood rules the island of Skurvash. Hugh Blackthorn is a member of the Brotherhood and travels to Skurvash with Iridal, where they obtain a map of the elven emperor's palace. Hugh needs the map to effect a rescue of Prince Bane, who is held by the elves. Members of the Brotherhood have a deeply-scarred hand which they acquire in a gruesome ceremony. A petitioner must squeeze the blade of a knife until it cuts through his hand and touches the bone. The Brotherhood was founded by elves, who soon extended membership to humans. See "Blackthorn, Hugh" and "Skurvash" for more information. (HC)

Btohar'in

Lieutenant to Captain Zankor'el on the elven dragonship *Carfa'shon*, he is wrongly disciplined and embarrassed in front of the crew. He later kills the captain in a duel and becomes the new captain of the flying ship. Btohar'in takes Hugh, Haplo, Alfred, Bane, and Jarre on board. (DW)

Cathedral of the Albedo

An elven holy place, the cathedral is maintained by the Kenkari. It is an impressive octagonal building made of crystal and coralite. In the center is the Aviary, the chamber for the dead. Albedo is an ancient Earth word, the meaning of which has been changed to refer to the "light of elven souls reflecting back to their people." When members of the elven royalty die, weeshams take their souls to the cathedral. See "weeshams" for more information.

Hugh the Hand and Iridal travel to the citadel in their search for Bane. In exchange for help, Hugh promises the Kenkari there that they can have his soul when the matter is finished. When Iridal slays Bane, she believes Hugh is safe from the citadel. However, the Kenkari expect Hugh to keep his promise, after the assassin fulfills one last contract—killing Haplo. See "Blackthorn, Hugh" and "Bane" for more information. (HC)

Caragans

These are large, squirrel-like animals that are used as mounts. They bound swiftly on all fours and can glide from treetop to treetop. Paithan, Roland, Rega, and Drugar rode caragans from Griffith to the Quindiniar estate, just ahead of the marauding tytans. (ES)

Chamber of the Damned

The chamber is found in the network of corridors and tunnels beneath Abarrach's city of Necropolis. Alfred, Haplo, and the lazar Jonathan discover the chamber when they attempt to escape from the king and his undead minions. Alfred and his companions return to the chamber later in search of the Seventh Gate. (FS, SG)

Chaodyn

These insectlike beasts with thick carapaces roam the Labyrinth. Chaodyn are cunning and dangerous, known to use captured Patryns as bait to lure even more Patryns to them. "A chaodyn must be struck directly, die instantly, or else an attacker will find himself facing two where one stood before." (FS, HC, IL, SG)

Chelestra

According to the dolphins, "Chelestra is a globe of water existing in the vastness of space. Its exterior, facing out to the frigid darkness of the Nothing, is

The Hand of Chaos, Volume V KEITH PARKINSON

made of ice, fathoms thick. Its interior, comprising the Goodsea, is warmed by the seasun, a star whose flames are so extraordinarily hot that the water of the Goodsea cannot extinguish them." The islands of Chelestra are called seamoons, and they include Kranque, Phondra, Mnilishi, Ulishan, and the New Worlds. The saltwater of the realm neutralizes the magic of Patryns, by temporarily washing away the runes that cover their skin. The Sartans are also unable to cast magic if they've been doused by the water. To stay dry is to remain powerful. (SM, IL)

Ciang

The elven word meaning merciless was taken by the head of the Brotherhood. Her real name is a mystery. The elven assassin is one of the oldest beings on Arianus, and is believed to come from royalty. She killed her weesham because the attendant would not leave her side. "Her face was a mass of lines, the skin drawn taut over high cheekbones, the fine-boned, beaked nose white as ivory . . . Her head was bald, her hair having fallen out long ago." Hugh the Hand visits her on the island of Skurvash. She refers to him as her old friend and thinks to herself that years ago she considered taking him as a lover. See "weesham" for more information. (HC, IL)

Colossus

Magical thick columns of stone called colossuses were constructed to keep the cold of the Void at bay in Kairn Telest. The columns transfer heat from the lower caverns to the higher ones. The necromancer Baltazar explains that if the colossus fail, as he believes is happening, the ocean will no longer be heated and the river will stop flowing through the tunnel. When Baltazar, the king, prince, and others leave Kairn Telest, they discover a rune-covered colossus that appears inert, proving the necromancer correct. (FS)

Coren

Alfred reveals to Haplo that his Sartan name is Coren and that it means "to choose" or "the chosen." Alfred had refused to give his true name to the Sartans on Chelestra. See "Montebank, Alfred" and "Sartans" for more information. (IL)

Council of Seven

The ruling body in Sartan society which directed the Sundering and ordered that four separate worlds be formed: Arianus, air; Pryan, fire; Chelestra, water; and Abarrach, stone. The council also built the Labyrinth and imprisoned the Patryns in it, whom they considered their enemy. Sartans who opposed the council's plans were also thrust into the Labyrinth. Following the Sundering, the Council of Seven and the other Sartans who supported them "slept" in a chamber on Chelestra for hundreds of years. They were awakened by Alfred's arrival. See "Montebank, Alfred" for more information.

When Samah, head of the council, disappears and is later killed, his son Ramu is elected to take his place. Leadership is not hereditary—the council members elect their leader and council replacements. (SM, SG)

Cursed Blade

This is a shortened version of the dagger's true name: the Accursed Blade. It was given to Hugh the Hand to use against Haplo, and he named the weapon the Cursed Blade. See "Accursed Blade" for more information. (IL, SG)

Daidlus

A young lord who owns beautiful lake-front property, Daidlus is one of Aleatha Quindiniar's prospective mates. She is interested in him only because of his wealth. (ES)

Darby, John

The young man appears in the presence of Ciang, leader of the Brotherhood of the Hand. John petitions to join the Assassins' Guild, sponsored by Ernst Twist, and is accepted after a grisly ceremony where he must cut his own hand. See "Brotherhood of the Hand" for more information. (HC)

Deathgates

Deathgates are portals. Four lead to the Elemental Realms of Abarrach, Chelestra, Arianus, and Pryan. The fifth leads into the Labyrinth. (ES)

Death's Gate

The one portal that leads out of the Labyrinth, the prison of the Patryns, is called Death's Gate. Through it, those who escape the Labyrinth can reach the Nexus and journey to the four worlds created by the Sartans. "Death's Gate. A place that exists and yet does not exist. It has substance and is ephemeral. Time is measured marching ahead going backward. Its light is so bright that I am plunged into darkness." (DW, ES, FS, SM, IL, SG)

Devon

The good-natured young elf is Sabia's betrothed on Chelestra. When he learns that Sabia and her friends Grundle, a dwarf, and Alake, a human, are giving themselves up to the dragon-serpents in an effort to keep their world safe, he knocks his betrothed unconscious. Devon wears one of Sabia's dresses and masquerades as her, sneaking away with Grundle and Alake. See "Sabia," "Heavybeard, Grundle," and "Alake" for more information. (SM)

Delu

She is the wife of Dumaka, chieftain of the humans of Chelestra. Her voice is pleasing to listen to, rich and low. She is as tall as her husband. "Her graying hair, worn in a coif at the back of the neck, provided an attractive contrast to her dark complexion. Seven bands of color in her feathered cape marked her status as a wizardess of the Seventh House, the highest rank a human can attain in the use of magic." (SM)

Dog

Never given a name, the dog follows Haplo throughout his adventures in the Low and High Realms in Arianus, then to Abarrach, Chelestra, Pryan, and back to the Labyrinth. The dog is exceptionally intelligent for an animal, stepping in at appropriate moments to save people in Haplo's company or to pass judgment on the character of strangers. The dog appears to die when a guard-cadaver in Necropolis hefts him into a bubbling hot pool of mud. However, he miraculously comes back to life at an estate in Necropolis. The dog's appearance convinces the Sartan Alfred that Haplo is not dead.

In the final Death Gate novel, Alfred reveals what the dog truly is. Haplo had been fighting his way out of the Labyrinth, attempting to get through one of the gates. He was torn between his good impulses—pity, compassion, mercy, which he was taught were weaknesses—and his selfishness to survive and make it on his own. "Part of Haplo was determined to die, but another part—the best part of him—refused to give up. At that point, wounded and weak in body and spirit, angry with himself, Haplo solved his problem. He did so unconsciously. He created the dog." The dog is Haplo's soul, separated from his body. Haplo's soul finally joins his body when his companions reach the Seventh Gate. After closing the gate, Haplo, Marit, and Alfred find themselves in the Labyrinth once more. (DW, ES, FS, SM, IL, SG)

Dolphins

The dolphins of the water realm of Chelestra communicate with the dwarves, elves, and humans who live there. The dolphins are a great source of information. "Elves think dolphins amusing gossips, entertaining conversationalists, fun to have at parties." Dwarves consider them a good source of information for navigation, but they consider the dolphins simply as smart fish. The elves and humans, however, regard the dolphins as a species similar to themselves because the dolphins give birth in a like manner. (SM)

Dragon-serpents (also: Dragon-snakes)

Chelestra's great dragons are called dragon-serpents or dragon-snakes. "The serpents were huge, their skin wrinkled. They were toothless and old, older than time itself. And they were evil." The largest of the serpents is called the Royal One, king of his people. "Chaos is our life's blood. Death our meat and drink," the Royal One says. They are shape-shifters, able to appear as elves, dwarves, or whatever else strikes their fancy. They escape Chelestra when Samah opens Death's Gate. Revealing themselves to Haplo, they tell him they feed on fear and terror and that they intend to insinuate themselves in the societies of the four worlds and in the Nexus. See "Sang-drax" for more information. (SM, HC, IL, SG)

Dragonships

These vessels fly, rather than sail across the water. Haplo's dragonship, named *Dragon Wing*, was built by the Arianus elves and was enchanted with Patryn runes to protect Haplo from harm. Only the tytans seemed able to get through the magic. (DW, ES, FS, SM, HC, IL, SG)

Dragon Wing

Haplo's flying dragonship carries him to the worlds of Arianus, Pryan, and Abarrach, protecting him from various magics and the elements. However, when *Dragon Wing* carries him to Chelestra, the Realm of Water, the ship breaks apart. The runes that protect the vessel are washed away, and Haplo is forced to swim to safety. (DW, ES, FS, SM)

Drugar "Blackbeard"

"Slightly above average height for his people, he had ruddy brown skin and a shaggy mane of curly black hair and beard that gave him his nickname among humans. Thick black brows meeting over a hooked nose and flashing black eyes gave him a perpetually fierce expression that served him well in alien lands." The dwarf, fond of song, dresses in bright colors. He makes a deal to acquire elven-fashioned weapons from the human smugglers Roland and Rega of Griffith. Drugar says the weapons will be used against tytans—humans the size of mountains. However, before the weapons are delivered, the tytans reach his people and slaughter them.

The dwarf later manages to rescue Rega, Roland, and Paithan Quindiniar from the tytans and begins plotting to murder them. Drugar blames them for his people's deaths, as they did not bring the weapons in time. The dwarf changes his mind about killing the trio when they reach the floating citadel of Pryan. He discovers the races must learn to live together. (ES)

Duenna

On the watery world of Chelestra, Sabia's duenna, Marabella, constantly frets over the elven princess. A member of the royal court, a duenna is a chaperone to an unmarried woman. (SM)

Dumaka

Dumaka of Phondra is chieftain of the humans of the world Chelestra. He is tall and handsome, and he talks and walks quickly, using abrupt gestures, often seeming frantic. (SM)

Durnai

The Sartans of Chelestra call the watery-world's living islands durnai. Some of the islands are still in hibernation. However, the awakened ones drift and are terrorized from time to time by the dragon-snakes. "They attacked one, woke it, and have tormented the durnai ever since," says the Sartan Orla. (SM)

Durndrun

Not yet married, he is one of the highest-ranking lords in the elven court. Cool, withdrawn, and polite, he is also one of the wealthiest elves. He proposes to Aleatha Quindiniar at his estate. The ground is shaking at the time, from the gyrations of a dragon. "If, by some miracle, we escape this monster, I want you to marry me!" Aleatha says she will listen if he asks again under other circumstances. And when the circumstances are different, she agrees. However, Durndrun is killed when he makes a stand against the tytans. (ES)

Dynast Clock

A clay doll representing the dynast, or ruler, placed within a miniature replica of his palace, is used to keep time in Necropolis in the realm of Abarrach. The doll is attuned to the ruler and displays the current time by its position within the miniature palace. Thus, when the doll is in bed, it is the dynast's sleeping hour. And when the doll is at the table, it is the ruler's dinner time. However, as the magic of Abarrach is fading, the doll is keeping less accurate time. (FS)

Edmund

Son of the king of Kairn Telest, the young prince leads his people when his father is killed by a fire dragon. Edmund is disturbed by the state of his dying world. "No, you won't find homes here. This world is dying. Already our dead outnumber the living. If nothing changes, I foresee a time, and it is coming on us very soon, when the dead alone will rule Abarrach." Edmund and Haplo are captured and held in cells beneath the castle of Necropolis, the main city in Abarrach. Edmund is slain, and his corpse is animated. (FS)

Eliason

The elven king of Chelestra recently lost his wife. Eliason is a proud, resourceful, and cautious ruler, who prizes his daughter, Sabia. He is devastated when Sabia kills herself by jumping to her death when she believes her betrothed is dead. See "Sabia" for more information. (SM)

Elixnoir

Called a Master Astrologer and wizard, this elf is considered by Lenthan Quindiniar to be part of his family. The astrologer spends a considerable amount of time in Lenthan's laboratory engaged in scientific research. He is also known for eating a considerable amount of food, particularly sweets, at the Quindiniar dinner table. (ES)

Elmas

On Chelestra, elves are called Elmas, as is their country. The capital is Elmasia. (SM)

Elmasia

"The elven royal city of Elmasia is a place of beauty and enchantment. Its palace, known as the Grotto, is built of pink and white filigree coral and stands on the banks of the seamoon's many freshwater lakes"—so writes the dwarven princess Grundle of her impressions of the city on the water world of Chelestra. (SM)

Etherlite

A navigational device, an etherlite is a sliver or ornite suspended in a globe of enchanted glass. Ornite always points to a magnetic pole, which is called norinth. The device was developed by the Quindiniars. (ES)

Equilan

This is one of the major land masses on Pryan. Elves are the prominent race on the surface. Beneath the surface is the realm of the dwarves, which includes the kingdoms of Grish, Thurn, and Klag. (ES)

Factree

On Arianus, "the Factree was a sacred and holy place to the Gegs. Not only was it the Kicksey-winsey's birthplace, but it was in the Factree that the Gegs' most hollowed icon was located—the brass statue of a Manger." The Manger statue was of a tall, thin man dressed in a hooded robe. See "Kicksey-winsey" for more information. (DW, SG)

Fifth Realm

"Often called Limbo or simply the Nexus by those who are unfamiliar with its structure, it is divided into three concentric regions. The outermost region is called the Nexus and is the place where the Death-gates of all realms converge. Four of the Deathgates lead to the Elemental Realms, while the fifth gate leads into the Labyrinth. Beyond the Labyrinth lies the Vortex. It was in this place that the Sartan originally imprisoned the Patryns. After three millennia, the Patryns managed to escape the Vortex through the Labyrinth and gain control over the Nexus and all of its Deathgates." (ES)

Fire Dragons

They are known for their great intelligence and malevolence. Fire dragons were hunted practically to extinction by the people of Kairn Telest. The dragons have dagger-sharp spiked tails, blazing red eyes, and can withstand intense heat. Some live in molten lava. A fire dragon slays the king of Kairn Telest and some of his soldiers. Sated, the dragon allows the remainder of the Kairn Telest refugees to pass. (FS)

Fitzwarren

The baron holds land in the realm of King Stephen and Queen Anne of Arianus. Cousin to the queen and a wealthy Uylandian, Fitzwarren is considered a hothead. (HC)

Fricka

Grundle's Aunt Gertrude brings her daughter Fricka to the Heavybeard household after Grundle runs away to sacrifice herself to the dragon-snakes. See "Grundle" for more information. Grundle returns, expecting to find Fricka occupying her bedroom. Living space is at a premium on Chelestra, and traditionally when one dwarf moves out of a room, another immediately moves in. However, Grundle's mother threatens Aunt Gertrude, who believes Grundle is dead. Gertrude and Fricka leave, and Grundle returns to find her room intact. (SM)

Gareth

The captain of a dead liege's knights, Gareth swoops down on a dragon and prevents the crowd from killing Hugh the Hand. Described as "a paunchy middle-aged man with a fiery-red beard," Gareth claims to have temporarily saved Hugh so the assassin could meet his end on the executioner's block. Gareth says he wants to put Hugh's head on his murdered liege's bier. At one time Gareth had paid Hugh to avenge the death of the captain's daughter. (DW)

Gargans

The dwarves on the water world of Chelestra are called Gargans. They are a good-natured folk adept at building things, especially ships. (SM)

Gegs

The dwarves on Arianus are called Gegs, a short version of "gega'rega," an elven slang term for insect. They later begin to refer to themselves only as dwarves. (DW, HC, IL, SG)

Gatecrashers

Patryns who are driven mad by the hardships they endure in the Labyrinth are called gatecrashers. They run insanely into the wilderness, believing that they have reached the Last Gate. Often, they are just running to their doom. (ES)

Gertrude

Grundle's Aunt Gertrude visits the Heavybeards on Chelestra after Grundle's disappearance. Gertrude thinks Grundle's mother has lost her mind for believing that the young dwarf is still alive. Grundle had given herself up to the dragon-serpents in an effort to save her people. Aunt Gertrude decides to leave when Grundle's mother grabs the battle-ax off the wall and threatens her. (SM)

Glampern

This source of light the dwarves turn to when the Kicksey-winsey stops working is a castoff from the elves. "The glampern, hanging on a hook, served well enough, once one got used to the smoky flame, the smell, and the crack down the side that allowed some sort of obviously highly-flammable substance to drip out onto the floor." (HC)

Gorgon

Sinistrad's dragon, Gorgon, is huge, "with shining silver skin, a sinuous thin body, and flaring red eyes." Though wingless, the dragon is a fast flyer. The wizard holds the dragon under his tight control. When Sinistrad dies, Gorgon is freed. (DW)

Green Caverns

Kairn Telest in Abarrach is also called the Green Caverns because of the vegetation grown there. When the magma river cools and the vegetation dies, the Lord High Chancellor of Necropolis suggests the place instead be called the Bone-Bare Caverns, referencing a move in the game of rune-bones where an opponent is stripped of all his runes. (FS)

Gregor

The large, red-headed human is a caravanner and a friend of the elf Paithan Quindiniar. Paithan considers Gregor reliable, dependable, and fearless. They meet as Paithan leads his own caravan to a rendezvous scheduled with Roland and Rega Redleaf. (ES)

Grenko

Large beasts, the grenko of Arianus are prized for their teeth, which they shed annually. The animals are rare, and elven law protects them from being hunted. The grenko are highly intelligent and will attack anything that enters their caves. (DW)

Gushni

The dragon-snakes of Chelestra use a jellyfishlike creature called the gushni to spy for them. The gushni have a shared intelligence, and "each one contains all the knowledge of the entire group." The gushni are not able to speak and are linked to the dragon-serpents telepathically. (SM)

Hamish

He is a human Paithan Quindiniar and Quintin meet along the caravan route to the human lands. Hamish and his companions tell Paithan that strange people are washing up as refugees on the SeaKings' shores, fleeing their homes because of tytans—gigantic creatures. (ES)

Hamish, Peter

Formerly a squire to Lord Gwenned, Peter Hamish of Pitrin's Exile comes before King Stephen and Queen Anne. He reveals that when he was recently a prisoner of the elves he saw their son, Bane. "He warn't no prisoner. More like an honored guest, he was." Peter explains that when he and the other prisoners were plotting their escape, he offered to let Bane join them. However, Bane said he was being too closely guarded. King Stephen believes Peter was allowed to escape so he could report on Bane. (HC)

Haplo

Called an "emissary to an unsuspecting world," Haplo is a Patryn who exits the Labyrinth at the direction of the Lord of the Nexus. The name "Haplo" means single, or alone. His mission is to explore the four worlds created in the Sundering and bring back information and news of the Sartans.

After exiting the Nexus, Haplo first enters the Low Realm of Arianus, the World of Air. He is rescued by the Geg Limbeck and initially mistaken for a god because of his magical prowess and ability to heal himself. He travels in the company of Hugh the Hand, the Sartan Alfred, and Bane. His explorations of Arianus finished, Haplo takes his flying dragonship through Death's Gate, to the world of Pryan—Realm of Fire. He is able to guide the great flying vessel "with his eyes, his thoughts, his magic." His presence on the World of Fire is foretold by the wizard Zifnab.

Haplo also journeys through other gates, visiting the World of Stone, Abarrach, where he is reunited with Alfred. Here, Haplo is poisoned by order of the king in Abarrach's major city, Necropolis. The king wanted the Patryn out of the way. However, Alfred slips into Haplo's cell and manages to cure him in time. Haplo is furious at being saved by a Sartan, his enemy.

In Chelestra, the World of Water, Haplo discovers a fierce enemy of the Sartans—the dragon-snakes. The dragons pretend to regard the Patryn as their master, while they secretly plot to use him. When a gate is opened by Samah the Sartan, the dragon-serpents escape through it to the Labyrinth and other worlds.

Haplo returns to the Labyrinth, where he is reunited with Marit, the woman he loves and who bore his child. He is determined to search for the child, Rue, but a struggle with the dragon-snakes dash those plans. Haplo is wounded, and Xar, Lord of the Nexus, spirits him away to Abarrach. Xar intends to let Haplo die, then revive his body to gain information about the Seventh Gate. Xar is thwarted, however, when he discovers that Haplo's soul is not in his body. Haplo's soul—his dog companion—finally joins his body when his companions reach the Seventh Gate. After closing the gate, Haplo, Marit, and Alfred find themselves in the Labyrinth once more. See "Dog" for more information. (DW, ES, FS, SM, HC, IL, SG)

Harald

A townsman of Griffith, he opens the gate to let Roland, Rega, Paithan, and Drugar inside. The quartet is fleeing the tytans. (ES)

Hargast

Agah'ran, emperor to the elves of Arianus, has a pet hargast. The birds are considered rare, difficult to capture, and are very expensive. "Their song is quite exquisite." (HC)

Hartmut

Beloved of Grundle on the world of Chelestra, the dwarf Hartmut commands a rego, or unit, of four clans. This gives him the rank of fourclan master, which is considered a high honor for a dwarf who is not yet married. "His russet hair is long and thick, his side whiskers are auburn." (SM)

Headman

The title bestowed on the leader of a Squatter community in the Labyrinth is Headman. He or she is considered wiser than most. (ES, IL, SG)

Heavybeard, Grundle

The Princess of Gargan, Grundle, has had songs composed about her beauty. Versed in human and elven languages, the dwarven princess keeps a journal of her experiences on Chelestra. She considers Alake and Sabia her sister-friends. Grundle is in love with the fourclan master Hartmut and hopes he can win her hand so they can marry. The dwarf's plans

Serpent Mage, Volume IV   KEITH PARKINSON

for the future change, however, when a messenger from the dragon-snakes appears and demands Grundle, Alake, and Sabia—the eldest daughters of the rulers—in exchange for not starting a war. Their parents refuse, but the girls sneak away in the evening, bent on saving their families and friends. At sea, Grundle discovers that Sabia's betrothed, Devon, used a spell and switched places with the elf. See "Sabia," "Alake," and "Devon" for more information. (SM)

Heavybeard, Hilda

The mother of Grundle "was said to be the most beautiful woman in all the seamoon." Her honey-colored side whiskers came almost to her waist. Hilda is Muter, or Queen, of the Gargans. (SM)

Heavybeard, Yngvar

The Vate, or king, of the Gargans is devastated when his daughter Grundle leaves. She and her friends are giving themselves up to the dragon-snakes in an effort to save their people. Yngvar fears his daughter is dead, but is astonished to see her return in the company of Haplo. Yngvar was ready to go to war rather than risk the life of his daughter and the other rulers' children. The dwarf believed the children were just the first of the dragon-snakes' demands. (SM)

Iridal

At age sixteen she agreed to wed Sinistrad, who told her he was evil. "If you are evil . . . it is the world that has made you so by refusing to listen to your plans and thwarting your genius at every turn. When I am walking by your side, I will bring you to the sunlight." She later realizes he is every bit as evil as he claimed, and she considers herself his prisoner. Sinistrad takes their child shortly after its birth and switches it with the baby of King Stephen and Queen Anne. He gives Iridal the other child, but it could not adapt to the new atmosphere of the High Realm and dies.

Iridal is skilled in magic and initially intends to use it to escape Sinistrad. However, he reveals that if she leaves, her father's life will be forfeit. Her father eventually dies, but by then she has no way off the floating island until Haplo and his companions arrive.

She escapes with Alfred after Sinistrad's death and returns to Arianus. Appearing with Peter Hamish before King Stephen, she says she will go to the elves and rescue Bane—in the company of Hugh the Hand. The freed Bane tries to kill Stephen, and she steps in and saves the king by killing her own son. See "Hamish, Peter" and "Blackthorn, Hugh" for more information. (DW)

Ivor

The Sartan named Ivor lays unmoving and unresponsive inside a crystal cocoon. Haplo sees the image of the man, a friend of Alfred, when he and Alfred are passing through the gate to Abarrach, the World of Stone. (FS)

Jarre

A member of WUPP—Worshipers United for Progress and Prosperity, Jarre gives a fiery speech that results in her listeners attacking the Kickseywinsey, a great and mysterious machine. This also results in Limbeck, the love of her life and head of WUPP, being arrested for the deed. (DW, HC, IL)

Jera

A Sartan necromancer, who gives her public name as Jera, is a duchess in the Abarrach city of Necropolis. She has green-flecked eyes that hint at her quick mind and reflexes. "Her face, although not beautiful by any purity or regularity of feature, was made attractive by an expression of singular intelligence." Her husband is Jonathan, a duke of Necropolis. She is killed when she steps in front of her husband and takes an arrow meant for him. The pair was in the catacombs beneath the castle on a mission to rescue Haplo. Grief-stricken, Jonathan animates her corpse. However, he does so too soon, and Jera's spirit is trapped between the worlds of the living and the dead; she is a lazar. Jera's lazar later slays Kleitus when he ventures into the catacombs, and then proceeds to lead an attack against Abarrach's living, including Jonathan. See "lazar" and "Kleitus XIV" for more information. (FS)

Jonathan

Jonathan of the ducal House of Rift Ridge is a duke in the Abarrach city of Necropolis. His wife is Jera, a powerful necromancer. "We make a good team," Jonathan says of himself and his wife. "I'm subject to whim, to impulse. I tend to act before I think. Jera keeps me in line. But she, on the other hand, would never do anything exciting or out of the ordinary if I wasn't around to make her life interesting." When Jera is slain defending Jonathan in the catacombs beneath the king's castle, he animates her body, but does so too soon. Her spirit did not have time to leave her corpse, and she is trapped between the worlds of the living and the dead as a lazar. Jonathan leads Haplo and Alfred from the catacombs and to the flying ship *Dragon Wing*. There, he is slain at the hands of his dead wife.

Jonathan reappears as a lazar when Xar, Lord of the Nexus, comes to Abarrach. Xar wants to learn how to raise the dead. Xar successfully animates the corpse of Samah, who also was on Abarrach. However, when Xar is elsewhere, Jonathan grants Samah's spirit a final rest, and the corpse is permanently dead. Jonathan later grants Hugh the Hand's and Xar's spirits their rest. See "lazar," "Xar," and "Samah" for more information. (FS, IL, SG)

Kairn Necros

The pear-shaped realm of Abarrach is called Kairn Necros. The domain consists primarily of Necropolis, the largest city; Old Provinces; New Provinces; and the Fire Sea. Other landmarks of note include the Salfag Caverns, the Pillar of Zembar, Rift Ridge, and the Pillar of Thebis. An upward sloping passage connects Kairn Necros to Kairn Telest. (FS)

Kairn Telest

Once a major realm of Abarrach, Kairn Telest consists of Telestia, Emeth, Holden, Furth, and Point Gan. The River Hemo flows from the Celestial Sea into Kairn Telest. A downward sloping passage connects Kairn Telest to Kairn Necros. (FS)

Ke'lith

The assassin Hugh the Hand is escorted from Yreni Prison on the world of Arianus to the city walls of Ke'lith. Here he is to be executed in front of a considerable crowd. The execution is never carried out. See "Blackthorn, Hugh" for more information. (DW)

Kenkari

The Sartan brought the Kenkari, one of the seven original clans of elves, to Arianus after the Sundering. The Kenkari wizards are more powerful than the wizards of other clans. (DW, HC)

Khadak

Khadak is a term applied to a length of wood soaked in a resin that will flame quickly when the proper rune is spoken. It can also be applied to hot-tempered people. Drugar's father called him a khadak. "I said you would make a good king. And so you will. If! If you will keep the fire under control! The flame of your thoughts burns clear and rises high, but instead of keeping the fire banked, you let it flare up, blaze out of control!" (ES)

Kicksey-Winsey

A great machine built by the Sartan, they were not able to get it working before they began to die. The Gegs, or dwarves, of Drevlin on Arianus cared for the machine, almost to the point of worshiping it. In a speech, Limbeck, High Froman of the dwarves, states: "The Kicksey-winsey is a masheen. A masheen is a collection of wheels and turn-knobbies and lever-bangers and tube-zoomers that, when all put together, DO SOMETHING! That is a masheen. When you turn your turny-wheelie, you are helping the masheen do something . . . What do all the parts do? I have no idea. Neither do you." The machine consists of such parts as the Liftalofts, the 'lectriczingers, whirly-wheels, flashrafts, whistle-toots, bubble-boils, glimmerglamps, and more. It is the only source of water for those living in the Mid Realms, as it powers the Liftalofts, which collect water from the clouds. See "Liftalofts" for more information.

The Kicksey-winsey is key to making things right on the sundered realms, the wizard Zifnab tells

Haplo. The Lord of the Nexus is also interested in the machine, wanting it up and working so he can use it to help effect his plans of taking over the four worlds. The machine stops working shortly before Haplo returns to Arianus at the behest of the Lord of the Nexus. However, in the end the machine is coaxed into running. It sends energy to the citadels on the world of Pryan, which in turn sends the energy to the remaining worlds. (DW, HC, IL, SG)

Kinilan

He is a Sartan magical researcher. (FS)

Kir Monks

The monks of Arianus worship death. "They view life as a kind of prison-house existence, to be endured until the soul can escape and find true peace and happiness elsewhere." In their monastery in the Volkaran Isles in the Mid Realm, they take orphans under their wing. Hugh the Hand was one of these orphans, but he fled the monastery when he was sixteen. Years later, Hugh is believed slain by the wizard Sinistrad, who he in turn killed. However, Hugh had been revived by the Sartan Alfred and returned to the monastery. (DW, HC)

Klausten, Sendric

A Nexus Runner of considerable reputation, Sendric studied rune magic and its limitations. (ES, SG)

Kleitus

The first ruler of Necropolis is seen in a vision when Alfred and Haplo are in the catacombs beneath the city's castle. (FS)

Kleitus VII

An ancestor to the current ruler of Necropolis, Kleitus VII prevented the sorceress Bethel from leaving Abarrach. His men captured her as she and her followers were attempting to abandon the world. She escaped and flung herself into the magma. (FS)

Kleitus XIV

The ruler of Necropolis in the realm of Abarrach is Kleitus XIV, a Sartan of numerous titles who always speaks in the royal "we." He is called by his chancellor as "Dynast of Abarrach, ruler of Kairn Necros, regent of Old and New Provinces, king of Rift Ridge, king of Salfag, king of Thebis, and liege lord of Kairn Telest." Kleitus is a powerful wizard, his very words birthing images. The king leeched off other caverns in Abarrach to keep Necropolis going. However, he recognizes that his efforts are not enough and that the entire world is dying. Kleitus is killed in the catacombs beneath his castle after he and his entourage come upon the Chamber of the Damned. Here, the lazar of the Duchess Jera slays him. He becomes a lazar, and together with Jera and Abarrach's dead, they lead an attack on the living. When Alfred, Marit, and Hugh the Hand return to Abarrach, Kleitus attempts to steal their elven dragonship. He hopes to leave this world and bring death to other worlds he encounters. See "lazar" and "Jera" for more information. (FS, IL, SG)

Krenka-Anris

The revered elf is referred to as "Holy Priestess," and her name is often invoked by the elves of Arianus in prayer. (HC, IL)

Krishach

The dragon Krishach summoned through prayer and magic by the Kenkari elves "was a creature of cloud and shadow; insubstantial, yet granted a terrible substance. Its flesh was a pale, translucent white, the white of a long-dead corpse." Krishach's skeleton is visible through skin that drapes loosely over his bones. Called the phantom dragon, he carries Haplo and Iridal on Arianus. (HC)

Labyrinth

The Patryns were placed in the mazelike prison world constructed by the Sartan in the hopes they would be "rehabilitated" and stop their aggressive ways. According to the Lord of the Nexus, "Countless numbers of our people have died in the fearsome place. Entire generations have been wiped out, destroyed." The Sartan abandoned the Labyrinth, and the place took on a life of its own. Many beasts, such as wolfen and chaodyn, hunt the Patryns there. Some Sartans were also sent to the Labyrinth, upon order of Samah, leader of the Council of Seven. They opposed Samah or the council and had to pay a terrible price. "It is a cruel place, filled with cruel magic that delights not only in killing, but in killing slowly, torturing, tormenting you until death comes as a friend," says Haplo of the Labyrinth. (HC, ES, FS, SM, HC, IL, SG)

Lady Rogar

The wife of the deceased Lord Rogar, she is sedated with poppy syrup to prevent her from throwing herself on her husband's flaming bier. (DW)

Lathan

Sir Lathan is a royal commander who brings a regiment of knights to the town of Griffith. He is the younger brother of Reginald, the Liege Lord of Terncia. "He was handsome, with the black hair and black mustache of the Thillian lords. A jagged battle scar cut into his upper lip, giving him a slight, perpetual sneer." Lathan meets with the smugglers Roland and Rega Redleaf, the dwarf Drugar, and the elf Paithan Quindiniar. He pretends to order them to leave Griffith so they can return with elven weapons. He secretly tells them not to look back. Lathan knows he and his fellows will quickly fall to the tytans, who are thundering toward the town gates. (ES)

Lazar

On Abarrach, the term lazar is applied to individuals whose spirits have not had time to leave their bodies before their corpses are animated. The term is from the proper name Lazarus. In ancient times the term referred to a person with a loathsome disease such as leprosy—the walking dead. Kleitus, the king of Necropolis in Abarrach, and Jera, Duchess of Abarrach, become lazars when their spirits are trapped between the realms of the living and the dead. (FS, HC, IL, SG)

Lectric, Lof

A dwarf with the Lectriczinger scrift, he provides information about a bird contraption that is to be used in Limbeck's rescue. See "Bolttightner, Limbeck" for more information. (DW, IL)

Liftalofts

Located in the city of Wombe, the Liftalofts consist of nine steel arms that each have an outstretched golden hand that thrusts into the storm clouds. The Liftalofts provide water to the Mid Realm. (DW, HC, IL)

Little People

The dwarves in Abarrach are called Little People. The Sartans there believe the dwarves to be extinct. (FS)

Longshoreman, Darral

A shrewd Geg, or dwarf, Darral is the High Froman from the wealthiest and most powerful clan in Drevlin. Darral is the first to see Hugh, Alfred, and Bane when they come to the Low Realm of Drevlin. He is also the first to believe they are not gods—as some of the other Gegs had labeled them. (DW)

Lord of the Nexus

The old, powerful wizard escaped the Labyrinth and then returned to it to lead his people to safety. He is known to Haplo as Xar. See "Xar" for more information. (DW, ES, FS, SM, HC, IL, SG)

Lucilla

Lucilla is an elf who hung herself over Lord Kevanish. ". . . Lucilla was a fool for thinking that a man like Kevanish could really be in love with her," says Althea Quindiniar. (ES)

Lucy

According to records in the Kir Monastery, Lucy was the name of Hugh Blackthorn's mother. No last name is given. (DW)

Fire Sea, Volume III   KEITH PARKINSON

Maelstrom

An area of perpetual storms in the Low Realm of Arianus is referred to as the Maelstrom. Dragons refuse to fly into the Maelstrom. However, the elves of the Mid Realm, with their enchanted dragonships, can sail the area and therefore hold a virtual monopoly on the water collected there. (DW)

Magicka

A land magus, he dresses in browns, the color of the magic he favors. He understands the nature and power of all manner of rocks. Hugh the Hand is passed to this wizard, referred to only as Magicka, to confess his guilt of murdering Lord Rogar. The wizard's real name is not mentioned; "magicka" is a term applied to powerful wizards in general. Later, it

is revealed that Magicka is the one who slew Lord Rogar. (DW)

Marabella

She serves as the elven princess's duenna, or royal chaperone, on Chelestra. Marabella was known to fret over the Princess Sabia "like a hen with one chick." (SM)

Marit

She kept company with Haplo when he was a Runner in the Labyrinth. And after she left him, she gave birth to their daughter, who she abandoned in a Squatter community. An accomplished wizard, she pledged her life to the Lord of the

Nexus when he rescued her in the Labyrinth and carried her to safety in the Nexus. She rune-joins with Xar, Lord of the Nexus, becoming in effect his wife. See "rune-joining" for more information. Then he bids her to travel to Arianus in search of Haplo. Xar wants Haplo killed and his body brought back. He intends to animate it and gain information that he believes Haplo, in life, would keep from him. Marit follows his instructions, but her attempt on Haplo's life fails. (HC—though not named there, IL, SG)

Marta

She is an elderly woman, tired and angry, and one of the refugees of Kairn Terest. During the funeral service for the king, she cries that the people they're heading toward and planning to seek aid from—the people of Necropolis—"robbed us of all we possessed!" Marta believes the people of Necropolis took their heat and water and doomed them to die. The prince counters that if their neighbors did anything, they did it unknowingly. This mollifies her a little. (FS)

Masters of the Sea

The great dragon-snakes of Chelestra are called the Masters of the Sea when one of their messengers arrives and demands the eldest daughter from each royal house. The dwarven, elven, and human kings refuse. However, the rulers' daughters slip away during the night, board a ship, and prepare to sacrifice themselves so their families and friends can live. See "dragon-serpents" for more information. (SM, IL)

Mensch

The Sartans and Patryns used the word mensch when referring to what they considered lower races: humans, elves, and dwarves. (DW, ES, FS, SM, HC, IL)

Mikal

Mikal is a boy Hugh meets as he is working for the Kir monks. Mikal's mother dies, and Hugh leads the boy away. Mikal joins the other orphans in the monks' monastery. (DW)

Melista

Though intermarriage has weakened the clan lines, there are still elves who work to keep the Melista clan reasonably pure. Melista is one of the seven clans of elves in the Mid Realm on Arianus. (ES, HC)

Miklovich

The captain of King Stephen's guards stops Bane as he heads toward the castle. Bane is disguised as an urchin, but when he draws near, Captain Miklovich recognizes him and allows him to pass. Miklovich is unaware that Bane means to kill the king. (HC)

Mnarash'ai

The legendary elven hero fought a creature called the seven-eyed dragon. In the beast's eyes, Mnarash'ai saw seven deaths. She was forced to overcome her fear of each death before she was able to defeat the dragon. (HC)

Montebank, Alfred

The tall and gangly chamberlain follows Hugh the Hand and Prince Bane when they leave King Stephen. When Bane poisons Hugh, Alfred saves the assassin, claiming that all life is precious. Elderly, clumsy, and prone to fainting spells, Alfred doggedly keeps with the pair as they journey through the Low Realm, then travel by elven dragonship and head to the High Realm.

It is in the High Realm that Haplo accuses Alfred of being a Sartan, and Alfred does not deny it. When the wizard Sinistrad dies and the dragon Gorgon is freed, Alfred does a magical dance that is able to charm it, revealing that he is indeed far more than an elderly chamberlain.

Alfred reappears when Haplo enters Abarrach, the World of Stone. When Haplo is poisoned by the ruler of the realm, Alfred sneaks into his cell and saves him. Alfred parts company with Haplo when they escape Abarrach and enter Death's Gate.

By accident, the elderly Sartan emerges in Chelestra, and his appearance awakens the Sartan Council of Seven that was "sleeping" there. See "Council of Seven" for more information. On the watery world he manages to save Haplo and the royal children in the Patryn's company from the dragon-snakes by taking on the form of a huge dragon. Alfred remembers none of it, however.

He later is reunited with Haplo, Hugh the Hand, and Marit in the Vortex at the opening to the Labyrinth. Inside the Labyrinth, he reveals his true Sartan name to Haplo—Coren. With Haplo's help, Alfred is able to seal the Seventh Gate, keeping the four worlds separate and safe from each other. (DW, FS, SM, HC, IL, SG)

Mother Peytin

Considered the goddess of the elves, Mother Peytin had long white hair that was tinged brown at the very ends. Haplo sees an icon of the deity in the Quindiniar home and notes that the hair makes the deity look like a Sartan. Haplo considers it proof that the Sartans have been to this world. (ES)

Muter

Dwarven queens on Chelestra are called Muter, a term meaning *mother*. (SM)

Necropolis

The largest city in Abarrach, Necropolis consists of half-circles radiating from the main fortress. In the early days, its population was primarily mensch and Sartans, and as the population grew, so did the city. The ruler claimed the fortress as his castle. In the city's declining years, more dead than living occupy the various boroughs. (FS)

Nexus

Patryns who manage to escape the Labyrinth reach a place they call the Nexus, which they have made into a beautiful city. However, the city is set ablaze by the dragon-snakes, who come through the gate and attack the Patryns there. (DW, ES, FS, SM, HC, IL, SG)

Orla

When Alfred emerges into Chelestra, Orla, sometimes mentioned as Orlah, is one of the first Sartans he sees. She is a member of the powerful Council of Seven, and the wife of Samah. She is drawn to him, but stays faithful to her husband. However, when

Samah threatens to open Death's Gate, she defies him. In response, Samah casts her and Alfred into the Labyrinth. When Orla senses that Samah is dead and discovers just how he died, she wills herself to die so her spirit can join his. Her body is kept in a crystal coffin in the Vortex. See "Samah" for more information. (SM, IL)

Orstan

In his journal, Alfred the Sartan writes that a fellow named Orstan might have been a researcher in the field of necromancy. Orstan created runes that allow communication via the Table of Elders. (FS)

Patryns

In rune language, Patryn means "Those Who Return to Darkness." Patryns were originally brothers to the Sartan. Close-knit, they are fiercely loyal to each other. The Patryns were close to taking over their world and are convinced that their enemy, the Sartan, destroyed the world to prevent the takeover. Then the Sartans cast the Patryns into the Labyrinth. Xar, the Lord of the Nexus, states, "The Sartan hoped that prison life would 'rehabilitate' us, that we would emerge from the Labyrinth chastened, our domineering and, what they term 'cruel,' natures softened." Patryns are born with brown hair, the ends of which later turn white. Patryns in the Labyrinth share food, children, lovers—everything. The Patryns magic is tied to the runes that cover their bodies. Shortly after birth, Patryns are tattooed with these runes, and as they age tattoos are added. The Patryns endure the pain of tattooing without flinching. Various runes on their skin glow to indicate danger. (DW, ES, FS, SM, HC, IL, SG)

Pauka

Snout-horned beasts called pauka are used for labor and to pull carriages in the city of Necropolis in Abarrach. The broad-backed animals are strong, with beady eyes and a considerable number of teeth. (FS)

Paxaria

Paxar Kethin was said to have founded the elven clan Paxaria. The name means "Souls at Peace," and the clan is the dominant one in the elven realms. Paxaria is also the name of the land belonging to the elven clan. Paxaria's greatest city is Paxaua. (ES, HC)

Phondrans

The elves on the water world of Chelestra are called Phondrans, and their island home is Phondra. (SM)

Pons

Lord High Chancellor Pons serves the king of Necropolis in the realm of Abarrach. Pons dies in the chambers under the king's castle when the undead royal guards turn on him. (FS)

Pullstarter, Dunk

He is the legendary dwarf who led the first dwarves of Arianus. The dwarves arrived in Drevlin in the Low Realm, where the dwarven homeland was established and where the Kicksey-winsey was started. (HC)

Pundar

A caravanner, he is an associate of Paithan Quindiniar. (ES)

Purgeflusher, Balin

He is mentioned in a speech about the Kicksey-winsey by Limbeck, High Froman of the Arianus dwarves. "No one told us what the lever twisting did when we twisted or why bolt tightening was of any consequence. My old friend Balin Purgeflusher—a fine and dedicated dwarf until his untimely accident—had no concept of what he was flushing when he was purged." (HC)

Pushpuller, Throtin

A dwarf who studied the Kicksey-winsey of Arianus, Throtin postulated various theories about the masheen, including one that stated the Conveyer was meant to be an alternate transportation system. Throtin "was tragically disproved by his own tests near the Erm Melty-vat only last year." (HC)

Preserver

The skilled individuals in Abarrach maintain cadavers that are to be brought back to life. The preservers help keep the corpses' flesh from rotting. (FS)

Pricklebulb Fish

Found on the water world of Chelestra, these spherical-shaped fish have razor-edged fronds. They emit a bright light to lure victims close. When the fish are threatened, they intensify the light, blinding the predator. (SM)

Pryan

The sun never sets on Pryan, which is called the World of Fire. Elves, humans, and dwarves live on the world and constantly fight each other. The world itself is a gigantic hollow sphere of rock with a sun burning in the center. The people live in countries on the inner crust. The vegetation is thick, and few on Pryan have seen the ground. Cities have been built on the branches of great trees.

The Sartan built citadels on Pryan, floating cities that were intended to gather energy from the sun. The energy was to be transferred to the other three worlds via the Kicksey-winsey and the Death's Gate. However, the citadels are empty, as the Kicksey-winsey does not work, and Death's Gate is closed. This situation changes at the end of the saga when the Kicksey-winsey functions, the tytans operate one of the citadel's Star Chambers, and the Seventh Gate is sealed. See "Star Chamber" for more information. (ES, IL, SG)

Queen Mother

The duke and duchess of Necropolis, in the company of the Sartan Alfred, pretend to be visiting the Queen Mother as a way to sneak into the castle. The Queen Mother was gracious in life, but demanding in death. Her cadaver kept interfering at court functions, and they had to eventually lock her away beneath the castle in the main city in Abarrach. The Queen Mother had her own personal necromancer, the one case of the living serving the dead in Abarrach. "The corpse was clad in robes of silver thread, and gold and jewels glittered on waxen fingers. Her silver hair was beautifully coiffed and cared for." (FS)

Quindiniar, Aleatha

Nicknamed Thea by her brother and sister, the elf-maid is known for her rich, throaty voice and heavy-lidded purple eyes. She ignores fashion, favoring dresses that show off her figure. And she enjoys the company of several men, including Lord Kevanish and Lord Durndrun, the latter of whom she decides to marry because of his wealth and lakefront estate. She flirts with humans, "but at least her dalliances were with men of her own kind." She initially believes humans are beneath elves and should be enslaved by them.

As the tytans overrun the Quindiniar property, Aleatha is carted off to safety by the human smuggler Roland Redleaf, whom she later admires and begins to care for. They set sail on an elven dragonship, landing in an ancient Sartan citadel-town. There, she admits the approaching tytans, who are no longer warlike. The tytans get the Star Chamber at the citadel to function. Aleatha is named High Priestess of the Tytans, and she marries Roland. (ES, IL)

Quindiniar, Calandra

The eldest of Lethan Quindiniar's children, Calandra runs the family business with a little help from her brother, Paithan. Her forte is manipulating people and numbers. "Calandra had never been pretty. . . . Now, in her fading youth, it appeared as if her entire face had been caught and pinched. She wore her hair pulled back in a tight knot at the top of her head, held in place by three lethal-looking, sharp-pointed combs. Her skin was dead white, because she rarely went out of doors and then carried a parasol to protect her from the sun." It is said Calandra did not care that she wasn't pretty, as she had no desire to catch a man. She speaks sharply and considers humans "ugly and boorish, little more than brutes and savages." She is appalled that her brother Paithan returns from a caravan trip with a human woman he wants to marry, and says that the woman can sleep with the Quindiniars' human slaves. Paithan unsuccessfully tries to change her mind and then later unsuccessfully tries to get her to leave the estate when the tytans come. She dies during the giants' onslaught. (ES)

Quindiniar, Elithenia

Wife of Lethan, she was a factory wizardess uneasy around the high-born elves. She emphasized education to her children, hiring a governess to teach them. She died of a mysterious illness, and her husband, Lethan, never got over her death. Her spirit is reunited with his when he dies on one of Pryan's floating citadels. (ES)

Quindiniar, Lethan

A wealthy elf, and father of Calandra, Aleatha, and Paithan, Lethan is an inventor and a dreamer. "The man was short, for an elf, and had obviously once been robustly plump. The flesh had begun to sag lately; the skin had turned sallow and slightly puffy. Though it could not be told beneath the soot, the gray hair standing up around a large bald spot on his head revealed that he was in his middle years." Paithan calls him "guvnor," though his sisters address the elf as Father or Papa. All of them consider Lethan a touch mad. Lethan is most interested in rockets and other experiments he works on in his laboratory. His home is on the highest hill in Equilan; the location was a status symbol among the middle class.

Lethan summons a human priest to his home, but instead receives the old wizard, Zifnab. The pair decides to use his rockets to attract the attention of a savior to rescue them from what Zifnab says is impending doom. The savior is Haplo, and the doom Zifnab foretells is the coming of the tytans who overrun Lethan's estate. Zifnab tells Lethan that by taking Haplo's flying ship to the stars, the elderly Quindiniar will be reunited with his dead wife. Lethan believes him and dies on one of those "stars," a citadel, where indeed his spirit is reunited with hers. (ES)

Quindiniar, Paithan

"Paithan's education came from the world, not from books." He traveled throughout Thillia, negotiating deals and making sure shipments were delivered. He and his older sister, Calandra, were in charge of the family business. Paithan stocks up a

Dragon Wing, Volume I   KEITH PARKINSON

caravan with "magical toys"—actually elven weapons, and travels to a rendezvous with the humans Roland and Rega Redleaf. He is initially duped into believing the Redleafs are husband and wife, and he curses himself for falling for another man's woman. When he learns the truth—that they are brother and sister who planned on scamming him—he thrusts her away. He cannot get her out of his heart, however, and later professes his love. He asks her to marry him, and the two, in the company of Roland and the dwarf Drugar, travel back to the Quindiniar estate. He refuses to give up Rega, even though his sisters Calandra and Aleatha object to a union with a human.

As the Quindiniar estate is overrun by tytans, he, Rega, Roland, Aleatha, and Drugar escape on an elven dragonship. They land in an ancient Sartan citadel-town, which they name Drugar. He and Rega wed and become rulers of the place. And he picks up the study of rockets, finally following in his father's footsteps. (ES, IL)

Quindiniar, Quintain

Father of Lenthan, he was said to be a legendary inventor and explorer who helped establish the elven city of Equilan. When Lenthan was old enough, Quintain turned the family business over to him and went off exploring again. Never heard from, Quintain was presumed dead. (ES)

Quintar

Intermarriage throughout the seven elven clans has weakened the various lines. However, there are still elves who are pure Quintar. (ES, HC)

Quintin

The elf "of much sense and worldly experience" serves as foreman to Paithan. Quintin rides at the head of Paithan's caravan to the human lands, and inspects all the merchandise they were carrying—"enchanted toys." In truth, they were carrying elven weapons. Quintin has been with the Quindiniar family for many years. (ES)

Raef

He is one of the Kairn Telest residents who flees his dying home with Prince Edmund. (FS)

Ramu

The son of Council of Seven members Samah and Orla is instructed to be friendly to the Sartan Alfred when he appears on the water world of Chelestra. Though Ramu is curious and questions much of what goes on around him, he is loyal to his father and the council. He is later named head of the council after his father is slain. (SM, IL, SG)

Ravenlark

Never seen, she was only talked about—touted as a minstrel who was said to have defeated the elves during the Battle of Seven Fields by bolstering the spirits of the other captives' with a song. (DW)

Redleaf, Rega

Introduced as a young woman sitting across from Roland of Griffith in the Jungleflower Tavern, Rega of Griffith is a smuggler and con artist. Short and muscular, she has dark hair and dark eyes shadowed by long lashes. She is careful never to drink to excess. Partnered with her brother, Roland, she masquerades as his less-than-faithful wife. Their intent was to make the elf Paithan Quindiniar fall for her, then Roland was to catch the pair at an opportune moment. Roland intended to gain riches from Paithan in exchange for keeping quiet the elf's indiscretion. However, Rega falls in love with Paithan and confesses the plot. The elf initially spurns her for it, then later reveals that he truly loves her and asks that she marry him. She travels with him to the Quindiniar estate, just ahead of the marauding tytans, and then leaves for the stars with him on Haplo's flying ship. The ship lands at an old citadel, into which they eventually welcome the tytans. Rega marries Paithan, and the two become rulers of the citadel-town, which they name Drugar, after their dwarven friend. (ES, IL)

Redleaf, Roland

A smuggler and consummate con artist, Roland of Griffith is a tall, muscular man with long blond hair. As part of their latest ruse, he pretends to be married to his sister Rega. The "husband and wife" team intends to sell weapons to the dwarf Drugar "Blackbeard." The weapons are to be acquired from the elf Paithan Quindiniar. Roland hatches a scheme to catch Paithan in a romantic moment with his "wife," after which he will force wealth out of the elf in exchange for not publicizing the elf's indiscretion. Then the Redleafs will gain money from the dwarf and the elf, walking away rich. Roland is frustrated when his sister actually falls for Paithan. In the end, Roland ironically begins to fall for Paithan's sister. He eventually marries her, and he becomes High Priest of the Tytans on one of Pryan's floating citadels. (ES, IL)

Reesh'ahn

He is the son of the elven emperor, and a rebellion leader. When a conflict erupts and Emperor Agah'ran disguises himself and slips away, the factions surrender peacefully to Prince Reesh'ahn. (DW, IL)

Reginald

Reginald is a half-mad knight found on the road leading away from Griffith. He reports to the Redleafs and Paithan Quindiniar that Reginald, the Liege Lord of Terncia, was killed by the tytans. (ES)

Rethis

Sage Rethis of the Vortex is credited with establishing some of the basic laws of rune-magic. Initially greeted with skepticism, his laws were later recognized as the standard foundation regarding understanding magic. (ES, SG)

River of Anger

The deep, fast river runs through the Labyrinth. Haplo says of the river: "According to legend, this river is the one thing in the Labyrinth we Patryns created. When the first of our people were cast into this prison, their rage was so terrible that it spewed forth from their mouths, became this river." (IL)

Rolf

He is a young boy who lived at the Kir monastery with Hugh. He died of an illness, which the monks would do nothing to treat. (DW)

Royal One

The king of the dragon-snakes of Chelestra is designated the Royal One. Ages past when the king met with the Sartan Council of Seven, he told the council leader that he wanted to destroy the Sartans. "Where did you come from?" the council leader asked. "Who created you?" The dragon replied, "You did." The Royal One led one attack after another against the Sartan city. The Sartans did their best to keep the king and his dragons away. In the end, the dragons gave up their assault and the Sartans "slept." See "Sartan" and "Samah" for more information.

When the Royal One appears before Haplo in a great sea cave, he tells Haplo that the Patryns created the dragon-snakes. The Royal One later captures Haplo on Arianus, after the dragon-serpents escape Chelestra through Death's Gate. Haplo escapes while the Royal One busies himself in the company of Xar, manipulating the wizard. The Royal One, calling himself Sang-drax, feigns loyalty to the Lord of the Nexus and offers to help him.

When Sang-drax and Xar travel to Abarrach to learn the necromantic secret of raising the dead, they capture Samah and Zifnab. Zifnab escapes their clutches; however, Sang-drax tortures Samah to death. See "Sang-drax," "dragon-serpents," and "Xar" for more information. (SM, HC, IL, SG)

Rue

Marit named the child Haplo fathered Rue, abandoning her in a Squatter village in the Labyrinth. (IL)

Rune-Bone

In the caverns of Abarrach, the Sartans play a game called rune-bone. The game is similar to the pre-Sundering game called mahjongg. (FS)

Rune-Joining

Patryns tattoo themselves with a complicated pattern, a magic sigla which binds them together. Their heart-runes become entwined, and they are in effect married. "We are one," the Lord of the Nexus tells Marit following their rune-joining. "No matter that we are apart, our thoughts will fly each to the other as we desire." As long as a rune-mate is alive, the partner cannot join with another. (IL, SG)

Runestate Boundary

The concept regarding the point beyond which magic will not function is called the Runestate Boundary. (FS)

Elven Star, Volume II KEITH PARKINSON

Runners

The Patryns in the Labyrinth are either considered Runners or Squatters. Runners, such as Haplo, are constantly on the move in an attempt to escape the Labyrinth. Escape is their primary goal. Though they sometimes cross paths with Squatters, Runners choose to live apart from them. (DW, ES, FS, SM, HC, IL)

Sabia

The elven princess Sabia is best friends with the dwarven princess, Grundle, and the Phondra chieftain's daughter, Alake. When the dragon-snakes demand the eldest daughters of the rulers, and the rulers refuse, Alake, Grundle, and Sabia decide to sneak away and give themselves up to the dragons. However, Sabia's betrothed, Devon, knocks the elven girl unconscious, puts on one of her dresses, and takes her place. When Sabia comes to, she is distraught and confident Devon went to his death. She throws herself out a window and dies. (SM)

Samah

When Alfred is pushed from Haplo's ship as it passes through Death's Gate, he appears in a chamber full of fellow Sartans. Samah is the first to introduce himself, giving Alfred his real name—which Alfred considers an honor. See "Sartans" for more information on the importance of names. Samah is the head of the Council of Seven on Chelestra. He was the Sartan instrumental in bringing about the Sundering and forming the four worlds—Arianus, Abarrach, Chelestra, and Pryan. He and the council also cast the Patryns, and rebellious Sartans, into the Labyrinth.

When it appears the humans, dwarves, and elves of Chelestra will attack the Sartan land, Samah threatens to open Death's Gate. His wife openly defies him, and he hurls her and Alfred into the Labyrinth. Samah eventually opens Death's Gate and is captured by the Lord of the Nexus and his seeming ally, Sang-drax. He is tortured in an attempt to gain information about the Seventh Gate. He dies, revealing nothing of use. The Lord of the Nexus revives Samah's corpse. However, the lord's efforts are for naught: Samah dies again. (SM, IL)

Sang-Drax

The Tribus elf captain Sang-drax brings his lieutenant, Ban'glor, and a contingent of elves to Drevlin in the Low Realm of Arianus. The elves wanted to gain the secret of the Kicksey-winsey. Captain Sang-drax is not loved by his men, and is considered a harsh taskmaster. In reality, he is the Royal One, a dragon-snake who came through Death's Gate.

He keeps company with the Lord of the Nexus, feigning loyalty, and travels with the lord to Abarrach to learn the secret of raising the dead. In elven, *sang* means *snake*, and *drax* means *dragon*. See "dragon-serpents" and "Royal One" for more information. (HC, IL, SG)

Sartans

In the rune language, Sartan means "Those Who Bring Back Light." Sartans are born with white hair that eventually turns brown at the ends. Ages past they split the universe into four worlds to prevent their enemy, the Patryns, from taking it over. The result was Abarrach, Realm of Stone; Arianus, Realm of Air; Chelestra, Realm of Water; and Pryan, Realm of Fire. The Sartan placed the Patryns in a prison called the Labyrinth, hoping the hardships there would "rehabilitate" them.

Sartans have two names. A private name is told to those individuals they love or trust, as a private name affords a measure of power. A public name is what a Sartan refers to himself as when he is in the general public. For example, Alfred is the Sartan Coren's public name. The Sartan language is embued with magic, and it can summon up images, visions, and emotions to enhance what the speaker is saying. (DW, ES, FS, SM, HC, IL, SG)

Savag

Though intermarriage has weakened the clan lines, there are still elves who work to keep the Savag clan intact. Savag is one of the seven clans of elves in the Mid Realm on Arianus. (ES, HC)

Screw, Dirk

Drunk on the job, this Geg allowed the Kicksey-winsey to be damaged. He was executed. (DW)

SeaKings

The SeaKings are humans feared by many of those on Equilan. Andor is the only SeaKing encountered during Paithan Quindiniar's travels. (ES)

Seamoon

The small, habitable islands formed by the Sartan on Chelestra are called seamoons. They orbit the sea-sun of Chelestra—albeit on the inside rather than on the outside. (SM)

Serpent Mage

Alfred the Sartan is called the Serpent Mage because his magic allows him to assume the form of a dragon. See "Montebank, Alfred" for more information. (SM, SG)

Seven-Eyed Dragon

This refers both to the ship that Hugh the Hand and Iridal take from Skurvash and to a legendary elven beast. The beast was defeated by the elven warrior Mnarash'ai after she overcame the seven deaths displayed in its eyes. (HC)

Seven Worlds

Though the Patryns and Sartans generally speak of four worlds resulting when their universe was sundered, there are technically seven: the Vortex, the Labyrinth, Nexus, Abarrach, Arianus, Chelestra, and Pryan. (IL)

Seventh Gate

"The Seventh Gate was a room with seven marble walls, covered by a domed ceiling. A globe suspended from the ceiling cast a soft, white glow." Here, Samah and the Sartan Council of Seven sundered the world and imprisoned the Patryns in the Labyrinth. Alfred, Marit, and the lazar Jonathan journey to the Seventh Gate. The Lord of the Nexus, Xar, and the dragon-snake, Sang-drax, are quick on their heels. A battle erupts in which Xar dies and the Seventh Gate is closed, sealing the worlds off from each other. (SG)

Sinistrad

A powerful wizard and mysteriarch of the High Realm, Sinistrad is Prince Bane's true father. When Bane falls overboard from a flying dragonship, Sinistrad magically speaks to the boy. As the child plummets through the air, Sinistrad teaches Bane to float using magic. A wizard of the Seventh House, Sinistrad came to King Stephen and Queen Anne's home on Bane's first birthday, congratulating the couple on their heir. His gesture convinced the king and queen that Bane was his son, not theirs. The evil wizard intended to take over Stephen and Anne's realm through Bane. He is slain by the assassin Hugh the Hand. (DW)

Skurvash

The Mid Realm island is home to cutthroats and thieves and is said to be more dangerous than the haunted islands of the Seven Mysteries. The rulers of Skurvash are called the Brotherhood, or the Brotherhood of the Hand, and they care little whether a man is an elf, dwarf, or human. "The rulers of Skurvash don't care about the slant of a man's eyes, only the glint of his money." Iridal and Hugh the Hand travel to the island as they begin to search for Iridal's son, Bane. Hugh is a member of the Brotherhood, which is an assassins' guild. (HC)

Snogs

These Labyrinth beasts killed Haplo's parents when he was a child. The intelligent creatures have hulking bodies, razorlike claws, and sharp fangs. The parents deaths are played out when Haplo and Alfred pass through a gate to the World of Stone. Alfred shares Haplo's consciousness and witnesses the grisly act. (FS)

Sparanga, Delsart

The elderly Sartan researcher discovered the necromantic theory of a spiritual state called the Delsart Near State or the Delsart Similitude. (FS)

Stadion

The dwarves of Chelestra measure distance in stadions. One stadion equals 520 dwarven feet. A stadion is also called a footrace. (SM)

Stalagma

A fiery liquor called Stalagma is the ruler of Necropolis' favorite drink. The red liquor is considered very potent. (FS)

Star Chamber

The chamber on one of the floating citadels of Pryan is manned by seven tytans. The massive Star Chamber brings power, heat, and light to the sundered realms. "The Star Chamber's lower area houses Seven Thrones, which surround and face the Well of the World. These thrones are immense, so that tytans may sit comfortably in them." Only the blind tytans are able to withstand the light of the Star Chamber. (IL)

Stardial, Groth

The Arianus dwarf studied the Kicksey-winsey and developed various theories about the masheen. "Groth Stardial's theory, popularly called Bloodwinsey, though crude, was not far from the truth." The theory postulated that raw materials moving through the Kicksey-winsey was like the blood that moved through a dwarf's veins. (HC)

Stephen

Together with his wife, Anne of Winsher, he is said to have formed an army that overthrew the elves and literally hurled them off Volkaran and Uylandia. He and Anne proclaimed themselves king and queen of the Volkaran Isles and the Uylandia Cluster. Stephen offers Hugh the Hand his life in exchange for a task—killing Prince Bane. Stephen knows Bane is not his true son. He directs Hugh to take the child far away and then kill him. A year passes from that time, and Stephen believes Bane is dead. He and Anne have another child, a daughter. He is surprised to see Bane reappear, and he is wounded when Bane attempts to kill him. Iridal, Bane's true mother, saves Stephen by slaying Bane. (DW, HC)

Squatters

Patryns in the Labyrinth are considered either Squatters or Runners. Squatters, though nomadic, establish temporary communities. Survival, not escape, is foremost in their minds. Like all Patryns in the Labyrinth they share lovers, food, and children, though they have a greater semblance of society. They hold binding ceremonies, vows held between individuals that signify a strong bond of friendship. They are often held between a man and a woman. Haplo's parents had been bound by such a ceremony. (DW, ES, FS, SM, IL, SG)

Stergo

The fungus on Tytan, an isle of Arianus, is used as a healing balm and as pipe tobacco. The elves grow it on their own plantations. However, the flavor and aroma of stergo grown on Tytan is far superior. (DW)

Sun-chasers

The dwarves of Chelestra build ships called sun-chasers, which resemble black whales. The ships are made of the drywood of Phondra and covered with a resin to protect it from water damage. (SM)

Sundering

When the Sartan Council of Seven split the Earth, four worlds were created, representative of the four basic elements: Arianus, air; Abarrach, stone; Pryan, fire; and Chelestra, water. The split was called the Sundering. Thousands were killed in the Sundering, and the mensch—the humans, dwarves, and elves—who survived were placed on these four worlds. The Patryns, the Sartans' enemy, were thrown into a realm called the Labyrinth. There, the Sartans believed their enemy would be rehabilitated.

According to the writings of Alfred the Sartan, the Sundering involved thus: "The Earth was destroyed. Four worlds were created out of the ruin. Worlds for ourselves and the mensch: Air, Fire, Stone, Water. Four Gates connect each world to the other: Arianus to Pryan to Abarrach to Chelestra. A house of correction was built for our enemies: the Labyrinth. The Labyrinth is connected to the other worlds through the Fifth Gate: the Nexus. The Sixth Gate is the center, and permits entry to the Vortex. And all was accomplished through the Seventh Gate. The end was the beginning." (DW, ES, FS, SM, IL, SG)

Surunan

This Sartan city on Chelestra is artistic. It is home to the Sartans who "slept" through the Sundering and the hundreds of years since. The Council of Seven meets in Surunan. (SM)

Table of Elders

It was found by Alfred and Haplo in sacred catacombs beneath the Necropolis castle on Abarrach. The table was made of wood brought through Death's Gate at the time of the Sundering. (FS)

Thillia

These are the major human lands on Pryan, consisting of the towns of Griffith, Terncia, Maloria, Strethia, Dourglasia, Barsport, Marcinia, and other villages closer to the elven land of Equilan. (ES)

Three-Chop-Nick

The executioner wears black robes and a black hood so the people of Dandrak will not recognize him. He gained his name because "he's never yet managed to sever a head from a neck at the first blow." He is frustrated when Hugh the Hand is spared and he has no one to behead. (DW)

Tier

These enormous birds are used as beasts of burden in Arianus. One was used to pull the cart carrying Hugh the Hand in the city of Ke'lith. They are poor flyers, though they are extremely fast runners because of their powerful legs. In the wild, dragons consider the tier their favorite prey. The elves consider the tier unclean and repulsive. (DW)

Tiger-Men

Taller than most humans, tiger-men have thick fur and long tails. They can run on two legs or four, are able to leap great distances, and are among the fierce predators in the Labyrinth. Equally at home on the ground and in the trees, they can also use weapons and are proficient in rune-magic. Haplo, Marit, Hugh the Hand, and Alfred run into a tiger-men hunting party. They narrowly escape with their lives. (IL)

Tomas

He is a messenger bringing bad news to the estate of the earl of Necropolis. Tomas, a young man dirty from his fast ride, tells the earl, duke, and duchess—and the Sartan Alfred who is staying with them—that the king has killed Haplo and Edmund, prince of Kairn Telest. Tomas assures Alfred that the bodies of the two men will be well preserved. (FS)

Torb

A descendant of the pig, torb is the Sartans' primary source of food in Necropolis and throughout Abarrach. Torb graze on the kairn grass. (FS)

Tretar

The flying dragonships are crafted by the Tretar, one of the clans of elves. The Tretar joined with the warlike Tribus elves, which might have faded into nothingness without them. (ES, HC)

Tretar, Count

The count is head of the Tretar clan and is Emperor Egah'ran's adviser. (HC)

Trian

King Stephen's magus, Trian, is sent to stop Hugh the Hand's execution. Trian, a wizard of the Third House who is alleged to dabble in rune magic, brought Hugh to King Stephen on Lord Rogar's dragon. Trian is unswervingly loyal to the king and to Queen Anne. "He knew their every secret and could have made his fortune ten times over by selling out one or the other. He would have as soon jumped into the Maelstrom." (DW, HC)

Tribus

The warlike Tribus were a fading clan until the Tretar banded with them. The Tribus descend on Drevlin in Arianus when the Kicksey-winsey stops working. Here, they are lead by Captain Sang-drax, who only appears to be a Tribus elf. He is, in fact, a shape-shifting dragon-snake. The Tribus elves in his company are true elves, however. (ES, HC)

Raistlin in the Tower of High Sorcery JEFF EASLEY

Twist, Ernst

A member of the Assassins' Guild on Skurvash, Ernst sponsors the young John Darby, who is trying to join the group. Ernst looks the part of a bumpkin, dressed in baggy clothes and broken shoes. "This was no bumpkin, however; those who took him for such probably never lived long enough to regret their mistake." His cold eyes have a peculiar red cast to them. See the "Brotherhood" for more information. (HC)

Tytans

Forest giants, the tytans are described as human in shape, but sightless. Their bodies are covered with leaves and vines, and their skin looks like tree bark, allowing them to effectively hide in the forest. Andor the SeaKing reveals that the tytans destroyed the Kasnar Empire. "Wiped it out. Not a building left standing, a person left alive except those who managed to flee ahead of them." Then the tytans moved south through the dwarven kingdoms, the human kingdoms, then to the land of the elves. The tytans were searching for the citadel, where they believed their sight could be restored. It was there, they claimed, that the Sartans stole their eyes. The Sartans had endowed the tytans with great strength and rune-magic for physical labor. They were blinded so they could work in the incredibly bright starlight. Eventually the tytans find their way to the floating citadel, where Paithan, Rega, Alethea, and Roland are living. The tytans have reached their goal and take their place in the Star Chamber. See "Star Chamber" for more information. (ES, IL)

Ulaka

The caravanner is an associate of Paithan Quindiniar. (ES)

Umbar

He is in the company of Ulaka and Gregor when Paithan Quindiniar's caravan stops for a rest. (ES)

Unseen

An elite unit of elven soldiers was established by the emperor to hunt down rebel elves. They are called the Unseen because they can make themselves nearly invisible. (HC)

Usha

In the Labyrinth near the seventh gate, Marit, Hugh the Hand, and Alfred cross paths with Usha. A Squatter, she reveals that their tribe's Headman is dead—along with several of her people. She leads her tribe, but has not yet been declared a Headman. Only the tribal council can officially appoint a Headman. (SG)

Vassa

The Squatter Headman hides Haplo and his companions from the dragon-snakes in the Labyrinth. He is half-Sartan, his lineage dotted with Sartan-Patryn intermarriages. (IL, SG)

Vate

Dwarven kings on the water world of Chelestra are called Vates, a term that also means *father*. (SM)

Vortex

One of the death gates leads to the Vortex, a place Alfred the Sartan calls safe. "All our wants and needs are provided. The magic sees to that." There are crystal coffins in the Vortex, and the body of Orla rests in one of them. Alfred explains that an empty coffin is for him when his time comes. The Vortex leads into the Labyrinth. (IL, SG)

Weesham

Elven wizards who take the souls of dying elven royals to the Cathedral of the Albedo are termed weeshams. They are linked to a royal child, following the child through its life and waiting for its death. Sometimes they are called geir, a slang elven word for vulture. The weesham are skilled in spirit magic and study at the side of Kenkari to perfect their craft. (HC)

Welves

The Gegs of Arianus refer to the elves of the Mid Realm as Welves. However, when the Gegs stop calling themselves Gegs, and instead use the word "dwarves," they also begin calling their neighbors elves. (HC)

Whispering Sea

This is the body of water, connected to the Terinthian Ocean, that separates Equilan from the Kasnar Empire. The Bay of Chothax and the Sea of Stars are off of the Whispering Sea. (ES)

Wolfen

Man-sized furry beasts that hunt in the Labyrinth are called wolfen. They have yellow eyes, formidable fangs, claw-fingered hands, and thick hides. Wolfen hunt in packs of thirty or forty, attacking Runners and Squatters in the Labyrinth. (ES, IL, SG)

Wombe

The city in Drevlin on Arianus is where Limbeck sets up his power base when he became leader of the dwarves. (DW, HC)

Xar

When Haplo returns from Abarrach, the Lord of the Nexus refers to himself as Xar. "Xar was not his real name. It is not a Patryn name at all, in fact, and is undoubtedly one he devised himself, possibly a corruption of the ancient word *tsar*, derived from Ceasar." Xar was the first Patryn to escape the hor-

Dragons of Triumph CLYDE CALDWELL

rors of the Labyrinth. He returned to help others escape and made Haplo one of his followers. He strikes up a partnership with Sang-drax and decides he wants to learn the secret of raising the dead. Sang-drax volunteers to aid him, and travels with Xar to Abarrach and Pryan.

At first the Lord of the Nexus believes Sang-drax and trusts his counsel. However, Xar begins to question the dragon-snake's intent after Sang-drax appropriates the lord's elven ship and sets sail, Sang-drax says, in search of Haplo the traitor. Zifnab warns Xar that Sang-drax intends to impersonate the lord. Xar is not overly concerned, he has his own plans to worry about—controlling the worlds of Stone, Air, Water, and Fire.

Eventually Xar finds his way to the Seventh Gate, where he expects to gain dominance over the worlds. However, the violence he brings with him is his downfall, and he dies after a battle with Sang-drax. (SM, HC, IL, SG)

Zankor'el

Captain of the elven ship *Carfa'shon*, Zankor'el is a member of the royal family. "Tall, slender, and handsome, Captain Zankor'el has a great personal regard for himself and none at all for those who have the distinct misfortune not to be of high rank, not to be of royal birth, and—in short—not to be him." He is killed during a duel with Btohar'in, his lieutenant whom he treated none too kindly. (DW)

Zifnab

Introduced as a bumbling old man who has trouble remembering his own name—"Fiz—No, I can't use that. Furball. Doesn't seem quite dignified enough."—he calms his charmed dragon and prevents the beast from eating the elves on the grand estate of Lord Durndrun. Zifnab claims he was asked to come to Lethan Quindiniar's home, as the human priests "were all out fund-raising." However, he quickly adds that "I've come to announce the end of the world." The old wizard, who is quick to drop the names of such great mages as Gandalf and Merlin, and who said he once stayed in the same hotel as Clark Gable, foretells the coming of Haplo. He calls Haplo the savior with bandaged hands who would take them to the stars in his flying ship. He also foretells the coming of the tytans and predicts that Aleatha Quindiniar will not be marrying Lord Durndrun.

Zifnab accompanies an entourage of arguing humans, elves, and the dwarf Drugar to one of Pryan's floating citadels. There, Zifnab stages a battle in which his dragon companion eats him. The dragon chases the arguing entourage into an abandoned city, where the dwarf, elves, and humans decide they had better get along if they are to survive. In the end, the dragon and Zifnab secretly observe the group. "Do you think there's a chance?" Zifnab poses. "There has to be," replies the dragon, who claims that Zifnab is his familiar.

Zifnab continues to appear from time to time, saving various individuals as needed and luring others to travel to different realms, such as the Labyrinth. In one instance, he alters his visage and appears before Ramu, leader of the Council of Seven. He baits Ramu into heading to the Labyrinth. Among Zifnab's aliases are James Bond and Dorothy from Kansas. (ES, HC, IL, SG)

4 Characters, Places, and Things in the *Dragonlance*® Novels

by Margaret Weis and Tracy Hickman

A Concordance by J. Robert King

The Dragons of Chaos CLARETTE

ach entry in the concordance is followed by an abbreviation that indicates the novel in which it appears:

CI: Chronicles I (*Dragons of Autumn Twilight*), TSR, Inc., paperback, 1984

CII: Chronicles II (*Dragons of Winter Night*), TSR, Inc., paperback, 1985

CIII: Chronicles III (*Dragons of Spring Dawning*), TSR, Inc., paperback, 1985

LI: Legends I (*Time of the Twins*), TSR, Inc., paperback, 1986

LII: Legends II (*War of the Twins*), TSR, Inc., paperback, 1986

LIII: Legends III (*Test of the Twins*), TSR, Inc., paperback, 1986

SG: *The Second Generation*, TSR, Inc., paperback, 1994

DSF: *Dragons of Summer Flame*, TSR, Inc., paperback, 1995

ALL: Appears in most or all novels

Occasional citations from *Leaves from the Inn of the Last Home* are not noted.

Abanasinia

This region in west-central Ansalon is where the companions of the Lance originate. The peninsula, bounded on the east and north by the Newsea and on the west by the Straits of Schallsea, contains Solace, Gateway, Haven, Xak Tsaroth, and the land of the barbarian tribes of Que-shu, Que-kiri, and Que-teh. (CI, CIII)

Abyss, the

This outer plane is a place of shifting forms and shadows, its topography determined by the expectations of those within it. Takhisis, the Queen of Darkness, dwells here and continually seeks a Portal from this plane to Krynn.

Raistlin and Crysania enter the Abyss through just such a Portal, hoping to draw Takhisis through to Krynn, where Raistlin can defeat her. Caramon enters as well, convincing Raistlin to abandon his plan and block the Queen's emergence.

Palin Majere's Test takes place in an illusory representation of the Abyss, in which he contacts his "dead" Uncle Raistlin. He later appears in the true Abyss, is stabbed by his Aunt Kitiara, and rescued by Raistlin.

Tasslehoff Burrfoot is whisked away to the Abyss when the fiery mountain strikes Istar in the Cataclysm. There, he meets the gnome Gnimsh, who repairs the kender's time-travel device.

The final conflict of the war against Chaos occurs in the Abyss. Steel Brightblade and Palin, riding on Flare, reach the plane through a portal at the base of a fiery rift in the ocean. Usha, Tasslehoff, and Dougan Redhammer reach it by way of a spell word. (LI, LII, LIII, SG, DSF)

AC

After Cataclysm. (ALL)

Aesthetics

This order of monks, committed to scholarship and archiving, work in the Library of Palanthas. Bertrem and the other Aesthetics valiantly defend the library against a draconian attack during Kitiara's assault on the city. (CII, LIII)

Ages of Krynn

Age of Starbirth

The First Age exists before recorded history, extending backward from 9000 PC. During this time, the lesser gods conspire against Chaos, Father of All and Nothing, to create Krynn and the creatures of the world. During this time, stars are born, dragons are created, and the gods fight over control of the world—the All Saints War.

Age of Dreams

This, the Second Age, stretches from about 9000 to 1000 PC. During this period, the original races—elves (the children of Paladine), humans (the children of Gilean), and Irda (the children of Takhisis)—find their places in the world. The latter half of this age contains the first two dragon wars, the creation and arrival of the Graygem of Gargath, the Kinslayer Wars, the signing of the Swordsheath Scroll, and the founding of Thorbardin, Ergoth, and Qualinesti.

Age of Might

The Third Age encompasses the thousand years before the Cataclysm (1000 to 0 PC). Istar and its developing sense of self-righteousness dominates this age. The Temple of Istar is established by the Kingpriest. Edicts call for a genocidal war against "evil" races such as goblins, hobgoblins, ogres (and, later, by extension, kender, dwarves, and gnomes). Mages are persecuted. The Tower of High Sorcery in Istar is taken over by the Kingpriest, the Tower of Palanthas is sealed, two others are destroyed, and the Tower of Wayreth withdraws within the magical Forest of Wayreth. Thirteen Warnings presage the Cataclysm, Lord Soth refuses to sacrifice himself to save the world, and a fiery mountain falls from the sky to destroy Istar.

Age of Despair

This period, the Fourth Age, extends from the Cataclysm until the end of the Chaos War, (1 to 379 AC). During most of this time, the gods that had ruled the world before the Cataclysm are forgotten, the Knights of Solamnia are in disgrace, and steel currency replaces gold. Fistandantilus/Raistlin fights in the Dwarfgate Wars. In Neraka, Takhisis plants the foundation stone of the Temple of Istar. Berem and his sister Jasla prevent her return to the world; and eggs of good dragons are corrupted to make the first draconians.

After the War of the Lance, Raistlin and Caramon travel back in time and into the Abyss, and Kitiara makes war on Palanthas. Takhisis founds her new knighthood, and her Highlord Ariakan conquers most of the world. The Graygem is split, releasing Chaos, and bringing about the end of the Fourth Age.

Age of Mortals

This period, the Fifth Age, extends from the end of the Chaos War, at 379 AC, forward. Fizban speculates this age will be the last and longest.

Krynn, during this period, is markedly different from what it has been before. The gods have abandoned the world, and so the constellations have changed. The departure of the three gods of magic means the disappearance of the three moons, leaving one nonmagical moon. It means also the end of magic as it has been known on the planet, though Fizban hints there may be other magic that mortals must discover themselves. A red star appears, lit by Flint Fireforge. (DSF)

Aghar

See Gully Dwarves.

All Saints War

This war in the heavens, during the Age of Starbirth, pits god against god in a struggle for control of Krynn and the creatures living upon it. The result of this war is an agreement between the gods not to intervene directly in mortal affairs. It is this voluntary exile from Krynn that Takhisis strives ever to break. (DSF)

Amberyl

This Irda woman, according to legend, meets Raistlin at the Wayward Inn, joins with him according to the ogre state of *Valin*, and bears him a daughter. (SG)

Amothus, Lord of Palanthas

Amothus rules Palanthas from the royal house during the War of the Lance, the invasion of Kitiara, and the Chaos War. He is ever reluctant to fortify for war, which eventually leads to the city's conquest. (CII, LIII, DSF)

Ansalon

This continent is the setting of the Weis/Hickman stories of Krynn. A southern-hemisphere land mass, its climates grow colder toward the south. Though once a solid land mass with few islands, the land is shattered by the Cataclysm, new islands are formed, Blood Sea and Newsea are created, and the polar ice cap joins the base of the continent. (ALL)

Antrax

The contagion is feared to have infected the skin of the Dewar during the Dwarfgate Wars. In fact, Raistlin's cursed money infects them. (CII)

Apoletta

This sea-elf, lover of Zebulah, encounters Tanis and company when they enter sunken Istar through the Blood Sea Maelstrom. (CIII)

Argat, Dewar Thane

During the Dwarfgate Wars, Argat, the leader of the Dewar dwarves, betrays the mountain dwarves, defending Pax Tharkas for money and a promise of

General Caramon's head. He then betrays Raistlin as well, and suffers the rot-plague of his cursed money. (LII)

Ariakan

Son of Highlord Ariakas and sea-goddess Zeboim, Ariakan fights under his father during the War of the Lance. Captured by the Solamnic Knights, he is held captive in the Tower of High Sorcery, where he observes the knights' organization and loyalty. Takhisis provides him a vision of her new knighthood, which he establishes. He lures, among others, Steel Brightblade to their ranks.

During the Chaos War, Ariakan is fifty years old, strong, tall, with a hawkish nose and piercing eyes. Prior to the war, he conquers more of Ansalon than all the dragonarmies in the War of the Lance. He is reputed by friends and foes to be driven but fair, a knight of honor. He dies in the High Clerist's Tower, defending it against the daemons and shadow-wights of Chaos's army. His mother Zeboim appears beside his body. (SG, DSF)

Ariakas, Highlord

The highest-ranking Highlord in the War of the Lance, Ariakas is commander of all the dragonarmies. He and his consort Zeboim give birth to Ariakan, who will dominate the continent twenty-five years later.

Ruthless, thorough, brilliant, and magically adept, Ariakas wears the Crown of Power, making him the chief rival of the Dark Lady, Kitiara. During the Council of War in Neraka, Tanis stabs Ariakas and takes the Crown of Power. Ariakas dies, forsaken by Takhisis as a weakling. (CII, CIII)

Army of Fistandantilus

In the time after the Cataclysm, en route to Zhaman and the Portal there, Caramon, Raistlin, and Kitiara are attacked by a group of marauders: disfavored Solamnic Knights. Caramon defeats their leader, Steeltoe, and takes charge of the group. Word of a crusade spreads across the land, and by the time they reach Pax Tharkas, the ranks swell into an army. Caramon becomes the army's general and leads the men in the Dwarfgate Wars. (LII)

The Companions of the Lance LARRY ELMORE

Art, the

This is the name of magic, as practiced by White-, Red-, and Black-Robed mages. (ALL)

Astinus of Palanthas

This scribe is immortal, recording the history of Krynn from its first moment to its last. He is said to be all races and none, both genders and neither, an impassive scribe and a meddler who has committed black deeds and made noble sacrifices.

Among Astinus's deeds are providing succor to Raistlin, giving Caramon a volume of future history that allows him to rescue Ansalon, and saving Steel and Palin by preventing the Knight of Takhisis's execution.

Some have said that Astinus is a monk who serves Gilean, god of the book. Others have said he is Gilean himself. Whatever his other names, Astinus is most certainly an alter ego of Weis and Hickman. (CII, CIII, LI, LII, LIII, DSF)

Aurak

These wingless draconians are formed from the eggs of gold dragons. Rare, they are often used as special agents. They can move undetected among other races. (ALL)

Avril

This young Irda, just past her Year of Oneness, argues that her people should remain on their isle and fight the Knights of Takhisis. (DSF)

Baaz

These draconians are the most common type, with small wings and small minds. Baaz are the draconians used by Senator Rashas Aronthulas to lead Tanis away from his abducted son, Gilthas. (SG)

Bakaris, Highlord

This young dragonrider is a subordinate, and lover, of the Dark Lady, Kitiara. She quickly throws him over for Tanis when they meet in Flotsam. Thereafter Bakaris is captured in aerial combat by none other than Tasslehoff Burrfoot. He is held captive. Kitiara suggests a trade of hostages, Bakaris for Tanis Half-Elven (who is not actually a captive) as a ruse to capture Laurana, the Golden General. When he attempts to rape her, she kills him. (CII, CIII)

Balifor

This country has the dubious honor of bordering on Goodlund (kender country) in the east and the Blood Sea of Istar in the north. Here, the Red Wizard and His Wonderful Illusions road show tours, featuring Raistlin and Goldmoon. (CII)

Bas Ohn-Koraf

This minotaur is first mate of the *Perechon*, a boat captained by the sea barbarian, Maquesta Kar-thon. (CII, CIII)

Battle Box

This strategic device is developed by Ariakan to allow him to play out a battle in miniature before sending in his troops. (DSF)

Battle of Thoradin Bay

See Thoradin Bay, Battle of.

Bay of Balifor

A long, crooked inlet of the Courrain Ocean, this bay separates Silvanesti from Balifor. It is crossed by Tanis and companions when they leave Silvanesti. (CII)

Beggar's Alley

When Crysania, Caramon, and Tasslehoff go back in time, they arrive in this rough district of old Istar. (LI)

Berem, the Green Gemstone Man, the Everman

While hunting for food near Neraka, Berem and his sister Jasla discover a gem-encrusted stone (foundation from the Temple of Istar, planted by Takhisis to grow her temple). Berem and Jasla get into an argument, which results in her falling against the stone and bleeding profusely on it. The stone grows quickly thereafter, though the presence of Jasla's spirit prevents Takhisis from entering the world through the temple.

Berem, a jewel embedded in his chest, flees. He is first encountered by the companions at Pax Tharkas, where he is crushed by a stone. He later appears at the wedding of Goldmoon and Riverwind. He cannot die. Tanis and his party next encounter Berem as the helmsman of the *Perechon*. He returns with Tanis to Neraka and, called by his sister's ghost, reunites with her, bringing the temple collapsing down around them. (CI, CII, CIII)

Bertrem

This unassuming Aesthetic works in the Library of Palanthas, a right-hand man to the famous Astinus. Though rotund and mild mannered, he and his comrades repel a company of draconians in Kitiara's attack on Palanthas. (CII, CIII)

Black Lily

This plant purportedly grows from the heart of murder victims and bleeds when plucked. It is the sign of the Knights of the Lily, an order of Takhisis. (SG, DSF)

Black Robes

This order of mages practices evil magic, which originates from Nuitari, the invisible moon of magic. During the War of the Lance, the order is headed by Ladonna of the Black Robes. She is followed by Dalamar the Black, one-time apprentice to Raistlin. Raistlin switches from his Red Robes when the Black Robe mage Fistandantilus saves his life in the Library of Palanthas. Later, Astinus offers the Black Robes to Palin because he is about to allow Steel to die in his place. (ALL)

Black Swan, the

This inn, a day's ride from the house of Tanis and Laurana, is where Senator Rashas pledges to meet Gilthas, when in truth he plans an abduction. (SG)

Blood Bay

See Blood Sea of Istar.

Blood Sea of Istar

This body of water is a deep, perpetual blood color, due, it is said, to the sediments churned up by the maelstrom at its center. The maelstrom is caused by the impact of the fiery mountain on Istar, dragging the city of the Kingpriest to the floor of the sea. Tanis, Caramon, Raistlin, and companions travel this sea aboard the *Perechon*, enter the maelstrom, and end up in the sunken city. (CIII)

Bloodwatch

This city is a dragonarmy garrison in Balifor. The companions are allowed to leave Port Balifor only when the Red Wizard and his Wonderful Illusions road show promises to appear here. (CII)

Blue Crystal Staff

This staff, brought back from his quest by Riverwind, is given as a gift to Goldmoon. The staff is made of a solid piece of blue crystal. It channels the healing powers of Mishakal, allowing Goldmoon to heal even the wicked Highseeker Hederick. It is part of the statue of Mishakal from her temple outside of Xak Tsaroth.

Goldmoon uses the staff to slay the black dragon Onyx in Xak Tsaroth, sacrificing herself to save Raistlin. When she is resurrected, she is a true cleric, and the staff rejoins the blue crystal statue. (CI)

Bozak

These draconians are created from corrupted bronze dragon eggs. They are expert gliders (a contingent of them lands atop the High Clerist's Tower during Ariakan's attack), fighters, and mages. Caramon and Tanis fight a Bozak wizard on the flying citadel. (LIII, DSF)

Bracelet, Antimagic

This bracelet, provided to Lord Gunthar by Dalamar, protects its wearer from magical attack, including Lord Soth's power word kill. Tanis wears it to battle the death knight, but Tasslehoff, seeing that Soth will kill Tanis's dragon mount and Tanis afterward, steals the item to prevent the encounter. (LIII)

Bridge of Passage

This smooth, white bridge leads from Foghaven Vale to Silver Dragon Mountain and the Tomb of Huma. The bridge crosses a wide swath of steaming, boiling hot springs. Silvara guides her companions across the railless expanse, much to Flint's trepidation. (CII)

Brightblade, Steel

Son of virtuous Knight of Solamnia Sturm Brightblade and treacherous Dragon Highlord Kitiara Uth Matar, Steel is from early days torn apart by the two halves of his nature. Unwanted by his mother, he nearly kills her in childbirth, and she leaves him while he is yet an infant. A twenty-year-old weaver, Sara Dunstan, raises the boy, with monetary help from Kitiara.

When Steel has come of age, Ariakan seduces him into the Knighthood of Takhisis. His uncle Caramon and Tanis Half-Elven intervene, taking the young man to his father's grave in the High Clerist's Tower. There, the ghost of Sturm bestows upon his son the sword of the Brightblades, and the starjewel given him by Alhana Starbreeze. Steel joins the knights anyway, though the priestess at the induction recognizes that his soul does not belong to Takhisis.

At the Battle of Thoradin Bay, Steel discovers Palin Majere among the few Solamnic survivors, and Tanin and Sturm Majere among the dead. In repayment of his debt to Caramon, Steel takes Palin and his brothers back to Solace, with Palin's oath he will return with Steel as a prisoner. Palin's ransom is to open the Portal for the Dark Queen's emergence.

Instead of taking this demand to the Tower of Wayreth, however, Palin and Steel go to the Tower of Palanthas to open the Portal themselves. Palin enters the Portal and they are separated, and Steel is called back to the ranks of the Knights of Takhisis. There, Steel is to be executed if Palin does not return. He fights in the storming of the High Clerist's Tower, his life spared by Tanis Half-Elven, who is killed in the fighting.

Afterward, Steel is held captive, awaiting execution, until Palin returns, fulfilling his vow. When the Knights of Takhisis are massacred at the High Clerist's Tower by the minions of Chaos, Steel and Palin band together to fight the new threat. They ride together into the Abyss and battle Chaos. Steel is killed, battling bravely against the giant. (SG, DSF)

Brightblade, Sturm

His father a Knight of Solamnia lost in battle, Sturm sets out from Solace to find him. His traveling companion, Kitiara Uth Matar, is intent on breaking the virtuous young knight and seduces him. This is only the beginning of Sturm's disillusionment. He discovers in Solamnia a country that reviles the knights. Worse, the knights themselves are vicious, conniving, and back-biting, at best unbendingly strict and at worst rife with corruption.

Sturm does not find his father, but does claim the armor and sword that have been in the Brightblade family since before the Cataclysm. Mustachioed and grim, Sturm reunites with the companions at the inn. He quests with them north to Xak Tsaroth, his vision of the white stag guiding them through Prayer's Eye Peak to an encounter with the Forestmaster.

Later, after Xak Tsaroth, Qualinesti, and Pax Tharkas, he meets and falls in love with Alhana Starbreeze in Tarsis. When they are separated, she grants him a starjewel as emblem of her love. Sturm adventures further with the companions, to Ice Wall, and Qualimori.

Afterward, he travels with Derek Crownguard to Sancrist, where the Rose Knight accuses Sturm of crimes punishable by death, specifically impersonating a knight. Gunthar Uth Wistan, recognizing which is the true knight, inducts Sturm into the Knighthood and sets him in charge of the Knights of the Crown.

Sturm battles bravely at the High Clerist's Tower, but is slain by Kitiara, his one-time lover. Entombed in the Chamber of Paladine, Sturm's ghost reaches out to grant his sword and starjewel to his son (by Kitiara), Steel Brightblade. He also appears to Tanis in a vision, telling him to defend his son. (CII, SG, DSF)

Brutes, the

Ariakan used these men among his shock troops. They come from a continent to the east of Ansalon

The Dragons of Krynn LARRY ELMORE

and are six to seven feet tall, as muscular as men, as lithe as elves, and as sturdy and war-loving as dwarves. (DSF)

Bulps

See Sluds, Bulps, Glups.

Bupu

The companions encounter this female gully dwarf in Xak Tsaroth, among the creatures upon whom Raistlin casts a love spell. Her devotion outstrips all others, though, and she provides him the spellbook he seeks in the ruins—a spellbook of Fistandantilus—and an emerald. Her love of Raistlin and his compassion toward her comes to represent his human side, his tiny store of compassion.

Bupu accompanies Caramon and Crysania to the Temple of Wayreth to plead the case for Raistlin's humanity. In the future, Caramon discovers her dead body, victim of Raistlin's ravages of Krynn. Due to this sighting Raistlin abandons his plan to ascend to godhood. Bupu appears later to him in a vision during his sojourn in the Abyss. (CI, LI, LIII, DSF)

Burrfoot, Tasslehoff

More than the Graygem of Gargath or even Chaos himself, Tasslehoff Burrfoot and his kender kin are perhaps the greatest source of chaos in the world of Krynn. Tasslehoff, infected with kender wanderlust, adventures from the heights of Mount Nevermind to the depths of the Blood Sea, hangs out with Raistlin in the Abyss and Fizban in Whitestone Glade, turns undead with a mundane spoon and captures Chaos himself with a pocketknife called *Rabbitslayer,* changes the future in ancient Istar and changes the past in the desolated Solace of the future. By his own reckoning, he has been killed three times over and lived to tell about it.

Tasslehoff's favorite companions are Flint Fireforge, whom he uses as a straight man, and Fizban the Fabulous, to whom *he* is the straight man. He also likes Usha a great deal, and seems happy when she and Palin fall in love.

Over the years, this nonmagical fellow has gained command of some rather nifty magic. His glasses of true seeing allow him to read spells and ancient writings accessible only to the most learned scholars. His time/dimension-travel device allows him to escape the Abyss, take Caramon to the future, and send Tanis and Caramon to the flying citadel (it also triggers the destruction of Zhaman and the Plains of Dergoth, but let's not get picky). His polymorphing ring turns him into a mouse and lets him travel back in time. He destroys the Dragon Orb of Ice Wall only to discover the Dragon Orb of the High Clerist's Tower. He steals Tanis's antimagic bracelet, saving the man from Lord Soth. He even navigates Kitiara's flying citadel—right into Palanthas Bay.

For the favor of returning Chaos to his lovely gemstone home, Tasslehoff is squashed by the god. It seems to make little difference to him. He can finally meet his friend Flint again, be greeted as an old doorknob, and help the dwarf stoke a fire that becomes the red star of hope in the firmament of the Age of Mortals. (ALL)

Caergoth

Once a small farming village, this town is transformed by the Cataclysm into a deep-water port. Caramon establishes his command post here for the Army of Fistandantilus before crossing the Straits of Schallsea. (LII)

Canticle of the Dragon

This epic poem speaks of the history of Krynn from the time of Huma to the start of the War of the Lance. The companions discuss it at the Inn of the Last Home, just before Hederick's immolation. (CI)

Cat Pete

This brigand comes to Palanthas for the easy pickings, accidentally kills a city guard, and goes underground. He is considered the founder of the Palanthas Thieves' Guild, though it is truly established by his lover, Quick-hand Bet. (DSF)

Cataclysm

A fiery mountain, hurled down upon Krynn by the gods, changes the face of the planet forever and comes to be called the Cataclysm.

This devastation is brought on by the arrogance of the Kingpriest of Istar, a fanatical devotee to the cause

Lord Soth's Charge   KEITH PARKINSON

of right. His fascistic program includes genocide against nonhumans, suppression of magic, and aspirations to godhood. He and the world are provided Thirteen Warnings of the impending doom, including the removal of all virtuous clerics. Knight of the Rose Lord Soth is given the opportunity to avert the disaster, but turns his back on the world.

When the fiery mountain strikes, it plunges Istar to the bottom of the ocean, obliterating the Temple of Istar and creating a maelstrom that continually churns the Blood Sea. The coastlines of all Ansalon are altered, and the world's icecap extends to enclose the southern extreme of the continent.

After the Cataclysm, knowledge of the true gods is lost, the Knights of Solamnia are persecuted for failing to avert the calamity, steel money replaces gold, and the Age of Despair is ushered in. In this time, the Queen of Darkness begins to build her dragonarmies and grow her temple from the foundation stone of the Temple of Istar. (LI)

Catyrpelius, Great Worm

When taken captive by Fewmaster Toede and placed in the slave wagon, Raistlin devises this fictional worm, which will ravage anyone who touches his pack (which contains his spellbook and the Disks of Mishakal). (CI)

Chamber of Paladine

The honored dead of the Solamnic Knights are laid to rest in this large rectangular room. Tanis, Caramon, and Steel come here to pay homage to Steel's father, Sturm Brightblade, and Steel receives a vision. (CIII, SG, DSF)

Chamber of Seeing

At the base of the Tower of Palanthas, this room holds a still pool for scrying across time and distance. Raistlin creates the space, the twisted Live Ones that surround it, and the eternal blue flame above it. Raistlin consults the chamber to find out about Crysania. Dalamar uses it to find out about Usha, and Steel to receive a message from Subcommander Trevalin. (LI, LII, LIII, DSF)

Chaos, Father of All and Nothing

Before the rest of Krynn's pantheon exists, there is Chaos, Father of All and Nothing. He is belligerent and rapacious, and his children gods do much without his knowledge. They create and populate the world of Krynn. They battle across the face of the world. They even create the Graygem by trapping some of Chaos's essence. As it turns out, though, Chaos is completely trapped within the gem.

When the gem is cracked open by the Irda, Chaos escapes and pledges to destroy the "lovely plaything" of his children gods. A fiery titan, Chaos brings with him also flame dragons, shadow-wights, and daemon warriors.

Chaos is at last defeated in the Abyss by Steel Brightblade wielding a dragonlance from the back of his dragon Flare, Tasslehoff Burrfoot wielding his pocketknife *Rabbitslayer*, and Usha wielding the severed halves of the gem. (DSF)

Chaos War

This conflict is set off accidentally by the Irda who, fearful of the Knights of Takhisis, crack the Graygem to harness its power to protect their island. Instead, they release Chaos, the Father of All and Nothing, who sets about to destroy the world his children had built (without his approval). In the end, Chaos is defeated by the united efforts of the Knights of Takhisis, the Wizards of the White Robes, a child raised by the Irda, a famous kender, and the very gods themselves. (DSF)

Chapel of the High Clerist

This room, in the High Clerist's Tower, is devoted to the worship of Paladine and the pantheon of good. (DSF)

Charles

Loyal, professional, and deferential, Charles serves the royal house of Palanthas for over fifty years. It would crumble without him. Among other duties, he handles Tanis's letter to Laurana before Half-Elven confronts the Death Knight. (LIII, SG, DSF)

Chemosh

A member of the evil pantheon, Chemosh is god of the undead. Rarely mentioned in the novels, Chemosh is named in an oath of Steel Brightblade's in the Shoikan Oak Grove. (DSF)

Chislev

This good goddess of woodlands and nature is deceived by Hiddukel in the creation of the Graygem. She says so at the god's conference in the Beyond. (DSF)

Chronicles, A History of Krynn

This collection of books comprises all the volumes of history written by Astinus of Palanthas. Not coincidentally, Chronicles is the name of the first Weis and Hickman Dragonlance trilogy. Caramon and Tasslehoff bring one volume of Astinus's *Chronicles* back from the future and, by reading it, avert the death of Tanis at the hands of Lord Soth. (CII, LIII)

Code and the Measure, the

This set of precepts, dating from the time of Vinas Solamnus, guides the Knights of Solamnia. The Code (sometimes called the Oath) is *Est Sularus oth Mithas*, or "My honor is my life." The Measure is an extensive set of writings that elaborates the meaning of the Code. (ALL)

Conclave of Wizards

When great danger threatens magic or Krynn, the three orders of magic meet in the Tower of Wayreth for a Conclave. Of the twenty-one mages in attendance—seven from each order—only the head of the orders is visible. Par-Salian of the white robes presides over the Conclaves held during the War of the Lance. Justarius of the Red Robes presides over the Conclaves held thereafter, until he is slain at Stone's Keep. (ALL)

Council of Thanes

During times of crisis, this ruling body of dwarves meets in Thorbardin. Composed of the rulers (thanes) of each clan—mountain, hill, deep, and gully dwarves—this council meets during the Dwarfgate Wars, and during the influx of refugees caused by the dragonarmy invasions. (CII, LII)

Council of Whitestone

This council is the decision-making body of the Knights of Solamnia. The council gathers beside an ancient Whitestone, where Vinas Solamnus had his vision of the knighthood, a stone blessed by the Kingpriest himself. Seated members can vote and advisory members can attend. A council convenes in response to the dragonarmy attacks, and another to determine the fate of the Dragon Orb brought from Ice Wall. At the latter, Tasslehoff destroys the orb, Fizban speaks for unity, and Theros Ironfeld reintroduces the dragonlances. Gunthar Uth Wistan presides. (CII)

Courrain Ocean

This large body of water wraps the eastern edge of Ansalon. (ALL)

Cristyne

A small island between Southern Ergoth and Sancrist, Cristyne is created by the Cataclysm. (ALL)

Crown of Power

This diadem, the outward manifestation of the blessing of Takhisis, is worn by Highlord Ariakas in the War Council called at Neraka near the end of the War of the Lance. The Dark Lady, Kitiara, covets it, for "Whoever wears the Crown, rules." At her bidding, Tanis slays Ariakas and takes the crown, though he surrenders it to her only after using it to win his (and Laurana's) freedom. (CIII)

Crown, Knights of the

The Order of the Crown is the lowest of the three orders of Solamnic Knighthood. When instated into the knighthood by Gunthar Uth Wistan, Sturm Brightblade becomes head of the Order of the Crown. (CII)

Crownguard, Derek, Knight of the Rose

This knight, with comrades Sword Knight Brian Donner and Crown Knight Aran Tallbow, encounter the companions in Tarsis. He aids them in recovering the Dragon Orb from Ice Wall and attempts to escorts it to the Council of Whitestone, only to be escaped by most of the companions at Qualimori. Instead, he takes Sturm to Sancrist for trial.

There, Derek testifies against Sturm Brightblade for aiding the enemy and posing as a Knight of Solamnia. Gunthar Uth Wistan makes Derek High Commander of the Order of the Rose. In the battle at the High Clerist's Tower, he leads a suicide charge onto the field and is hauled back, dying. He is entombed with his rival/nemesis Sturm Brightblade in the Chamber of Paladine. (CII)

Crysania of the House of Tarinius

Daughter of the ancient and wealthy royal family of Tarinius, Crysania grows to be strong-willed, idealistic, ambitious, and a bit cold and aloof. She has long black hair, often worn severely pulled back, and skin as pale as Solinari's glow. Elistan's preaching converts her to Paladine's church, and she soon becomes a Revered Daughter. Though she attempts to warn Raistlin away from his aspirations to godhood, she is drawn to him like a moth to a candle. She journeys to the Tower of Wayreth, seeking the advice of Par-Salian about stopping Raistlin, but is struck down by Lord Soth, sent by Kitiara.

At the Tower, Par-Salian and the others determine that Crysania must be taken back to the time of Istar to find a powerful enough cleric of Paladine to rejoin her soul to her body. (Elistan has grown infirm.) While there, Crysania and Caramon intend to stop Raistlin, even if they must kill him. In fact, the Conclave hopes Crysania does not return, so that she cannot be used by Raistlin to open the Portal to the Abyss, which requires a Black Robe mage and a cleric of Paladine.

Crysania does not stop Raistlin, but joins him, campaigning with him later in the Dwarfgate Wars, and even following him into the Abyss, hoping for the overthrow of Takhisis. Ambition and love blind her. There, she is convicted in a surreal trial and burned at the stake. Surviving the blaze, she is physically blinded, but only in her blindness does she see the truth about Raistlin. Chastened, she learns compassion and gains humanity.

She is rescued from the Abyss by Caramon, and after recovering, takes the place of Elistan at the head of the Church of Paladine. She acquires the white tiger, Tandar, to guide her in her blindness. (LI, LII, LIII, DSF)

Crystalmir Lake

This large lake, just north of Solace, provides the companions escape from the goblin and draconian forces that invade the town. When Caramon and Tasslehoff travel to the future, they see a blasted, mud-crusted remnant of this lake. (CI, LIII)

Culof, Lord

This man is ruler of Kalaman during the siege of the city. (CIII)

Cursed Money

During the Dwarfgate Wars, Raistlin pays the Dewar traitor Argat with this money. It rots the skin of anyone who double-crosses the mage. (LII)

Cyan Bloodbane

A huge and cunning green dragon, Cyan Bloodbane guards the nightmare-haunted Silvanesti against invaders. After the companions end the dragon-orb's hold on Lorac and save the elven homeland, Bloodbane flies north to Neraka to join the Dark Queen's forces. He gets in a fight just outside the temple. (CII, CIII)

Daemon Warriors

These abyssal fighters are formed out of the terrors of mortals, appearing different to everyone they attack. They fight for Chaos. (DSF)

Dalamar the Black

Though apprenticed to Raistlin Majere, the dark elf Dalamar is in fact a spy in the employ of the Conclave of Wizards. His interest in black magic makes him an exile of his people, and a likely assistant to Raistlin. When his true allegiances are discovered, Raistlin sets his five fingers on the man's chest and sears five unhealing wounds into him.

The War of the Lance   LARRY ELMORE

Dalamar warns the Conclave they are playing straight into Raistlin's hands, but still maintains his allegiance to his master. During Raistlin's absence, Dalamar oversees the Tower of Palanthas and becomes a master in his own right. When Raistlin enters the Abyss, Dalamar contrives to slay him, recognizing the doom he is bringing about. Kitiara, temporarily in league with Raistlin, attacks Dalamar and is slain by him.

Dalamar becomes head of the Order of Black Robes after Ladonna; aids in the kidnapping of Gilthas; intercepts Usha, so-called daughter of Raistlin; becomes the lover of Jenna, daughter of Justarius; and arms the forces that at last confront and destroy Chaos. To the end, he considers Raistlin his *shalafi*, Elven for *master*. (LI, LII, LIII, SG, DSF)

Dalamar's Room

Unlike the horrific chambers of the Tower of Palanthas, this room is well-appointed, with thick tapestries, woven rugs, and beautiful furniture. During his master's rule of the tower, it is called Raistlin's Study. Tasslehoff Burrfoot and Usha wait, eat, and sleep here as Dalamar checks her story. (DSF)

Dale, Sally

A Palanthas Thieves' Guild member, Sally Dale saves the life of Widower when Raistlin shows up to confront his so-called daughter. Later, as an underling of the thief Jack Nine-fingers, Sally seizes Usha in the sewers beneath Palanthas. She wears a red tunic and leather leggings. (DSF)

Daltigoth

Capital of Ergoth before the Cataclysm, Daltigoth becomes a monster-plagued human city on the isle of Southern Ergoth. (ALL)

Dargaard Keep

Once a bastion of the Knights of Solamnia, this castle is burned during the Cataclysm. Home of Knight of the Rose Lord Soth, the castle is set ablaze by a falling candle chandelier, which also slays the lord's wife and son. He refuses to save the boy, and his wife curses him and the Keep. After the Cata-

clysm, it is a place haunted by banshees and undead, as well as the Death Knight himself. (CIII, LI, LII, LIII)

Dargonesti

These sea elves appear to air-breathers as dolphins. When Tanis and company end up in sunken Istar, they meet the Dargonesti Apoletta. (CIII)

Dark Elf

Unlike drow, a race of "dark elves," a dark elf such as Dalamar is simply an elf exiled by his or her people. Dalamar is exiled from practicing magic as a Black Robe. Alhana Starbreeze and Porthios Solostaran are made dark elves through the machinations of Senator Rashas, intent on blocking the Treaty of the Unified Nations of the Three Races. (LI, SG)

Dark Lady, the
See Uth Matar, Kitiara.

Dark One
See Fistandantilus.

Darken Wood

A forbidding forest, the Darken Wood is purported to be haunted by undead. Though undead do roam the land here, it is also home to the otherworldly Forestmaster, a powerful unicorn. The companions follow the white stag through the wood, en route to Xak Tsaroth. Tanis finds himself at the border of the Darken Wood after being expelled from Qualinesti. (CI, SG)

Darknight, Chief

This barbarian chief joins his warriors with Caramon's Army of Fistandantilus during the Dwarfgate Wars. He vies with Reghar Fireforge to retrieve a prize sword and battle-ax from atop a pole. (LII)

Day of Banishment

Following the Cataclysm, when Tarsis is cut off from insular Thorbardin and Silvanesti and loses all contact with Solamnia, the lord of the city declares this day, by which all Knights of Solamnia must leave, or be murdered.(CII)

Dead Ones

Undead creatures, from spectres and wraiths to zombies and mummies, who haunt the Shoikan Oak Grove and Tower of Palanthas. Compare to: Live Ones. (LI, DSF)

Decider, the

The leader of the Irda settlement from which Usha comes. The Decider determines that Usha must be sent away before he splits the Graygem, thus inadvertently saving her life. (DSF)

Denubis

A virtuous cleric of Paladine during a time of great corruption, Denubis spends his days in the Temple of Istar. As a result of Raistlin's time-travel, he is taken away on the night when all good clerics disappear. Otherwise, he would have accompanied Fistandantilus to the future and journeyed with him during the Dwarfgate Wars, helping him open the Portal. (In that continuity, he plays the role Crysania does with Raistlin.) (LI, LII)

Derkin's Tomb

This is the resting place of the fabled Hammer of Kharas until Tanis and his companions retrieve the artifact. (CII)

Dewar

This race of evil dwarves is driven deep into the earth by its cousins, and nearly exterminated. They become embittered, traitorous, and despicable. Arak Rockbreaker, trainer of Caramon the Victor in Istar, is Dewar. So, too, is Thane Argat, traitor to dwarves and Raistlin alike in the Dwarfgate Wars. (LI, LII)

Dezra

This faithful (if clumsy) waitress at the Inn of the Last Home should not be confused with Dezra Majere, youngest daughter of Tika and Caramon. (LI, DSF)

Dimensional/Time-traveling Device

Given to Tasslehoff by Raistlin, this bejeweled device is (unsuccessfully) used by Tas to escape doomed Istar. In the Abyss, it is modified by the gnome Gnimsh (his Life Quest centers around such devices), and it takes them to the army of Fistandantilus. It is next used to take Caramon and Tas forward in time to a point after Raistlin ascends to godhood. After getting them back to the present, the device is used to take Caramon and Tanis to the flying citadel. (LII, LIII)

Dimernesti

Kin to the Dargonesti, these sea elves take on the appearance of otters. (ALL)

Disks of Mishakal

These platinum disks, containing revelations about the true gods of good, are lost during the first centuries of the Age of Despair. Goldmoon rediscovers the disks in Xak Tsaroth, and they travel with the companions through the Sla-Mori and into Pax Tharkas. The revived faith in Paladine, led by Elistan, is developed on the basis of this holy book, which is kept in the Temple of Paladine in Palanthas. (CI, CII)

Donner, Brian, Sword Knight

This comrade of Rose Knight Derek Crownguard joins the companions at Tarsis. (CII)

Draconians

These reptilian shock troops of Takhisis are created during the first dark centuries in the Age of Dreams. Through clerical and magical manipulations, the eggs of good dragons are corrupted, each producing hundreds of scaly warriors. The types of draconians are determined by the type of dragon egg from which they emerge: Aurak from gold, Baaz from brass, Bozak from bronze, Kapak from copper, and Sivak from silver. (CIII)

Dragon Isles, the

These isles, located to the east of Ansalon, are home to most of the good dragons. They remain here during much of the War of the Lance due to the Oath, an agreement with Takhisis not to join the war, in exchange for return of their hostage eggs (which are already being corrupted into draconians). (CIII)

Dragon Orb

Created during the Second Dragon War, these five artifacts are fashioned to allow mortals to control dragons, though often they take over the minds of their users, as with Lorac (and Raistlin). The three Orders of Magic come together in the Tower of Palanthas to make these powerful items, and stationed one in each Tower of High Sorcery.

During the time of the companions, one Dragon Orb is recovered from Ice Wall and another from haunted Silvanesti. Tasslehoff destroys the former at the Council of Whitestone, and as if to replace it, discovers a third orb in the High Clerist's Tower in Palanthas. Raistlin carries with him the Silvanesti Orb, and uses it to escape the Blood Sea Maelstrom. (CII, LII)

Dragonbane, Huma

In ancient times, a thousand years prior to the Cataclysm, Huma seeks to end the suffering of his people under the firestorm of dragons. He prays to Paladine for an answer, but instead meets the woman Silvara in a glade in Ergoth and falls in love with her. A silver dragon, she prays to be allowed forever to keep her human form and remain with her beloved. Paladine offers her this boon, *or* knowledge of a way to stop the ravages of evil dragons—the dragonlances. Silvara chooses the latter.

Creating the first dragonlances, Huma and Silvara fly into battle, drive the Dark Queen back to the Abyss, and seal her there with Huma's sacrifice. Silvara later leads the companions to Huma's Tomb to gift Theros Ironfeld with the power to make more dragonlances.

During the Chaos War, Huma appears in a vision to blue and silver dragons guarding his tomb, telling them to go to the High Clerist's Tower to aid in the final conflict against Chaos. (CII, DSF)

Dragonfear

Attacking dragons emit this debilitating aura of dread, which prevents mortals from fighting back or even fleeing. (ALL)

Dragonlance

Used first during the time of Huma, these magical weapons allow dragon-mounted riders to fight aerial combat. The secret of their manufacture, lost for ages, is revealed to the companions by Silvara, the silver dragon, and includes metal retrieved from the Tomb of Huma, use of the fabled Hammer of Kharas, and the power of Theros Ironfeld's silver arm. That arm hurls one such lance to split the Whitestone in a demonstration of the lances' power. (CII)

Dragontraps

The lowest level of the High Clerist's Tower contains these portcullised gates. A Dragon Orb within lures the dragons through the gates, where they can then be engaged in close quarters by the knights. When the Knights of Takhisis are in charge of the tower, this section is used by Gray Robe mages, and is where Palin and Steel are held captive. (CIII, DSF)

Dumak/Dulak

This command word deactivates the light power of the Staff of Magius. Raistlin uses the former word, and Palin, untrained in use of the staff, the latter. (CI, CII, CIII, DSF)

Duncan, King of Thorbardin

Prior to the Dwarfgate Wars, Duncan unites the various clans into one kingdom, for the first time in ages. The schism between him and Reghar Fireforge makes the hill dwarves join the army of Fistandantilus during the war. His two sons are killed in the resulting battle. (LII, LIII)

Dunstan, Sara

At twenty years old, this weaver outside Palanthas nurses Kitiara back to health, helps her deliver her baby, and cares for the child—Steel Brightblade—as

Death of Sturm LARRY ELMORE

The Reign of Istar   LARRY ELMORE

her own. When he is grown and about to join the Knights of Takhisis, she enlists the aid of Tanis and Uncle Caramon to save him. (SG)

Dwarf Spirits

A strong liquor, this drink is used by Dougan Redhammer to abduct Sturm, Tanin, and Palin Brightblade. It is also almost the ruin of Caramon Majere, who briefly becomes a drunkard after the War of the Lance. (LI, DSF)

Dwarf(gate) Wars

This series of battles, fought between the mountain dwarves and a coalition of hill dwarves, barbarians, and Solamnic expatriates, sprawls from Pax Tharkas to Zhaman and Thorbardin. Originally led by Fistandantilus, the army named after him is (in another continuity) led by Raistlin and his brother Caramon. Reghar Fireforge, grandfather of Flint, leads the hill dwarves and Chief Darknight leads the barbarians. King Duncan and Kharas of the legendary hammer leads the mountain dwarves. Dewar Thane Argat betrays both sides to the other and, due to Raistlin's cursed money, introduces a rotting disease to his people.

The conflict ends with the great explosion at Zhaman, caused by the simultaneous activation of the Portal and Tasslehoff's dimensional/time-traveling device. (LI, LII)

Dwarves

These short-statured people are long-lived and pragmatic. They are among the best stone- and metal-workers in the world. According to the Irda creation myths, dwarves are created by the Graygem of Gargath, gnomes that lust after its value. (DSF)

Eben Sanderstone

Son of a once-wealthy merchant family from Gateway, Eben becomes a spy in the service of Lord Verminaard. He and his men—supposedly freedom fighters retreating from the dragonarmy in Gateway—joins Tanis and the companions on the way to Pax Tharkas. He diverts their suspicions to

Gilthanas, but betrays the party during their attempt to escape Pax Tharkas. He pursues the Green Gemstone Man and is killed with him by a boulder. (CI)

Elf Water

Dougan Redhammer uses this phrase for wine. (SG)

Elistan

Among the captives in Pax Tharkas, this tall, distinguished middle-aged man is healed by Goldmoon, demonstrating the truth of the old gods. He becomes a cleric of Paladine, adventures with the companions to Tarsis, and becomes the chief interpreter of the Disks of Mishakal. Laurana works closely with him in the early years, and Crysania later on. He establishes the Temple of Paladine in Palanthas. He dies just prior to its destruction by Kitiara's armies, and is buried in the caves beneath the ruined Temple. (CI, CII, CIII, LI, LII, LIII)

Elsa

Elsa is one of the leaders of the Revered Daughters of Paladine in Palanthas, before Crysania takes leadership. (LI)

Elves

Tall, slight, and long-lived, these creatures belong to one of the three original races, said in the Irda myths to be the children of Paladine, god of good. (DSF)

Ember (Pyros)

A gift from Takhisis to Dragon Highlord Verminaard, Ember is in fact charged with spying upon his master. This ancient, powerful, and enormous red dragon is also seeking the Green Gemstone Man. He resides in Pax Tharkas, interrogating (and sometimes eating) prisoners, when the companions arrive. He battles Matafleur (Flamestrike) above Pax Tharkas and is driven by her into a mountain peak, the collision killing them both. (CI)

Estwilde

It is on this wide, grassy wasteland that Fizban climbs onto the ancient gold dragon Pyrite to battle what he thinks are enemy dragonriders (who are, in fact, Tanis, Berem, Tas, and companions on their way to Neraka). Estwilde is also noted for the large northern city of Kalaman, besieged in the War of the Lance and later conquered by the Knights of Takhisis. (CIII, DSF)

Everman

See Berem.

Evil Dragons (chromatic)

Though all chromatic dragons are utilized by the forces of Takhisis, they have different strengths and weaknesses. Blue dragons are the favored mounts of the Knights of Takhisis due to their strong attachment to their riders and their appreciation of subtle battle strategy. Black dragons—small, devious, and selfish—make inferior mounts. Red dragons are used most extensively during the War of the Lance due to their vicious brutality, their enormous size, and their destructive fiery breath. They are especially good at razing cities. Green dragons, being adept magic-users, have little love for tooth-and-claw combat and even less love for military commanders. They prefer an arrangement like that enjoyed by Cyan Bloodbane in his magical domination of Silvanesti, with the Dragon Orb. White dragons, though used during the War of the Lance, cannot bear the heat of the world during the Chaos War. (ALL)

Fair Field

This town, a day's ride from the house of Tanis and Laurana, is where the Black Swan Inn is located, to which Senator Rashas lures Gilthas. (SG)

Feal-thas

This Dragonlord guards the Dragon Orb at Ice Wall. He is defeated by Flint, Sturm, Gilthanas, Laurana, Tasslehoff, and Derek Crownguard. (CII)

Fire Dragons

From a fiery cleft in the ocean, these massive wyrms emerge to spread the power of Chaos. With bodies of magma, obsidian scales, flaming wings, poison-breath weapons, and wakes of incinerating sparks, these monsters are mockeries of dragonkind and potent destroyers. (DSF)

Fireflash (Khirsah)

Among the first metallic dragons to answer the call to fight, this young bronze dragon is ridden by Flint Fireforge and Tasslehoff Burrfoot. In the Battle of the Vingaard Mountains, he assists in the capture of Bakaris by Tas. Later he meets Tanis outside the royal house of Palanthas. He completes many aerial spying missions during and after the War of the Lance. During Kitiara's assault on Palanthas, Khirsah carries Tanis toward combat with Lord Soth, and later conveys Tasslehoff to the flying citadel. (CIII, LIII)

Fireforge, Flint

One of the oldest of the original companions, Flint Fireforge is the grandson of Reghar Fireforge, who fought for the hill dwarves in the Dwarfgate Wars. Short, gray-bearded, and outwardly stern, Flint has a soft heart, an affection for a certain doorknob of a kender, and an abiding fear of open water and boat travel. He journeys with the companions to Xak Tsaroth, Pax Tharkas, Tarsis the Beautiful, the Tomb of Huma, Palanthas, Neraka, and, finally, Godshome, where his heart at last gives out.

From that time to the beginning of the Fifth Age, Flint waits beside a certain tree on another plane, expecting Tasslehoff's arrival (who dies three times over before actually joining him). Once the kender, stomped by Chaos, arrives, Flint starts a fire to draw in the other companions; that fire becomes a red star forever fixed in the night sky of Krynn, to let mortals know they are not alone. (CI, CII, CIII, DSF)

Fireforge, Reghar

Ancestor to Flint Fireforge, Reghar is leader of the hill-dwarf clans denied provision and shelter by the dwarves of Thorbardin. He joins with Caramon of the Army of Fistandantilus and Chief Darknight of the plains barbarians to fight the Dwarfgate Wars. He

The Cataclysm   LARRY ELMORE

Dragons of Spring Dawning   LARRY ELMORE

competes head-to-head with the chief to retrieve a sword and ax from the top of a pole—a test of cooperation. He later marches his dwarves on Thorbardin, falling into the trap of the Dewar. (LII)

Fistandantilus

The greatest Black Robe mage ever to live (before Raistlin), Fistandantilus is the first mage to seek egress through the Portal into the Abyss. Called the Dark One, he haunts the halls of the Temple of Istar before the Cataclysm, seduces the virtuous cleric Denubis to his side, sparks the Dwarfgate Wars in his hopes to gain the Portal, and is slain in the explosion that destroys Zhaman and ravages the Plains of Dergoth.

His ghost makes a pact with Raistlin during the young Red Robe's Test, giving Raistlin the power to overcome the Test in exchange for a portion of the mage's soul. Fistandantilus hopes eventually to take over Raistlin's whole being, but the Red Robe turned Black Robe travels back in time, slays Fistandantilus, and takes his place, becoming the master of past and present. (LI, LII)

Fizban the Fabulous

Though the flesh-and-blood presence of Paladine in the world, Fizban seems anything but a sharp-eyed platinum dragon. He is a befuddled old man with a long white beard, tattered, mouse-gray robes, and a patched hat, with a penchant for getting lost at the most inopportune times.

He first encounters the companions in Lord Toede's slave wagon, on the way to Pax Tharkas. In the Mechanism Room, he and Tasslehoff release the chain, preventing the doors from opening and the dragonarmies from entering the fortress. Unfortunately, Fizban is killed in a subsequent fall, due to a misfired spell.

He reappears next in the Tomb of Huma, and travels with the companions to the Council of Whitestone, where his impassioned speech helps meld together the disintegrating alliance. Later, aback Pyrite, he launches a misconceived aerial attack against the dragon-riding companions, saving them from certain death in Neraka.

He reappears briefly to attend to his old friend, Elistan, on his deathbed. Lastly, Fizban appears to Palin, Usha, and Raistlin to tell of the departure of the gods and magic, and the dawning of the Age of Mortals. (CI, CII, CIII, LIII, DSF)

Flamestrike (Matafleur)

This ancient, toothless red dragon dwells in Pax Tharkas, a virtual prisoner of Highlord Verminaard. Senile, the create has become sweet, doting on the children of the human slaves as her own offspring. To defend them, she attacks and kills Verminaard's mount, Ember, but she also dies. (CI)

Flare

A large and cunning blue dragon, Flare is the favored mount of Steel Brightblade. Mistress Sara, Steel's surrogate mother, rides this dragon to fetch Tanis and Caramon and to take Steel to his father's grave at the High Clerist's Tower. After the Battle of Thoradin Bay, Flare bears Steel and Palin with the bodies of Tanin and Sturm Majere back to Solace for burial.

During Steel's incarceration and disgrace, Flare becomes incorrigible, faithful only to her original rider. Even after Takhisis has abandoned the world, the Knights, and Steel, Flare remained true, bearing Steel through the rent in the ocean to battle Chaos in the Abyss. He is killed in the fight. (SG, DSF)

Flotsam

This city on the edge of the Blood Sea is a staging ground for the dragonarmies, specifically Kitiara's troops. Here, she discovers and seduces Tanis. From here, she launches the dragon flight that drives Tanis, the companions, and the crew of the *Perechon* into the Blood Sea Maelstrom and to the lost city of Istar. (CIII)

Flying Citadel

Created for use in the War of the Lance, these massive war machines are used in the siege of Kalaman, in Kitiara's attack on Palanthas, and later in the campaigns of the Knights of Takhisis. Each flying citadel is a castle that is ripped, summit and all, from its mountaintop and set afloat on clouds of black magic and clerical might.

During Kitiara's attack on Palanthas, Tanis and Caramon use the dimensional/time-traveling device to board a flying citadel, and Tasslehoff boards by dragonback. Together, the kender and a gully dwarf he meets in the citadel steer it into the bay. (CIII, LIII, DSF)

Foghaven Vale

A valley of hot springs and bubbling pools, Foghaven Vale guards the path to the Tomb of Huma. (CII)

Forestmaster, the

This unicorn guards the haunted Darken Wood, protecting it and its sacred inhabitants. Fleeing Solace, the companions encounter this beast. (CI)

Gakhan

A draconian assassin, Gakhan is Kitiara's personal "aide." He raids and ravages the Que-shu village of Goldmoon, seeking the blue crystal staff. He nearly captures the companions in Tarsis, but is driven off by the griffons of Alhana. He follows the companions to Ice Wall, later follows Tanis in Flotsam after his tryst with Kitiara, and rides dragonback to stop the companions' escape. (CIII)

Games of Istar

These gladiatorial matches allow the citizens of Istar to vent their violent urges, and allow noble slave-owners to take out vengeance against each other. Though much of the combat is staged, at other times the matches are deadly. Caramon the Victor fights in the games with Kiiri and Pheragas. (LI)

Garad

An underling to the ailing Elistan, Garad is a cleric whose righteousness reminds Elistan of the Kingpriest's. (LIII)

Gargath, Castle of

Home of Gargath of legend, this castle houses the Graygem. The chaotic effects of the stone cause the castle to constantly change, in a surreal progression of styles, floor plans, and materials. In ancient times, the gnomes mount a series of attacks on the castle, most ending in fire and explosion. In recent times, Dougan Redhammer and Palin, Sturm, and Tanin Majere mount a more successful attack, freeing the stone with the very hammer that made it. (SG)

Gargath, Isle of

Far west of Ansalon, this isle holds the Castle of Gargath. It is a tropical locale, reached by Dougan Redhammer and the three Majere boys aboard the gnomish ship *Miracle*. (SG)

Gargath, Lord

This human, in ancient times, captures the Graygem and holds it through newly acquired magical means. He repulses two gnomish attacks, only to lose the gem in the third. He builds a boat and follows the drifting stone west from Ansalon. He is lost to history until the gnomish ship *Miracle* reaches his island.

Though originally the captor of the gem, Gargath becomes its captive, his shape constantly and chaotically changed by the stone that holds him in thrall. Once he is freed from this slavery, he vows to reform his ways, cease seeking the stone, and give up being a renegade mage. (SG)

Garibanus

This dragon Highlord, acting commander while Bakaris is a prisoner of war, is slain by Ariakas when he is found in bed with Kitiara. (CIII)

Garic

Son of a Solamnic Knight, Garic flees when his family is killed by mobs after the Cataclysm. He joins Steeltoe's marauders and then the Army of Fistandantilus. He distinguishes himself, guarding Raistlin and fighting beside Caramon. (LII)

Garnet Mountains

This range in southern Solamnia is passed by the Army of Fistandantilus en route to Caergoth. (LII)

Dragons of Autumn Twilight LARRY ELMORE

Gateway

Central town of Abanasinia, Gateway lies between Solace and Pax Tharkas. (ALL)

Gilean

Neutral god of the book, Gilean struggles to maintain the balance of good and evil. His constellation is a scale. He is the middle child of Chaos, quiet and contemplative, and has no consort. During the Chaos War, he sides with Takhisis, believing a peaceful world under the hand of darkness is better than no world at all. Some say Astinus is Gilean's fleshly manifestation. (CIII, DSF)

Glasses of True Seeing

These glasses, "found" by Tasslehoff, allow him to read ancient and foreign languages. Among other texts read by him is one in the ancient library of Tarsis describing the coming armies of chromatic dragons. (CII)

Glob

This hobgoblin stablehand of the Knights of Takhisis gets in a row with Sara Dunstan, surrogate mother of Steel Brightblade. (SG)

Globe of Present Time Passing

A glass globe, this artifact allows one to peer into distant places. Made by Raistlin for Astinus (in exchange for help in finding the Portal), the globe lets the scribe record all Krynn's history from his desk. (LII)

Glups

See Sluds, Bulps, Glups.

Gnimsh

Met by Tasslehoff in the Abyss, this gnome repairs the kender's time-travel device with what he knows of dimensional travel devices (his Life Quest). He is killed by Raistlin when the mage reads that the explosion at Zhaman is caused by a gnomish device. Tasslehoff never forgives Raistlin. (LII)

Gnomes

Short, inquisitive, and irrepressible, gnomes are humans smiths cursed by Reorx because they forgot to honor him, their teacher. Each gnome has a Life Quest, usually to create some elaborate, dangerous (and useless) machine. (DSF)

Gnosh

This gnome, from Mount Nevermind, aids Fizban and Tasslehoff in determining the (nonexistent) mechanical use of a Dragon Orb. He inherits the pieces of the globe after Tasslehoff shatters it against the Whitestone. (CII)

Goblin and Ogre Wars

In the third century after the cataclysm, the Knights of Solamnia stationed at Vingaard fight these battles against goblins and ogres from Throt and Estwilde. They defeat the monsters, though outnumbered fifty to one. See also Great Goblin Wars. (CII)

Godshome

This strange igneous formation is purported to be a terrestrial meeting point for the gods—a desolate circle of irregular standing stones and jagged mountains around a smooth mirrorlike expanse of obsidian. Here, Flint catches the escaped Berem, only to suffer a heart attack. In a rage afterward, Tanis kills Berem, only to have the Everman return to life. (CIII)

Golden General, the

See Laurana.

Golden Key

In the gladiatorial Games of Istar, this item is the object of a championship match. It is placed upon a prominence, and the gladiators compete to gain the key and their freedom. Caramon the Victor defeats the Red Minotaur to gain the prize. He uses it to reach his brother just before the Cataclysm. (LI)

Goldmoon, Princess

Daughter of the chief of the Que-shu, Goldmoon is dark-skinned with silver-gold hair, and statuesque features. She falls in love with a poor man's son, Riverwind. Among the gifts he bestowed upon her is a blue crystal staff, given him by Mishakal in a vision. When the chief calls for Riverwind to be stoned, Goldmoon joins him in his escape and together they travel to Solace.

Goldmoon heals Hederick the Theocrat, thus demonstrating the truth of the old gods. She and Riverwind join the companions, trekking with them to Xak Tsaroth, where she slays the black dragon Onyx with the staff, killing herself in the process. She is returned to life by the power of Mishakal, her goddess, and made into a true cleric. The companions retrieve the Disks of Mishakal.

In Pax Tharkas, Goldmoon heals the slave-prisoner Elistan, thus providing the world its first new priest of Paladine (and eventually the high priest). Traveling with Tanis and his companions through Silvanesti, Goldmoon sings in Raistlin's traveling road show in Port Balifor and thus gains more converts to the new gods.

She and Riverwind accompany the group through Flotsam, Old Istar, and Palanthas. There, they depart the company to care for the child Goldmoon will have in the autumn, a symbol of hope for all the companions. They keep in contact with Tanis and Laurana, even inviting the couples' children out for visits. (CI, CII, CIII, DSF)

Good Dragons (metallic)

Like their chromatic cousins, these five types of dragon—gold, silver, brass, bronze, and copper—are sent to sleep when Takhisis is driven by Huma from the world. When the Queen of Darkness begins to reemerge, shortly after the Cataclysm, she awakens the evil dragons, but lets good wyrms sleep while she steals their eggs.

At last awakening, the good dragons are kept from interfering with Takhisis's plans due to their hostage eggs. The metallic dragons take an oath not to interfere, and break that oath only when they learn their eggs are being corrupted to produce the five races of draconians. (ALL)

Goose and Gander Tavern, The

This triangular tavern in Palanthas has bad food and wine, and so is ignored by Knights of Takhisis. Tasslehoff brings Palin here to contact Usha, who waits tables. They meet also Dougan Redhammer. (DSF)

Gray Knights

Though Knights of Takhisis (Order of the Thorn), Gray Knights are actually magic-users. Nightlord Lillith leads this contingent during the conquest of Ansalon by the Knights. They first alert the knighthood to great danger from the isle of Irda, thereby accidentally touching off the Chaos War. They capture Palin during the battle of Thoradin Bay, requiring negotiation from Knight of the Lily Steel Brightblade to gain the prisoner. (DSF)

Graygem (Graystone) of Gargath

At the goading behest of Hiddukel (trickster god of bad deals) Reorx creates this gem, with either explicit or tacit approval of the other gods. In doing so, he captures what he thinks is a tiny essence of Chaos, Father of All and Nothing, in the stone. In fact, he has imprisoned the entire god.

The Graygem is given to Lunitari, but then stolen from her by a gnome with a ladder that climbs through the heavens. It escapes, wandering the world and creating havoc until captured by the human Gargath and held through newly acquired magical means. Gnomes mount a series of ill-fated assaults on the castle. In defense of itself, the stone transforms the gnomes who finally breach the wall, making those who lust after its value into dwarves and those who desire it out of curiosity into kender. The gem escapes again and is pursued by Gargath and the gnomes west from Ansalon.

Dougan Redhammer and Palin, Sturm, and Tanin Brightblade sail aboard a similar gnome ship, the *Miracle,* to the Isle of Gargath to regain the stone. Redhammer gains the stone only to lose it again in a card game.

The Graygem eventually ends up among the Irda, who split it in hopes of harnessing its power to protect themselves from the Knights of Takhisis. In doing

Dragons of Winter Night   LARRY ELMORE

so, they release Chaos, Father of All and Nothing, and initiate the Chaos War. The gem is at last repaired by Usha and Tasslehoff in the Abyss, who capture a drop of Chaos's blood and close the two halves together. (SG, DSF)

Graystone Gem Races

These races are said to be created by the gem, specifically dwarves and kender (some also include gnomes). *See* Graygem of Gargath. (SG, DSF)

Green Gemstone Man

See Berem.

Great Goblin Wars

Prior to the Cataclysm, the Kingpriest of Istar fomented these battles between the dwarves of Thorbardin and goblins and ogres from Bloden and the Plains of Dust. The legendary Kharas fought in these wars. *See also* Goblin and Ogre Wars. (LII)

Grubb, Sergeant

This is one of four Palanthas harbor guards who accosts the gully dwarf Slug, in the employ of the Knights of Takhisis. He is likely named after Jeff Grubb, one of the world builders and author of *Lord Toede*. (DSF)

Gully Dwarf (Aghar)

These creatures, of the lowest caste of dwarven society, live in squalor and rags in sloughs across Ansalon. One gully dwarf, Bupu, changes history by providing Raistlin the spellbook of Fistandantilus. He holds a strange sympathy for them and mourns their deaths in the Dwarfgate War. (ALL)

Haarold

This Istar nobleman makes a bid on Caramon in the slave market, but loses him to Arak Rockbreaker, acting for Fistandantilus (Raistlin). (LI)

Habbakuk

Called the Fisher King, Habbakuk is god of living creatures. (ALL)

Half-Elven

See Tanis Half-Elven.

Hall of Audience

In the Temple of Istar, this room is where the King-priest receives petitions. Engineered to impress visitors with their own insignificance, the large round room has walls shaped like opening rose petals, reaching to a dome of frosted crystal that absorbs sunlight and moonlight and sends them gleaming through the chamber. An elevated throne dominates the room, emitting a magical aura of brilliant light and ceaseless love. (LI)

Another Hall of Audience, in Thorbardin, contains seven carved thrones, one each for the members of the dwarven clans. The largest and finest is reserved for the King of Dwarves. In this hall, Hornfel receives the recovered Hammer of Kharas from the companions. (CII)

Hall of Justice

On the way to this judicial hall in Tarsis the Beautiful, Sturm Brightblade and companions are pelted with rocks and garbage, due to the city's hatred of Solamnic Knights. Once within the imposing edifice, they meet Alhana Starbreeze, and Sturm is immediately smitten. When they leave, Derek Crownguard and his two companions rescue them from the guard. (CII)

Hall of Thanes

In this stately chamber of granite in Pax Tharkas, King Duncan of Thorbardin convenes the Council of Thanes, consisting of himself and representatives from each of the six dwarven clans. This is just before the outbreak of the Dwarfgate Wars. (LII)

Hall of the Ancestors

One room left intact when Xak Tsaroth slides downhill after the Cataclysm, the Hall of Ancestors contains crypts of priests and kings. (CI)

Hall of the Ancients

This huge hall in the Sla-Mori is held up by seven grand columns along each side. At the end of the hall stands an ornate granite stone where sits the skeletal remains of Kith-Kanan, flanked by two huge marble statues. The companions arrive here only to be attacked by a giant slug. Tanis finds the ancient elven king's sword, *Wyrmslayer*, suddenly in his hand and slays the beast. Afterward, he recalls Kith-Kanan granting it to him. (CI)

Hall of the Sky

This meeting chamber occupies the top of the Tower of the Suns in Qualinost. Hundreds of feet tall, the room rises to a dome at the very peak of the tower, where mosaics represent sun, moons, and constellations. Hidden windows and mirrors fill the hall with light at all times. No seats, columns, or supports mar the elegant simplicity of the space. Here the companions report to Solostaran, Speaker of the Sun. (CI)

Hammer of Kharas

This ancient artifact, from the time of Huma, is a large war hammer blessed by the gods to be used in creation of the dragonlances. It is given by the Knights of Solamnia to a valorous dwarf whom they call Kharas (Solamnic for *knight*). This dwarf fights in the Dwarfgate Wars for King Duncan, and even attempts to assassinate Fistandantilus/Raistlin.

When the hammer is retrieved from Derkin's Tomb by the companions, they grant it to the dwarves of Thorbardin in thanks for sheltering the refugees of Pax Tharkas. Later, the hammer is used by Theros Ironfeld to forge new dragonlances. (CII)

Haven

Located on the southwest corner of the Darken Wood, Haven is one of the three major towns of Abanasinia, with Solace and Gateway. The Seekers are based in this town. (ALL)

Havenswood, Slegart

Owner of the Wayward Inn, this man hires Amberyl and aids in the delivery of her child, according to the legend of Raistlin's daughter. (SG)

Hederick, Highseeker

This self-important, self-righteous man is head of the order of Seekers in Solace. Like all Seekers, Hederick purports to seek knowledge of the new (false) gods after the Cataclysm. In fact, he seeks only power, and does not care if that comes from the forces of good or those of evil. He wears the gold and brown robes of his order, is heavyset, sour-minded, and petulant.

In the Inn of the Last Home, he is burned by the fire, but healed by Goldmoon. In repayment, he brands her a blasphemous witch and instigates the hunt that sends the companions from Solace. Eventually, he is rounded up with others from Solace and taken to slavery in Pax Tharkas. Once rescued, he repays the companions again by stirring up trouble in the refugee camps in Thorbardin. In the end, the truth of the old gods shows him to be a fraud. (CI, CII)

Hiddukel

This god of corrupt wealth and bad deals is behind the creation of the Graygem of Gargath. Though he says he seeks to assure the balance of power on Krynn by introducing chaos, he in fact further unbalances it. He is roundly condemned by the council of gods held during the Chaos War. He is the first god to abandon the world of Krynn. (SG, DSF)

High Clerist's Tower, the

Built by Vinas Solamnus in ancient times, this structure is the greatest land defense of Palanthas. It repels two large-scale attacks during the War of the Lance, thereby sparing the city the ravaging dragon-armies. Sturm Brightblade is slain in one of these battles, and he is buried among the honored dead in the Chamber of Paladine. Kitiara's later attack upon Palanthas is successful only because her flying citadel allows her to bypass the tower.

Seemingly designed by an idiot, the tower's lower curtain wall is pierced by no fewer than six portcullised gates. In fact these are dragontraps, which lure dragons inward through use of a Dragon Orb to allow them to be destroyed in close-range combat.

Tanis, Caramon, and Sara Dunstan bring Steel Brightblade here to visit his father's grave, and Sturm's ghost grants the boy his ancestral sword. Tanis later promises this same ghost to look after his son, and so Half-Elven dies in the subsequent invasion by the Knights of Takhisis. Steel Brightblade and Palin Majere are both captives in the Tower thereafter.

The Knights of Takhisis are decimated in the tower when the forces of Chaos attack. (ALL)

High Priestess of Takhisis

Leader of the clerical arm of Takhisis's army, this woman leads other clerics in the Knights of the Skull. Disturbed by the prophecies spoken by Palin, the high priestess accidentally spills holy oil across the altar to Takhisis, and the resulting fire destroys the sacrifices prematurely. The priestess dies before the blaze, apparently considering it a sign of the fiery end of Krynn. (DSF)

Highbulp

See Phudge I, Highbulp.

Highgulg

Leader of a group of gully dwarves, the Highgulg (or High Private) meets with the thanes in the Hall of Thanes before the Dwarfgate Wars. The Highgulg and his people are slaughtered in the fall of Pax Tharkas, and Raistlin is grieved. (LII)

Highseekers

These leaders of the Seekers are false clerics seeking new gods. (CI, CII)

Hornfel, Thane of the Hylar

By receiving the Hammer of Kharas from the companions, this dwarven leader gains the opportunity to unite the six clans of Thorbardin dwarves into one nation again, as in the time of King Duncan. (CII)

Huma's Tomb

The companions reach this secret spot with Silvara as their guide. They pass through Foghaven Vale and cross the Bridge of Passage to a lawn decorated by larger-than-life images of the Heroes of the Lance. They come to a rectangular building of obsidian. Within is a single bier of obsidian, empty save for a sword and shield. At the far end is a small altar. In hidden subterranean passages, Tasslehoff encounters Fizban, and the rest of the companions discover stores of the metal used to make dragonlances. (CII)

Humans

The most short-lived of the original races, humans are said to be the children of Gilean, neutral god of balance. (DSF)

Hylar

The most ancient clan of mountain dwarves, Hylar are the traditional rulers of Thorbardin, with such members as Duncan, King of Thorbardin, and Hornfel, Thane of the Hylar. (ALL)

Ice Wall

After the company is sundered at Tarsis the Beautiful, half of them continue on to Ice Wall in the far south of Ansalon. Among them are Goldmoon, Riverwind, Flint, Gilthanas, Sturm, Laurana, Tasslehoff, and Derek Crownguard and his comrades. Here, they enter Ice Wall Castle, slay Dragonlord Feal-thas, take the Dragon Orb, and retrieve the severed part of an ancient dragonlance. Fighting white dragons and Thanoi, they escape to Sancrist aboard a ship. (CII)

Inn of the Last Home, the

This arboreal tavern and inn is the favorite meetingplace of the companions in the years before they go their separate ways to seek their fortunes in the world. It is here that they have sworn to return. All do so, except Kitiara.

The original inn is run by Otik Sandath until it is destroyed by a dragonarmy that razes the town. It is rebuilt after the War of the Lance, eventually taken over by Tika Waylan (former waitress) and Caramon Majere. It is in this rebuilt inn that Alhana Starbreeze and Porthios Solostaran give birth to their baby. This is also the place to which Raistlin returns after he emerges from the Abyss, calling the inn "home." He has a room there, a broom-closet turned shrine by magic-using adventurers who have come to pay homage. (ALL)

Irda

Among the three original races (elves and humans being the others) Irda are the primal ogres before they are turned ugly by avarice. They are the beautiful children of Takhisis who forsake their queen, their brethren, and the world to escape the monstrous transformations caused by greed. They live apart from the rest of the world, with an occasional individual foray into the world at large. Amberyl of legend purportedly meets Raistlin on one such sojourn.

When Knights of Takhisis land on their isle, the Irda decide to crack the Graygem and use its powers in defense. They thereby accidentally start the Chaos War. (SG, DSF)

Ironfist, Darren

This messenger is sent by King Duncan of Thorbardin to Fistandantilus/Raistlin to declare the dwarves' intention to fight. (LII)

Istar

Once a trade city, Istar grows though the millennium before the Cataclysm to become the political, spiritual, and economic center of the world. Headed by the Kingpriest, the city-state becomes convinced of its own righteousness and destiny to rule the world. Its campaign against evil races becomes a full-fledged war against all impure races (see Graystone Gem races). It also wages war on Ansalon's mages, capturing one Tower of High Sorcery and destroying two others. Soon, the Kingpriest outgrows even the gods and ceases listening to them. The Cataclysm results.

Raistlin, Caramon, Crysania, and Tasslehoff travel back in time to Istar just before the Cataclysm, where Raistlin murders and takes the place of the court mage (Fistandantilus), Caramon fights in the Games of Istar, Crysania is welcomed into the priesthood of Paladine as a true healer, and Tasslehoff is left behind with a nonfunctioning time-travel device.

Caramon, Tanis, and companions visit the city sometime later, beneath the Blood Sea of Istar. There, they meet Apoletta and Zebulah. (CIII, LI)

Jack Nine-Fingers

This member of the Palanthas Thieves' Guild helps a Solamnic Knight's widow and baby escape the Knights of Takhisis, and aids Usha, Palin, and Tasslehoff in the city's sewers. (DSF)

Jasla

This younger sister of Berem is accidentally slain against the foundation stone of the Dark Queen's temple. Her ghost prevents Takhisis's return. Her reunion with her brother destroys the Dark Queen's temple at Neraka. (CIII)

Jenna

Daughter of Justarius and lover of Dalamar, Jenna owns a mage-ware shop (a Three-Moons Shop) in Palanthas. She is approached by Senator Rashas in his plot to abduct Gilthas Solostaran, aids Dalamar in his work during the wars with the Knights of Takhisis and Chaos, and helps Palin when he arrives in the occupied city, even though her shop has been taken over by Gray Knights. (SG, DSF)

Jetties, the

At this run-down inn near the edge of Flotsam, Riverwind, Goldmoon, Caramon, and Raistlin await Tanis's return from his tryst with Kitiara. (CIII)

Justarius of the Red Robes

Long-time head of the Order of the Red Robes, Justarius succeeds Par-Salian as head of the Con-

Dragons of Desolation   LARRY ELMORE

clave just after Kitiara's attack on Palanthas. He leads the Conclave during the decades of peace, and fathers Jenna of Palanthas. He aids in creating the Test for Palin Majere.

After the opening conquests of the Knights of Takhisis, Justarius orders an assault on the renegade Gray Robes at Storm's Keep. There, he is slain, and the other members of his team routed. (LIII, SG, DSF)

Kaganesti (or Kagonesti)

Known as Wilder elves, these feral cousins of the Silvanesti and Qualinesti extensively tattoo their bronze-skin. The original residents of the southern end of Southern Ergoth, the Kaganesti are displaced and subjugated by Silvanesti and Qualinesti refugees during the first part of the War of the Lance. Silvara, the silver dragon, first joins the companions as the Kaganesti druidic healer Silvart. After the war, Kaganesti warriors are used to keep Alhana and Gilthas captives of Senator Rashas in Qualinesti. (CII, SG)

Kalaman

Positioned in north central Ansalon, Kalaman is a key overland and maritime city, and so is besieged during the War of the Lance by dragons and flying citadels and conquered during the campaigns of the Knights of Takhisis by a vast armada. Tanis and his companions are bound to Kalaman aboard the *Perechon* when they are driven by dragons into the maelstrom. (CI, CII, CIII, DSF)

Kal-thax

During the Age of Dreams, this race of dwarves achieves perfection in stone- and metal-working, and are taken up by Reorx to live beside the forges of heaven. All dwarves afterward strive for this level of perfection. (LII)

Kapak

Theses draconians, created from corrupted copper dragon eggs, are voracious, powerful, and stupid. They make good brute squads and occasional assassins. (ALL)

Karthay

This Blood Sea Isle is the largest and northernmost of the group. (ALL)

Kar-thon, Maquesta

With black skin, curly black hair, and brown eyes that flash with steel, Maquesta is unquestioned captain of the *Perechon*. She takes Tanis and companions toward Kalaman, only to be dragged into the maelstrom. (CII, CIII)

Kender

These slight, childlike creatures have an irrepressible curiosity and no sense of private property. According to Irda legend, they are gnomes overcome with curiosity about the Graystone of Gargath, and thus transformed by it. (ALL)

Kender Spoon of Turning, the

A mundane spoon from Dalamar's table service, this spoon is used (apparently effectively) by Tasslehoff to turn the undead guardians of the Tower of High Sorcery. (DSF)

Kendermore

Capital of the kender homeland of Goodlund, Kendermore is defended against the dragonarmies by Kronin Thistleknot, who even managed to slay Dragon Highlord Fewmaster Toede. (CIII)

Keryl

This is one of two Irda sent to claim the child of Amberyl, according to the legend of Raistlin's daughter. (SG)

Khalkist Mountains

The literal spine of Ansalon, this long, high range of rugged mountains runs from Nordmaar in the north to Silvanesti in the south. The range includes the dragonarmy strongholds of Sanction and Neraka. (ALL)

Kharas

This dwarven warrior is named Kharas (Solamnic for *knight*) by the Knights of Solamnia due to his honor and valor in battle. Kharas keeps the name and the golden hammer used to forge Huma's dragonlances. He further distinguishes himself in battle and survives the Cataclysm only to be drawn into the nasty Dwarfgate Wars. He fights for King Duncan of Thorbardin, but under protest, shaving his beard. After a failed attempt at assassinating Fistandantilus/Raistlin, he survives the conflagration of Zhaman and bears the bodies of Duncan's sons back to him. (CII, LII, LIII)

Kharolis Mountains

Extending from Abanasinia in the north to the Plains of Dust near Tarsis in the south, this mountain range includes Thorbardin and Pax Tharkas. (ALL)

Khirsah

See Fireflash.

Khisanth

See Onyx.

Khur

This land bridge joining the Balifor Peninsula to the rest of Ansalon is a grassland populated by nomadic humans. It is early dominated by the Green Dragonarmy. (ALL)

Kiiri the Sirine

Though she looks like a young human woman, Kiiri is actually a shape-changing Sirine, from a warlike sea-dwelling people. She fights beside Pheragas of Northern Ergoth and Caramon the Victor in the Games of Istar. (LI)

King of the Mountain Dwarves

See Duncan, King of Thorbardin, or Hornfel, Thane of the Hylar.

Kingpriest of Istar

This human establishes a fascistic state in the city of Istar. Through his programs of racial genocide, magical suppression, and religious intolerance, he brings down the Cataclysm upon Krynn. His presence within the Hall of Audience in the Temple of Istar is dazzling, compassionate, embracing, and life-changing due to clerical and magical spells. None who visit him come away with the same impression of his appearance.

Just before the Cataclysm, though, this glamour is stripped away, and he appears only as a weary, frail man, still holding blindly to belief in his own righteousness. *See also* Istar. (LI)

Kinslayer Wars

More than two thousand years before the Cataclysm, the elves of Silvanesti come into border conflict with Ergoth. The elven general Kith-Kanan does much to keep these conflicts from becoming full-scale war until his father, the Speaker of the Stars, is accidentally slain by humans. The resulting war splits the elven nation, and at its conclusion, half of them repair to the forest of Qualinesti, granted them by Ergoth in the Swordsheath Scroll, treaty document of the war.

Kiri-Jolith

Son of Paladine, Kiri-Jolith is the god of virtuous warriors. He and Sargonnas lead the divine battle against Chaos on their immortal plane. (DSF)

Kith-Kanan

Elven hero of the Kinslayer Wars, Kith-Kanan leads his people from the homeland of Silvanesti to the forest of Qualinesti, granted to them by Ergoth in the Swordsheath Scroll. He oversees the building of Pax Tharkas, and is credited with the peace between humans, elves, and dwarves, a peace represented by the fortress. Entombed in the Hall of Ancients, he grants his fabled sword *Wyrmslayer* to Tanis Half-Elven to slay the giant slug that attacks them. (CI)

Knight of the Black Rose

See Soth, Knight of the Black Rose Lord.

Epic Quest Larry Elmore

Knights of Solamnia

This ancient order of knighthood is founded by Vinas Solamnus two thousand years before the Cataclysm. Consisting of three orders—Crown Knights, Sword Knights, and Rose Knights (see separate entries)—the Knights of Solamnia pledge themselves to Code and Measure. The Code is *Est Sularus oth Mithas,* ancient Solamnic for "My honor is my life." The measure is a lengthy set of volumes explaining the meaning of the Code. Famous Solamnic Knights include Huma Dragonbane, Gunthar Uth Wistan, and Sturm Brightblade.

Due to the failure of the knights to avert the Cataclysm (and perhaps specifically due to such negligence as shown by Rose Knight Lord Soth), the Knights are reviled, persecuted, and exiled in the Age of Despair. Only during the War of the Lance do they regain the trust and love of the public. (ALL)

Knights of Takhisis

This knighthood is established by Ariakan after the War of the Lance. During his incarceration among the Knights of Solamnia, he witnesses the value of honor, cooperation, and dedication and recognizes that the queen's dragonarmies have defeated themselves by being divisive. After a vision of Takhisis, he creates a knighthood of three orders—Lily Knights, Skull Knights, and Thorn Knights (see separate entries)—that makes room not only for warriors, but also for clerics and magic-users. Famous Knights of Takhisis include Ariakan, Steel Brightblade, and Nightlord Lillith.

Under Ariakan's leadership, the Knights of Takhisis conquer more of Ansalon than did all the dragonarmies during the War of the Lance. They capture, among other sites, the High Clerist's Tower and Palanthas, which had not fallen previously. They are swiftly decimated, though, by the forces of Chaos. (SG, DSF)

Kothas

This Blood Sea Isle is the smallest and the farthest south, home to minotaurs. (ALL)

Krynn

This is the name of the planet created by the children of Chaos, a jewel all the gods are desirous of owning, saving, and protecting. The true measure of their love of the world is their self-banishment to draw Chaos away from it. (ALL)

Ladonna of the Black Robes

Head of the order of the Black Robes, Ladonna helps defend magic during the War of the Lance and the subsequent troubles. She is succeeded by Dalamar. (CI, CII, CIII, LI, LII, LIII)

Life Quest

Every gnome has a Life Quest, some technological inquiry that, if uncompleted, is passed on to offspring. Gnosh's Life Quest is a study of Dragon Orbs. Gnimsh's is a study of dimensional-travel devices. (CII)

Lillith

See Nightlord Lillith.

Lily, Knights of the

These forces compose the fighting arm of the Knights of Takhisis, made up of warriors such as Steel Brightblade. They wear the emblem of the black lily, a plant purported to grow from the heart of a murder victim. Those who enter the order pledge their bodies, hearts, and souls to Takhisis. Known for efficiency, valor, and utter dedication to the Dark Queen, these warriors overcome the previous tendency of evil to turn upon itself. (SG, DSF)

Live Ones

These pitiful creatures slouch around the pool in the Chamber of Seeing, oozing, living remnants of creatures abortively created by Raistlin's magical experimentation. *See also* Dead Ones. (LI, DSF)

Lorac, Speaker of the Stars

This ruler of Silvanesti seeks to save his land from the ravages of the coming dragonarmy. He enters into communion with the Dragon Orb of Silvanesti, believing he can use the power to keep dragons at bay. In fact, the orb uses him, calling the great green dragon Cyan Bloodbane to guard the wood and twisting it into a hideous nightmare landscape. He is liberated from his imprisonment by his daughter Alhana and Tanis and the companions. (CII)

Loralon

Greatest of the elven clerics before the Cataclysm, Loralon fights the rise of Quarath. He prophesies about the Thirteen Warnings and even carries out the first of these: Loralon appears to all virtuous clerics, including Denubis and Crysania, and invites them to leave Krynn and go with him to another realm, where they can escape the coming Cataclysm. (LI)

Lords of Doom

Three active volcanoes, the Lords of Doom surround the city of Sanction and send rivers of lava down through it. Beneath them, Silvara and Gilthanas discover that good dragon eggs are being corrupted into draconians. (CIII)

Lost Battles

During the suppression of magic by the King-priest of Istar, the three Orders of Magic join forces as they have not since the creation of the Dragon Orbs. The result of these battles is the destruction of two Towers of High Sorcery, the capture of the Tower of Istar, the sealing of the Tower of Palanthas, and the withdrawal of Wayreth into its magical forest. (CII, LII)

Lunitari

The neutral god of magic, Lunitari appears to folk on Krynn as the red moon, smaller and closer to the planet than the white moon, Solinari. Red Robe Mages draw their power from Lunitari and are more powerful when the moon is present. The Graygem is entrusted to Lunitari (by Reorx), only to be stolen by a gnome (sent by Reorx). (All volumes)

Lynched Geoffrey

Guildmaster of the Thieves' Guild of Palanthas, Lynched bears the rope burn of a previous execution attempt. Tall, lank, with twitching hands, he dies once and for all when Lord Ariakan sentences him to hang. (DSF)

Magius

The greatest war mage to ever live, Magius trained and fought beside Huma. Raistlin and, in turn, Palin, inherit his staff and spellbook. (DSF)

Majere

This is a good god of healing, after whom the Majere family is named. *See also* Majere; Caramon, Dezra, Laura, Palin, Raistlin, Sturm, Tanin, or Tika Waylan. (ALL)

Majere, Caramon

Described as a giant of a man with a booming voice, biceps as big as most men's thighs, and a torso like a tree trunk, Caramon is the physical opposite of his slight and sickly twin brother, Raistlin. Open, optimistic, and straightforward, he is also Raistlin's psychological opposite.

From childhood, Caramon protects his brother, defends him against other children, and soothes away his nightmares. Sons of an impoverished woodcutter and a frail woman given to trances, the twins are raised largely by their half-sister, Kitiara Uth Matar, eight years their senior. Caramon learns his sword skill from her. When the boys are about ten, she takes them on adventures, and the twins learn to fight side by side, one with steel and the other with staff.

Caramon accompanies Raistlin to Wayreth to take the Test. During the harrowing experience, Caramon witnesses Raistlin killing a facsimile of him, an image that haunts both brothers and foretells Raistlin's betrayal.

They continue the tradition of fighting side by side—through Xak Tsaroth, Tarsis, Silvanesti, and Flotsam—until Raistlin uses the Dragon Orb to escape the Blood Sea Maelstrom, abandoning his brother to death. From that point on, Caramon pursues his brother, intent on protecting him—perhaps even saving him.

When Raistlin returns to Istar just before the Cataclysm, Caramon follows him to stop him. Sold into slavery, Caramon fights in the Great Games of Istar and follows his brother to Zhaman, becoming general of the "Army of Fistandantilus." Attempting to return to the present time, Caramon arrives in the future, finds his own corpse, and witnesses a world ravaged by his brother's ascent to godhood. Taking this vision and a volume from Astinus's *Chronicles* with him back in time, Caramon enters the Tower of Palanthas by way of the flying citadel. From there, he enters the Portal to the Abyss, confronts his brother with a vision of the future, and convinces him to forsake his plans for deification.

Prior to the journey back in time, Caramon marries Tika Waylan, and they take over management of the Inn of the Last Home. They have five children: Tanin and Sturm, the eldest, who become Solamnic Knights; Palin, the third child, who becomes a White Robe mage; and the two youngest, daughters Laura and Dezra. He has a fourth "son" in his half-sister's boy, Steel Brightblade, whom Caramon fights beside in the High Clerist's Tower. (ALL)

Majere, Dezra

Youngest child of Tika Waylan and Caramon Majere, Dezra is only four when her brother Palin takes his Test, and only a few years older when her brothers Sturm and Tanin are buried near the Inn. (SG, DSF)

Majere, Laura

Fourth child of Tika Waylan and Caramon Majere, Laura is eleven years younger than Palin and one year older than Dezra. She and her little sister are sent to stay with Goldmoon and Riverwind just prior to the revelation about Sturm and Tanin's deaths and Palin's imprisonment and impending execution. (SG, DSF)

Majere, Palin

Third son of Tika Waylan and Caramon Majere, Palin is tall and thin but well built. Unlike his warrior elder brothers, he studies magic, and is summoned to the Tower of Wayreth under the pretext that he is in danger of his uncle Raistlin's influences. Through this ploy, the Conclave provides the young man his Test without Caramon knowing (though, in fact, Raistlin does get involved, granting to Palin the Staff of Magius). Palin takes the White Robes.

Palin later accompanies his brothers, Sturm and Tanin, and Dougan Redhammer on a quest for the Graygem of Gargath. Palin throws the hammer of Reorx, thereby unseating the stone and rescuing Gar-

gath from centuries of imprisonment to the stone.

When Sturm and Tanin are made Knights of Solamnia, Palin accompanies them, and survives them in the Battle of Thoradin Bay. He travels with Steel Brightblade to return the bodies to Solace, then takes the Knight of Takhisis to the Tower of Palanthas to enter the Portal.

In the Abyss, Palin is stabbed by Kitiara, but saved by Raistlin, who emerges to carry the young man forth. In Palanthas, he falls in love with Usha, but leaves her, intent on keeping his word to Steel Brightblade (and preventing the knight from being sacrificed in his stead).

Later, Palin is granted the spellbook of Magius by Raistlin. The White Robe mage accompanies Usha and Tasslehoff to the isle of Irda to retrieve the halves of the Graygem. He travels dragonback with Steel to the Abyss to capture Chaos once again. With his uncle Raistlin and his beloved Usha, Palin hears the final words of Fizban (Paladine) about the Age of Mortals. (SG, DSF)

Majere, Raistlin

Twin to Caramon Majere and half-brother to Kitiara Uth Matar, Raistlin is born to a poor woodcutter and a peasant woman whose health is ruined by the pregnancy. Raistlin's health is little better. If not for the ministrations of his half-sister (eight years his elder), Raistlin would have died. If not for his brother's constant protection, companionship, and nurturing, Raistlin might not have survived childhood. Frail but brilliant, Raistlin wins his few childhood friends by performing sleight-of-hand tricks. When he and his brother are about ten, they begin adventuring with their sword-swinging sister.

A decade later, the twins travel together to the Tower of Wayreth for Raistlin's Test. During the deadly experience, Caramon witnesses his brother slaying him, and knows ever after that the mage is capable of great treachery. At his lowest moment, Raistlin abjures the spirit of Fistandantilus to save him, trading a part of his already-fragile health. Raistlin triumphs over the Test, but emerges more sickly than before, with golden skin, a chronic cough, and hourglass eyes that see only death and decay in all things. This provision is meant to teach him humanity and compassion, but it only hardens his spirit to evil.

Raistlin journeys with the companions to Xak Tsaroth, where he is almost slain by Onyx, saved only by Goldmoon's sacrifice. He meets also the gully dwarf Bupu and receives from her a spellbook of Fistandantilus.

He continues with the group through ruined Solace, Qualinesti, and Tarsis. Raistlin battles the Dragon Orb in Silvanesti and masters it, claiming it for himself. In Port Balifor, Raistlin's descent into evil has a momentary reprieve as he performs in the Red Wizard and His Wonderful Illusions road show. It is like old times, until one night Raistlin is almost slain by the Dragon Orb.

Later, Raistlin successfully uses the device to escape the *Perechon*, bound for the Blood Sea Maelstrom. The feat nearly kills him, though, and he appears, bloodied and dying, on the steps of the Library of Palanthas. After ravaging a room of the library in search of a means of saving his life, he discovers the Key, heals himself, takes on the Black Robes, and proceeds to the Tower of Palanthas. As prophesied master of the past and present, he takes it over.

His attentions turn toward the Portal in his laboratory, a gateway to the Abyss that can be opened only by a Black Robe mage and a virtuous cleric of Paladine. He begins a seduction of Crysania of Paladine, and his plans are unwittingly aided by his traitorous sister Kitiara, the Conclave of Wizards, and Crysania herself.

Raistlin travels back to Istar before the Cataclysm to slay Fistandantilus and take his place, thus reversing the deal he struck with the archmage during his Test. He discovers Caramon, Crysania, and Tasslehoff have followed him, intent on stopping him. Tasslehoff's presence convinces Raistlin time can be altered, but fearing the kender will foul up his plans, sticks him with a nonfunctioning time-travel device.

Raistlin, Caramon, and Crysania leap forward some three decades after the Cataclysm, when Crysania will be the most powerful cleric of Paladine, but discover the Portal has moved from the Tower of Palanthas to Zhaman. Raising the Army of Fistandantilus, the three march south in the Dwarfgate

Wars. Tasslehoff reappears, rescued from the Abyss by Gnimsh, a gnome with dimensional-traveling devices as his Life Quest. Learning that a gnome's meddling would cause the attempt to enter the Portal to fail, Raistlin slays Gnimsh.

The meddling is already done, though. Tasslehoff's activation of his gnome-repaired time-traveling device fouls Raistlin's attempt to enter the Portal, causing the explosion that ruins the Plains of Dergoth and transforms Zhaman into Skullcap. Raistlin and Crysania, however, escape to their own time, and both enter the Portal in his laboratory.

There, they battle Takhisis, the Queen of Darkness, Raistlin's intent being to draw her through the Portal into Krynn, where he can slay her and take her place. After a surreal tribunal in the Abyss, Crysania is burned at the stake—not killed, but blinded. Raistlin leaves her for dead. When Caramon appears in the Abyss, though, bringing with him a tome from the future that shows Krynn destroyed if Raistlin ascends to godhood, Raistlin gives up his aspirations and instead remains in the Abyss to block Takhisis's emergence.

It is from the Abyss that Raistlin reaches out to Palin during his Test, gifting the Staff of Magius to the boy. Later, when Palin enters the Abyss and is stabbed by Kitiara, Raistlin gives up his twenty-five-year vigil to carry his dying nephew out of the Portal to save his life. Thereafter, Raistlin has no true magic, but he still manages to fool Nightlord Lillith with sleight of hand. Before Palin enters combat with Chaos, Raistlin grants the young White Robe the spellbook of Magius, which Palin uses to save Krynn.

In the end, Raistlin, his nephew, and Usha have an audience with Fizban—Paladine himself in his last appearance on Krynn—and learn from him about the coming Age of Mortals. (ALL)

Majere, Sturm

This second son of Tika Waylan and Caramon Majere is tall and well-muscled, with red curly hair and dancing green eyes. He becomes a warrior and travels with Dougan Redhammer to the Isle of Gargath to retrieve the Graygem. By the time of the invasion of the Knights of Takhisis, he is a

Time of the Twins   LARRY ELMORE

Knight of Solamnia and fights at the Battle of Thoradin Bay, where he is slain. (SG, DSF)

Majere, Tanin

Eldest son of Tika Waylan and Caramon Majere, Tanin has his father's build and his mother's red curls and flirting eyes. He travels with his brothers to the Isle of Gargath in search of the Graygem and, as a knight, fights and dies in the Battle of Thoradin Bay. (SG, DSF)

Majere Symbol

Designed by Caramon for the admittance of his sons into the Knights of Solamnia, this emblem is a rose (symbol for the god Majere) submerged in a flagon of ale. Tanis thinks it looks like the sign for an inn. (DSF)

Majere, Tika Waylan

Teenage waitress at the Inn of the Last Home when the companions are young, Tika is a full-grown woman when they return for their reunion. Red headed, buxom, and lethal with a frying pan, she travels with them to Xak Tsaroth, Qualinesti, and Pax Tharkas. Her long-standing attraction to Caramon grows, though they do not act upon it until after Silvanesti, Port Balifor, and Flotsam. By the end of the War of the Lance, she and Caramon marry and assume the day-to-day running of the inn.

Tika puts up with much from Caramon—first his long period of drunkenness and dissolution, then his pursuit of his brother back in time and forward in time. In the future, he sees her grave in a ruined Solace. Tika bears him five children, Tanin, Sturm, Palin, Laura, and Dezra. She also aids in the birth of Alhana Starbreeze's child on the same day she buries her two eldest sons. (ALL)

Mammoth

Though Tasslehoff Burrfoot often hopes to see one of these furry elephants, he probably would not have been happy to see them used in the Knights of Takhisis's attack on the High Clerist's Tower. (DSF)

Mapete

Laurana's pet name for Gilthas, her son, this word is Elven for *child*. (SG)

Maritta

Among the female captives in Pax Tharkas, Maritta helps the companions reach the imprisoned children. (CI)

War of the Twins   LARRY ELMORE

Marjoram

This spell-component spice is used by Raistlin to enhance trail rations. It becomes a symbol of his and Caramon's lost camaraderie. (LII)

MarKenin, Sword Knight Lord Alfred

Appointed by Lord Gunthar Uth Wistan to head the Knights of the Sword in the War of the Lance, Lord Alfred is continually caught between the corrupt Rose Knight Derek Crownguard and the virtuous Crown Knight Sturm Brightblade. He witnesses Sturm's unwillingness to commit his men to the suicidal mission Derek has planned. Alfred follows Derek to both of their deaths. He is entombed beside these two comrades in the Chamber of Paladine in the High Clerist's Tower. (CII)

Markham, Knight of the Rose, Sir

During the War of the Lance, Sir Markham and Sir Patrick are the Knights of the Crown with the greatest seniority.

Later, Markham is the highest-ranking Solamnic Knight left in Palanthas during Kitiara's attack. This easy-going, undependable nobleman is called in to conference with Tanis and Dalamar. He accompanies Tanis on his abortive attempt to confront Soth and his Death Knights. (CIII, LIII)

Markus

This nineteen-year-old intern works at Jenna's Three Moons Shop (and is in love with her) when the elven Senator Rashas arrives. (SG)

Master of Past and Present

According to a prophecy uttered by the Black Robe mage who seals the gates to the Tower of Palanthas by impaling himself on the spiked front gate, the tower will open again only when the master of past and present arrives. Raistlin, already tied to Fistandantilus, fulfills the prophecy, opening the gates and taking over the Tower. He later *becomes* Fistandantilus. (CIII)

Mastersmate, Dunbar, of Northern Ergoth

This robust black man makes for an unconventional wizard in his bare chest, brightly colored, loose-fitting trousers, and white sash. He succeeds Par-Salian as head of the White Robes, and helps oversee the Test given to Palin. (SG)

Mechanism Room

Fizban and Tasslehoff fight the dragon Ember in this room in Pax Tharkas. The resulting conflagration melts the gate chain preventing the doors from opening and allowing the dragonarmies to flood inward. Fizban dies here in a long fall, landing in a great cloud of feathers that saves Tasslehoff. (CI)

Michael

This young Solamnic Knight, a friend of Garic, joins the Army of Fistandantilus in his search for treasure. During the Dwarfgate Wars, Caramon puts him in charge of conquered Pax Tharkas. (LII)

Miracle

This is the shortened name of the gnome ship Dougan Redhammer uses to take Sturm, Tanin, and Palin Majere to the Isle of Gargath. Its sail can move aft above the gunwales only to roll up and return to the front of the ship underwater. (SG)

Mishakal

Consort of Paladine, this healing goddess of good reintroduces the old gods to the world after the Cataclysm. Through her blue crystal staff and the Disks of Mishakal, she converts Goldmoon and Elistan, and from them much of Ansalon. (CI, DSF)

Mithas

This is the central, medium-sized Minotaur Isle in the Blood Sea. (CIII)

Morgion

God of decay, Morgion is blamed by Dougan Redhammer for tricking Reorx into creating the Graygem in order to spread his power. During the gods' meeting witnessed by Raistlin and Palin, the blame is placed squarely on Hiddukel. (SG)

Margoyle, Palas

This is the false name Jenna uses for Palin Majere to disguise him from the Knight of the Thorn in her Three Moons Shop. (DSF)

Mount Nevermind

This homeland of the gnomes is located on Sancrist. Its true gnomish name is so long that when an unsuspecting visitor asks it, he cuts short the resulting oration with "never mind." So came the name.

Recognizing the power potentials in a semidormant volcano, the gnomes built this city within Mount Nevermind's cone-shaped interior. (CII, LII, SG, DSF)

Muralasa

Elven name for Alhana Starbreeze, *Princess of the Night*. (CII)

Murf

This gully dwarf, a member of the Thieves' Guild of Palanthas, is the first to notice Raistlin's arrival, and comes to find Usha. (DSF)

Neraka

Just after the Cataclysm, Neraka is only a small village, home of Berem and Jasla. Nearby, though, the Dark Queen plants the foundation stone of the Temple of Istar and grows her temple of evil from it.

During the War of the Lance, the tall, twisted temple dominates the landscape and is surrounded by encampments of dragonarmies. It is here that Berem and Jasla are reunited, Tanis kills Ariakas, and Laurana escapes Kitiara. The temple's fall heralds the end of the War of the Lance. (CI, CII, CIII)

Newsea

Created by the impact of the Cataclysm, this large, branched inland sea stretches from Southern Ergoth in the west to Sanction in the east, from Lemish in the north to Skullcap in the south. It includes the Isle of Schallsea. (ALL)

Night of Doom

This is the night before the Thirteen Warnings commence, the Eve of Yule, when the good clerics disappear from Krynn. (LI)

Night of the Eye

Considered a powerful night of magic by the three orders of magic, the Night of the Eye is the time when the three moons of Krynn line up, forming an eye. The Gray Robes, whose magic is not drawn from the moons, scoff at the event as a time when costumed children go door to door for treats. (DSF)

Nightflight

This coal-black charger is the horse of Ariakan. (DSF)

Nightlord (Lillith)

Head of the magely Knights of the Thorn, this forty-year-old woman has dark hair and startlingly green eyes. Because her knights capture Palin Majere, she has charge of him. Suspicious and impractical, she argues against letting Steel Brightblade take charge of Palin. She desires Palin's Staff of Magius. When Steel returns without his prisoner, Lillith demands his execution.

Later, the Nightlord and her renegade followers attempt forcibly to attend a Conclave called by Dalamar. Raistlin prevents them with an ominous prophecy and some stage magic.

After regaining Palin, Lillith takes the Staff from him, only later to trip over it and fall beneath a lowering portcullis. She is killed instantly. (DSF)

Nordmaar

This large cape includes the northernmost point on continental Ansalon. It is largely a tropical rain forest and swampy wasteland. Its two major fortifications—North Keep and Valkinord—fall early to the invasion of the Knights of Takhisis. (DSF)

Northern Ergoth

This island, created by the Cataclysm, is home to the dark-skinned races of seafarers from which Maquesta Kar-thon and Theros Ironfeld come. (ALL)

Test of the Twins   LARRY ELMORE

Nuitari

The black moon, Nuitari is detectable only to Wizards of the Black Robes and on the Night of the Eye. God of evil magic, Nuitari is sanguine and mysterious. (ALL)

Oath and the Measure, the

See the Code and the Measure.

Old City Wall

Built when Palanthas is much smaller (and less proud) the Old City Wall does not enclose much of the city, is in ill repair, and is poorly manned. Tasslehoff knows a route through the wall, discovered when kender are forbidden entry into the city. Laurana and Bakaris cross the barrier to make the hostage trade for Tanis. During Kitiara's invasion, this wall is the only defensive work that stands between Lord Soth's Death Knights and the city proper. (CI, CII, CIII, LI, LII, LIII)

One-eyed Kate

This eye-patch-wearing fishmonger works in Palanthas as an agent of the Knights of Takhisis. She ushers Steel and Palin into the city. Her name is perhaps an homage to author Kate Novak. (DSF)

Onygion, Lord

This lord of Istar, angry with the cleric Quarath, arranges for the priest's gladiator to get killed in the games by Caramon the Victor. (LI)

Dragons of Winter Night   LARRY ELMORE

Onyx (Khisanth)

Resident of Xak Tsaroth when the companions arrive, this sleek black dragon is charged by Verminaard to stop the adventurers with the blue crystal staff. She confronts the companions within the sunken city and even captures Raistlin beneath her claw. Before she can slay him, however, Goldmoon shatters the blue crystal staff against Onyx, killing dragon and Goldmoon both. (CI)

Paladine, the Platinum Dragon

Head of the pantheon of good gods, Paladine is the creator of elves, and harborer of the Irda that flee Takhisis. His human form is Fizban, the distracted mage. He provides the vision that makes Vinas Solamnus establish the Knights of Solamnia. Paladine fights Chaos to the end, and appears last to explain the dawning age to Raistlin, Usha, and Palin. (ALL)

Palanthas

One of the greatest cities of Ansalon, Palanthas is guarded in the south by the High Clerist's Tower, the east and west by high mountain ranges, and the north by the ocean. Because of these fortifications, natural and otherwise, Palanthas does not fall in the War of the Lance. It is attacked afterward, though, by Kitiara and her flying citadel, which bypasses these troubles, and is completely taken over by the Knights of Takhisis during the Chaos War.

Notable sites in the city include the Library of Palanthas (base for Astinus), the Tower of Palanthas (Raistlin and Dalamar's abode), the Temple of Paladine (built and tended by Elistan and Crysania), and the royal house of Palanthas (home of Lord Amothus and tended by Charles). (ALL)

Par-Salian of the White Robes

This venerable wizard is head of the Conclave of Wizards (and of the Order of the White Robes) in the years before and during the War of the Lance. He oversees the Test given to Raistlin. Later, he sends Crysania and Caramon back to Old Istar to stop Raistlin, knowing even if they cannot, Crysania will be killed in the Cataclysm, keeping Raistlin from using her to enter the Portal. Through such actions, he makes an enemy of the Black Robe, and in the end is tormented in his Tower by the Abyss-bound mage. Shortly thereafter, Justarius replaces him as head of the Conclave. (CI, CII, CIII, LI, LII, LIII)

Paths of the Dead

This is the name of a slippery stairway to the top of a column in Xak Tsaroth, known to Raistlin but none of the other companions. (CI)

Patrick, Knight of the Crown, Sir

Along with Sir Markham, this knight has the greatest seniority in his order after the death of Sturm Brightblade in the War of the Lance. (CIII)

Pax Tharkas

Built by Kith-Kanan after the signing of the Swordsheath Scroll, this mountain fortress is originally a stone-and-mortar embodiment of the peace between the Qualinesti elves, the Thorbardin dwarves, and the Ergoth humans. During the Dwarfgate Wars, this fortress is captured by the Army of Fistandantilus. During the War of the Lance, it is held by the Dark Queen under Lord Verminaard.

The companions travel here through the Sla-Mori, heal the slave-captive Elistan, and rescue the slaves. The dragon Flamestrike slays Ember above the fortress, and Sturm slays Lord Verminaard within. (CI, LII)

PC

Pre-Cataclysm. (ALL)

Perechon, the

This ship is captained by Maquesta Kar-thon, helmed by Berem, the Green Gemstone Man, and crewed by first mate Bas-Ohn Koraf. It takes Tanis, Caramon, Goldmoon, Riverwind, and companions into the Blood Sea Maelstrom, and thereby into sunken Istar. (CII, CIII)

Pheragas of Northern Ergoth

A dark-skinned gladiator, Pheragas fights beside Caramon the Victor and Kiiri the Sirine in the Games of Istar. He dies in the arena just before the Cataclysm. In the Fistandantilus continuity, he is taken forward in time, past the Cataclysm, to be a general in the Dwarfgate Wars, slain in the end by the Dewar. (LI, LII)

Phudge I, Highbulp

This gully dwarf, ruler of the Bulp clan in Xak Tsaroth, provides a map that leads the companions to the lair of the black dragon Onyx. (CI)

Pig and Whistle, the

Run by William Sweetwater, this tavern in Port Balifor serves watered-down ale and wine to draconians in order to keep them out. It becomes a surrogate for the Inn of the Last Home for Raistlin and companions. (CII)

Plains of Dergoth

This grassland surrounding the ancient fortress of Zhaman is blasted into blackness by the explosion that melts the fortress down, creating Skullcap. (LII)

Plains of Dust

A large, cold expanse of grassland and glacial tundra, the Plains of Dust isolate Tarsis the Beautiful from the rest of Ansalon. The companions cross it to reach Tarsis. After the party is sundered, Laurana and Gilthanas's group traverses it heading toward Ice Wall, and Tanis and Raistlin's group crosses it to reach Silvanesti. (CII)

Polymorph Ring

Tasslehoff discovers this item in the Tower of Wayreth and is changed into a mouse. Believed to be a familiar, his presence is suffered long enough that he can be sent back in time with Caramon and Crysania and change history. (LI)

Portal, the

This rift in the fabric of Krynn leads to the Abyss. It hovers within a five-headed-dragon frame in Raistlin's Laboratory. To keep anyone from using it, the Orders of Sorcery enspelled it so it can be opened only by a virtuous cleric of Paladine working in concert with a powerful Black Robe Mage. Raistlin seduces Crysania (eventually to help him open the Portal), and even draws her after him to Istar so that he can gain all the power of Fistandantilus.

Upon their trek past the Cataclysm, the Portal is relocated to Zhaman, requiring Raistlin to fight the Dwarfgate War in Fistandantilus's stead. Raistlin's attempt to enter the Portal is fouled by Tasslehoff's use of his time-travel device, causing an explosion that sears the Plains of Dergoth.

At last returning to his own time, Raistlin and Crysania successfully enter the Portal. Caramon follows them and convinces his brother not to seize god-

hood, but instead to sacrifice himself to keep the Dark Queen within the Abyss.

Palin passes through the Portal in an illusion during his Test, and in reality later, during the Chaos War. Wounded in the Abyss, he is carried out by Raistlin, who emerges without his magic. (LI, LII, LIII, SG, DSF)

Prayer's Eye Peak

This mountain, shaped like a pair of hands pressed together in prayer, stands above the Darken Wood. The companions travel between the "hands," led by Sturm's vision of the white stag. (CI)

Protector (Prot), the

This Irda is assigned to care for Usha, the orphan human child brought among the Irda. (DSF)

Pyrite (Fool's Gold)

Fizban rides this ancient, senile gold dragon into "battle" against Tanis, Berem, and companions, flying to Neraka. Through this attack, Pyrite and Fizban save the companions from certain death by the waiting dragonarmies. (CIII)

Pyros

See Ember.

Qualimori

This city is capital of the forest realm established on Southern Ergoth by the refugees of Qualinesti during the War of the Lance. The capital is built on the east side of the Thon-Tsalarian by displacing and subjugating the native Kaganesti elves. Laurana, Gilthanas, and companions arrive here en route to Sancrist. Here they meet Silvart, alter ego of silver dragon Silvara. (CII)

Qualinesti

This land and these elven people are created by the Kinslayer Wars. A thousand years before the Cataclysm, Kith-Kanan, ashamed of the atrocity of elves slaying elves, leads a band of refugees west to a forest granted them by Ergoth. The capital of Qualinesti is Qualinost, in which the trees and natural forms are gently coaxed into beautiful and useful buildings.

Dragons of Autumn Twilight   LARRY ELMORE

The companions are rescued from Lord Toede's slave wagon by Qualinesti elves. Among them, Tanis confronts his homeland, and Laurana and Gilthanas join the party. Qualinesti is later besieged by the dragonarmies, its people fleeing to Southern Ergoth to establish Qualimori. (CI, SG, DSF)

Qualinost

Capital city of Qualinesti, this beautiful elven enclave is typified by natural forms gently guided into new structures. The Tower of the Suns stands in the center of the settlement. Within, the companions give a report to Solostaran, Speaker of the Sun, father of Porthios, Gilthanas, and Laurana, and adoptive father of Tanis.

Later, Gilthas, the son of Tanis and Laurana, is brought here against his will and imprisoned with Alhana Starbreeze. Here, he accepts the title of Speaker of the Sun and Stars, though he is merely a puppet of Senator Rashas. (CI, SG)

Quarath

A corrupt, high-level cleric in the Temple of Istar, Quarath's ascent is opposed by Loralon, greatest of elven clerics. Quarath discovers the letter from Par-Salian in Crysania's possessions and conspires to condemn her as a witch. He is, of course, left behind when such virtuous clerics as his underling, Denubis, are spirited by Loralon away from Krynn. (LI)

Que-kiri

This barbarian tribe of Abanasinia is kin to Goldmoon's Que-shu. (CI)

Que-shu

A tribe of plains barbarians, the Que-shu dwell in hilly eastern Abanasinia, near the ruins of Xak Tsaroth. Their chief is Goldmoon's father. (CI, CII, CIII)

Que-teh

This barbarian tribe of Abanasinia is kin to Goldmoon's Que-shu. (CI)

Quick-hand Bet

A dwarven thief, Quick-hand Bet is the founder of the Palanthas Thieves' Guild, unionizing so thieves would not steal from thieves. (DSF)

Quithain, Magius

Elven for *Congratulations, Mage*, this is said by Dalamar to Palin at the end of the young man's Test. (SG)

Quith-pa

Elven for *iron rations, quith-pa* is dried fruit. It is introduced to the companions as trail food by Gilthanas and received ruefully by Caramon. (CI)

Dragons of Spring Dawning   LARRY ELMORE

Rabbitslayer

Tanis is making fun of Tasslehoff's diminutive, nonmagical pocket knife when he names it *Rabbitslayer*. Even so, this small blade does some big things, including freeing Palin from the dungeon of the High Clerist's Tower and drawing the drop of Chaos's blood that allows the god to be captured again. (DSF)

Raf

Just after the War of the Lance, this gully dwarf works in the kitchens of the Inn of the Last Home. (LI)

Raag

An ogre gladiator, Raag fights with Arak Rockbreaker in the days when the games are real (and deadly). (LI)

Raistlin's Daughter

This legend, though widespread and compelling, lacks corroboration from Astinus of Palanthas, and is disbelieved by all the companions, including Raistlin himself. Usha, however, believes herself to be Raistlin's child, due to the legend she learned from her Irda guardians.

The story goes that the Irda Amberyl is rescued by Caramon and Raistlin at the Wayward Inn. Overcome by *Valin*, the mage and the Irda are joined, and she dies later in childbirth, the child carried away by two Irda strangers.

Raistlin relates a different story, that Usha is a fully human child, her parents shipwrecked on the isle of the Irda. After she is born, her parents attempt to leave, though the Irda forbid them. In the resulting struggle, her father is accidentally slain. Afterward, grief-stricken, her mother wanders out to sea. The orphan Usha is then raised by the Irda and told she is Raistlin's Daughter.

This story, too, is somewhat dissatisfying. It does nothing to explain Usha's golden eyes (Raistlin says her parents also have golden eyes, but this is unheard of among humans), or her native control of magic (which could come from being part Irda, part Raistlin, but not from two unmagical castaways). The truth of these stories may never be known. (SG, DSF)

Raistlin's Laboratory

Dominated by a vast stone table, this room is dark and filled with bubbling beakers, jars of spell components, mysterious artifacts, shelves of books with night-blue bindings, and of course the shimmering Portal to the Abyss. Here, the three Orders of Magic met to create the Dragon Orbs, and to devise their strategies to save magic from the Kingpriest. Here, too, Dalamar kills Kitiara, Palin comes for his Test, and Raistlin emerges to save his nephew's life. (ALL)

Raistlin's Room

This storage closet in the Inn of the Last Home is named Raistlin's Room by Laura and Dezra, daughters of Caramon and Tika. Hearing this, traveling mages begin leaving talismans and artifacts, turning the room into a shrine. Raistlin takes up residence here after returning from the Abyss. (DSF)

Raistlin's Study

Unlike Raistlin's daunting laboratory, this room is plushly appointed in fine carpets and fabrics and beautifully carved wood. Here, Raistlin entertains Kitiara after the War of the Lance. This room becomes Dalamar's Room. (LI)

Rashas, Senator

Wanting to prevent the Treaty of the Unified Nations of the Three Races, this member of the Thalas-Enthia kidnaps Alhana Starbreeze and Gilthas Solostaran, declaring the former a dark elf (outcast) and the latter ruler of the elves. The quarter-elf boy becomes his puppet. Rashas later signs Qualinesti's unconditional surrender to the Knights of Takhisis. (SG, DSF)

Red Dragon Inn, the

This Tarsis inn is the home base of the companions during the dragon attacks on the city. (CII)

Red Minotaur

Caramon the Victor, Kiiri the Sirine, and Pheragas of Northern Ergoth fight this gladiator in the Games of Istar on the day of the Cataclysm. (LI)

Red Robes

This order of magic-users is committed to neutral magic, province of Lunitari. Justarius heads this order through the War of the Lance and the years after, until he is killed at the siege of Storm's Keep. Raistlin begins as a Red Robe, and so can learn from any master, White, Black, or Red Robe. (ALL)

Red Wizard and His Wonderful Illusions

This traveling road show, featuring Raistlin, Goldmoon, and other companions, performs in Port Balifor, providing the company money and a means to spread news of the old gods. Margaret and Tracy have their own traveling road show, which goes to conventions. (CII)

Redhammer, Dougan

This flamboyant "young" dwarf (just over one hundred) is the mortal manifestation of Reorx. Taller than most dwarves, Dougan is rotund, with curly black hair and beard. He has a penchant for drinking and gambling, a combination that account for his repeated loss of the Graygem. He originally encounters the companions when he abducts Palin, Sturm, and Tanin Majere to recover the gem from the Isle of Gargath.

Later, he sells Usha into service in the Palanthas Thieves' Guild. He aids also in the final conflict with Chaos, fighting alongside Usha, Tasslehoff, and Steel Brightblade. (SG, DSF)

Reorx

Forger of the planet of Krynn and creator of the Graygem of Gargath, Reorx is the neutral god of manufacture and artifice. He elevates the Kal-thax dwarves to immortality due to their mastery of craft, and demotes his smiths to tinker gnomes in punishment for their shortsighted folly. He appears on Krynn as Dougan Redhammer. (ALL)

Riverwind

The "poor man's son" of the song of Goldmoon, Riverwind is sent on a long quest by the Que-shu Chief, who hopes he will never return. Riverwind does, however, bringing with him the blue-crystal staff as a gift for his beloved, the chieftain's daughter. When the people of the tribe try to stone him, Goldmoon joins him and the two flee. They arrive at the Inn of the Last Home on the night of the companions' reunion and are quickly befriended by them.

Tall, thin, dark-skinned and dark-haired, Riverwind strives to be just and honorable in all his dealings. His first thought is always toward Goldmoon, and he is her protector.

Riverwind travels with the companions to Xak Tsaroth and Pax Tharkas, lending his fighting prowess to a number of deadly battles, including the final showdown with Lord Verminaard. He follows Tanis's group from Tarsis into Silvanesti, Port Balifor, Flotsam, Istar, and Palanthas, but there he and Goldmoon depart. Their child is due the next autumn, and they must make preparations. He and Goldmoon later host Laura and Dezra Majere. (CI, CII, CIII, DSF)

Rockbreaker, Arak

This crusty dwarven trainer in the Games of Istar is given charge of Caramon the Victor. Once a slave gladiator himself, Arak suffers a disfiguring injury when he is hurled from the arena, his face split on the stones outside. (LI)

Rose, Knights of the

The highest order of Solamnic Knighthood, Rose Knights wear the emblem of the kingfisher, from Vinas Solamnus's own noble crest. Famous Knights of the Rose include Huma Dragonbane, Lord Soth, Gunthar Uth Wistan, Derek Crownguard, Sir Markham, and the father of Sturm Brightblade. (ALL)

Rounce

This gully dwarf ends up helming the flying citadel with Tasslehoff. (LIII)

Sageway East

This Abanasinian highway leads near Xak Tsaroth. (CI)

The Second Generation LARRY ELMORE

Dragons of Summer Flame   LARRY ELMORE

Sally Dale

See Dale, Sally.

Saltbreeze Inn, the

This Flotsam inn is where Tanis trysts with Kitiara. (CIII)

Samar of House Protector

Guardian and friend of Alhana Starbreeze, Samar overcomes her Kaganesti guards to save her and Gilthas from Senator Rashas. In the end, he fails, but is himself rescued by Tanis and Dalamar. He accompanies Alhana and Porthios to the Inn of the Last Home when they are exiled. (SG, DSF)

Sancrist

Westernmost island of Ansalon, Sancrist is home to Whitestone Glade, where Gunthar Uth Wistan holds his knightly council, and Mount Nevermind, dormant volcano and gnome homeland. (ALL)

Sanction

This city, on the easternmost edge of the Newsea, becomes a dragonarmy staging area. Three active volcanoes, the Lords of Doom, surround the city and send lava flows down through it. Silvara and Gilthanas travel here, learning of the creation of draconians from the corrupted eggs of metallic dragons. (CIII)

Sandath, Otik

Boisterous and welcoming, this man is proprietor of the Inn of the Last Home, and famous for his recipe for spiced potatoes. (CI)

Sargaron, Kargai

Elven name for Theros Ironfeld. (CII)

Schallsea

This island rests at the junction of the many arms of the Newsea. (ALL)

Sestun

A gully dwarf in the employ of Lord Toede, Sestun escorts the slave wagon toward Pax Tharkas and tries to help the companions escape. (CI)

Shadow-wights

Minions of Chaos, these shapeless warriors are rips in the fabric of reality. They take the form of their opponents, whisper killing words of despair, and at a touch disintegrate flesh. They massacre the Knights of Takhisis at the High Clerist's Tower. They can be killed by fireballs. (DSF)

Shalafi

Elven for *master*, this is Dalamar's term for Raistlin. (SG)

Shirak

This command word activates the light spell on the Staff of Magius. (ALL)

Shoikan Grove

This ancient grove of oaks is full of undead creatures and surreal horrors that guard the Tower of Palanthas, preventing entry to all but the master of the tower and those given a charm. Even fearless kender cannot pass the grove. (ALL)

Silvamori

This settlement is capital of the refugee camp of Silvanesti elves in Southern Ergoth. It occupies the western side of the Thon-Tsalarian River. (CII)

Silvanesti

Ancient nation of the elves, Silvanesti has been home to elves for four thousand years. Two thousand years before the Cataclysm, the realm is sundered after the Kinslayer Wars, losing much of its population. Even so, Silvanesti remains the spiritual homeland of most elves until Speaker of the Stars Lorac uses his Dragon Orb to repel the coming armies of dragons. The orb plunges the land into a twisted, haunted nightmare. Silvanesti is liberated by Tanis and his companions, and Alhana Starbreeze, daughter of Lorac, remains behind to heal the land. This task is nearly complete twenty-five years later, when the Chaos War begins. (CII, DSF)

Silvanost

Capital of Silvanesti, this city is a haunted nightmare land when the companions arrive. Even at its best, Silvanost's beauty and grandeur comes from the subjugation of nature rather than the subtle shaping of it. (CII)

Silvara

Disguised as Kaganesti healer Silvart, Silvara joins the companions at Qualimori and leads them to the Tomb of Huma. En route, she falls in love with Gilthanas Solostaran, and he with her. Only then does she reveal her true nature: she is a silver dragon, in fact *the* silver dragon who had been lover of Huma Dragonbane.

She teaches Theros Ironfeld how to forge dragonlances, and afterward travels with Gilthanas to Sanction, where they learn the truth about the origin of draconians. She is instrumental in bringing the good dragons into the War of the Lance, thereby saving Ansalon from complete domination. (CII, CIII)

Silver Dragon Mountain

This mountain on Southern Ergoth holds the Tomb of Huma. Silvara leads the companions here and teaches them how to construct dragonlances. During the Chaos War, Huma himself instructs the blue and silver dragons guarding the tomb to go to the High Clerist's Tower for the final conflict with Chaos. (DSF)

Sirrion Sea

This body of water embraces the western third of the continent of Ansalon. (ALL)

Sivak

Born from the corrupted eggs of silver dragons, Sivak draconians are large and powerful, deadly when directed by intelligent commanders. (ALL)

Skie

This large blue dragon is the mount of the Dark Lady, Highlord Kitiara. She rides him after the *Perechon*, and there almost captures Berem and Tanis. She rides him also in her attack upon Palanthas. Like most blues, Skie is utterly loyal to his mistress. (CIII, LIII)

Skullcap

This name is given to the fortress of Zhaman after Raistlin's attempt to enter the Portal melts Zhaman into the shape of a skull. (LII)

Skull, Knights of the

Clerical arm of the Knights of Takhisis, the Knights of the Skull are led by the High Priestess of Takhisis. They are in charge of healing, external intelligence, and internal security. (DSF)

Sla-Mori, the

Elven for the *Secret Way*, this catacomb of underground passages leads past the tomb of Kith-Kanan to Pax Tharkas. (CI)

Sleet

A white dragon, Sleet is away on a scouting mission when the companions enter Ice Wall, kill Fealthas, and take the Dragon Orb. Sleet pursues the companions aboard ship and attacks, encasing them in ice. When the boat sinks, she retreats, believing the Dark Queen's spies can recover the orb from the bottom. (CII)

Sluds, Bulps, Glups

These three tribes of gully dwarves live within ruined Xak Tsaroth. The Bulps rule (through the Highbulp) since they developed the lift. (CI)

Slug

This gully dwarf, on the docks of Palanthas, guides Steel and Palin to the workplace of One-eyed Kate. (DSF)

Solace

One of three towns in Abanasinia, Solace is the location of the Inn of the Last Home, the place from which the companions start their journeys. Early in the War of the Lance, Solace languishes under the tyranny of the Seekers, and then Fewmaster Toede and his goblins, and at last the dragonarmies themselves. Destroyed by dragons, the town and the inn are rebuilt after the War.

When Caramon and Tasslehoff travel to the future, they arrive at a desolate, ash-filled Solace and discover Caramon's body and Tika's tomb. Such sights, related to Raistlin, prevents him from destroying the world. When he returns from the Abyss, he heads for Solace, or more simply, "home." (ALL)

Solamnia

Created two millennia before the Cataclysm, Solamnia is the breakaway eastern half of Ergoth. Its knighthood defends the world for two thousand years before being disgraced during the Age of Despair. In the time of the War of the Lance, Solamnia holds the largest and most important human population centers, including Palanthas, Solanthus, and Caergoth. It is, understandably, considered the great prize of the campaign of the Knights of Takhisis, the object of attack on two fronts sweeping inward. (ALL)

Solamnic Death Chant

This song of mourning is sung when Knights of Solamnia die. It wishes the shade of the deceased to rise to join that of Huma. (CI)

The Soulforge   LARRY ELMORE

Solamnus, Vinas

Two millennia before the Cataclysm, this man leads a revolution against Ergoth, establishing the nation of the Solamnia and the knighthood. (ALL)

Solanthus

This major population center in southern Solamnia lies upon the main road linking Caergoth in the west to Lemish in the east. (ALL)

Solinari

Largest of the three moons, Solinari is the goddess of good magic. She joins with her sister and brother during the All Saints War to prevent magic from being destroyed and creates the Order of the White Robes. (DSF)

Solostaran, Gilthanas

Second son of Solostaran, Qualinesti Speaker of the Sun, Gilthanas is a childhood playmate of Tanis Half-Elven and his sister Laurana. When an attraction grows between his sister and his playmate, Gilthanas sides with those who would throw Tanis out.

When the Qualinesti elves rescue the companions from Lord Toede's slave wagon, Gilthanas joins the group and adventures with them through the Sla-Mori, Pax Tharkas, Tarsis, Ice Wall, and the Tomb of Huma. He falls in love with Silvara, before knowing she is a silver dragon. He travels with her to Neraka, where they discover the corruption of the good dragon eggs. His impossible love for the dragon at last softens his censure of his sister's love for a half-elf. (CI, CII, CIII)

Love and War   LARRY ELMORE

Solostaran, Gilthas, Prince

Son of Laurana Solostaran and Tanis Half-Elven, this quarter-elf is lured to Qualinesti by Senator Rashas of the Thalas-Enthia. There, threatened with the death of hostage Alhana Starbreeze, he is made the senator's puppet ruler of elves: Speaker of the Sun and Stars. Forced by Senator Rashas, he surrenders the elven kingdoms to the Knights of Takhisis. (SG)

Solostaran, Laurana (Lauralanthalasa, the Golden General)

Younger sister of Porthios and Gilthanas, Laurana is raised also with Solostaran's adopted nephew, Tanis Half-Elven. The two fall in love and even play at being betrothed, though Porthios and Gilthanas cannot stomach the idea of their sister marrying a half-breed.

Laurana, with brown skin, honeylike hair, full lips, and large liquid eyes, is an adult when Tanis and his companions are rescued by the Qualinesti elves from Lord Toede's slave wagon. She reiterates her love of Half-Elven, but he returns the "engagement" ring she had given him. She hurls it into the trees. (Tas retrieves it.) Laurana follows the party to Pax Tharkas, revealing herself only when the companions are at the point of death in the Sla-Mori.

After Pax Tharkas, Laurana continues with the companions through Tarsis, Ice Wall, and the Tomb of Huma, all the while proving a devoted helper of Elistan, priest of Paladine. Once she and the others arrive at Whitestone Glade with the dragonlances, she is sent by Gunthar Uth Wistan to deliver the lances and train the knights. After the death of Derek Crownguard (and Sturm Brightblade), Gunthar appoints Laurana to head up the Knighthood.

Distinguishing herself in battle, Laurana comes to be known as the Golden General, symbol of hope for the forces of good. Kitiara steals this hope by luring Laurana out of Palanthas for a prisoner exchange. Instead of freeing Tanis from imprisonment, though, the Dark Lady captures Laurana. She is rescued by Tanis himself during the collapse of the Temple of Takhisis. In time, these two are married and have a quarter-elf son, Gilthas.

Just prior to Kitiara's invasion of Palanthas, Tanis writes an impassioned letter to his wife. He survives that attack, but during the war against the Knights of Takhisis, Laurana repairs to Qualinesti to be near her son, the new ruler of elves, where she remains when Tanis is slain. (ALL)

Solostaran, Porthios

Eldest son of Qualinesti Speaker of the Suns Solostaran, Porthios is a man of virtue, but tends to be aloof, stern, and racist. He marries Alhana Starbreeze, daughter of the Silvanesti Speaker of the Stars, and thereby unites the kingdoms for the first time in a millennium. Though it is at first a loveless, political marriage, in the end Porthios grows to love his wife.

She is pregnant with their child, heir to the throne of elves, when they are cast out by a conspiracy of powerful elven senators and generals. Porthios and Alhana become dark elves. They have their child in exile, at the Inn of the Last Home. (ALL)

Solostaran, Speaker of the Sun

Father of Porthios, Gilthanas, and Laurana and adopted father of Tanis Half-Elven, Solostaran is the even-handed leader of the Qualinesti elves for well over a century. Tall, austere, and serene, his hair is only touched with silver. During the Dwarfgate Wars, Solostaran receives a message from Caramon, asking for elven aid in their cause. After being rescued from Toede's slave caravan, the companions report to Solostaran in the Tower of the Sun. His death at the end of the War of the Lance prevents Tanis from accompanying Crysania to the Tower of Wayreth. (CI, CII, CIII, LI, LII)

Soth, Knight of the Black Rose, Lord

Lord of Dargaard Keep, Soth is a powerful and well-regarded Lord Rose Knight before the Cataclysm. Despite his marriage, he falls in love with a beautiful elven priestess and takes her to his keep. In time, his wife dies under suspicious circumstances. Shortly thereafter, the elf woman is found to be pregnant with Soth's child. His knighthood is stripped and he is sentenced to death, though he escapes to his keep.

There, one night, he strikes his wife and realizes what a monster he has become. He prays to Paladine to regain his honor, and Paladine gives him the task of traveling to Istar to stop the Kingpriest and save Ansalon. En route, though, a troop of elf maidens jeer him, saying (untruthfully) that the child is not even his. Soth turns back from saving the world, returns to Dargaard Keep, and arrives during the Cataclysm. He sees a candle chandelier fall upon his mistress and child. He deigns to save them, and is cursed by her, becoming a death knight. He is attended, day and night, by banshees, keening the history of his misdeeds.

At the time of the War of the Lance, he allies with Kitiara and eventually falls in love with her. At her behest, he slays Crysania en route to the Tower of Wayreth and later leads a death-knight charge through the streets of Palanthas itself. When Kitiara is slain by Dalamar, Soth comes to collect her body and seeks to posses her soul. (CIII, LIII, DSF)

Soth, Quivalen

The greatest of elven bards, Quivalen Soth teaches Tanis dragonlore. (CI)

Southern Ergoth

This island on the western coast of Ansalon becomes home to the Silvanesti and Qualinesti refugees of the War of the Lance, with the settlements of Silvamori and Qualimori. In the latter, the companions meet Silvart (Silvara), and trekking northward on Southern Ergoth, they discover Silver Dragon Mountain and the Tomb of Huma. (CII)

Southgate

This southern district of Thorbardin opens its doors to the refugees of Pax Tharkas in exchange for the Hammer of Kharas. (CII)

Speaker of the Sun and Stars

This new position is created for Gilthas, son of Tanis Half-Elven and Laurana Solostaran, placing him in control of both Silvanesti and Qualinesti (if only as a puppet). *See also* Solostaran, Gilthas. (SG)

Speaker of the Suns

See Solostaran.

Spliced Jib, the

This is the ominous name of an ominous tavern in the town of Sancrist, where Dougan Redhammer meets Tanin, Sturm, and Palin Majere. (SG)

Spring Dawning

This annual festival in Kalaman serves also as a victory celebration for the Knights of Solamnia, led by Laurana. The festival is overshadowed by the Golden General's disappearance. (CIII)

Staff of Magius

This staff, gained by Raistlin after his successful Test, is a plain wooden staff topped by a golden claw clutching a crystal. Once belonging to the legendary wizard that fought alongside Knight of Solamnia Huma, the staff has untold powers, the most famous of which is its light ability, activated by the command "*Shirak*" and deactivated by the command "*Dulak*," or "*Dumak*." Raistlin carries it everywhere until he is lost in the Abyss, at which time Caramon returns with it and the light of the staff goes out.

Later, during Palin's Test, Raistlin grants the staff to him. When Palin is captured by the Knights of Takhisis, Nightlord Lillith tries to take it, is tripped by it, and slain by a falling portcullis. In the final battle with Chaos, Palin uses the staff to turn the shadow-wights. (LIII, SG, DSF)

Starbreeze, Alhana

Daughter of Lorac, Speaker of the Stars of the Silvanesti elves, Alhana joins the companions at the Hall of Justice in Tarsis. Ambassador from Silvanesti, she is in as much trouble as Sturm, the knight. Called *Muralasa*, Elven for *Princess of the Night*, Alhana is said to be the most beautiful of elf maidens. Her hair is black, her eyes purple, and her complexion as pale as the moon.

During the dragon assault on Tarsis, she expresses her love for Sturm Brightblade and grants him a star-jewel, a potent magic item that binds elven lovers together. Afterward, she travels with Tanis's party to Silvanesti and helps free the elven homeland of the nightmare caused by her father's Dragon Orb. She remains behind to help the elven homeland in healing.

Perhaps her greatest accomplishment in healing the elven homeland is her marriage to Porthios, son of Qualinesti Speaker of the Suns Solostaran, thereby uniting the kingdoms. (This is after Sturm's death.) Just prior to the birth of their son, who would seal the union, Alhana and Porthios are exiled and become dark elves. (CII, CIII, SG, DSF)

Starjewel

An emblem of love that binds elven lovers together, a starjewel is given by Alhana Starbreeze to Sturm Brightblade just before they are separated in Tarsis. The ghost of Sturm bestows this jewel upon his son, Steel Brightblade, and it becomes a symbol of his chance for salvation, that his soul does not belong to Takhisis. Nightlord Lillith sees the jewel as a sign of Steel's traitorous nature. (CII, SG, DSF)

Steeltoe

This peg-legged half-ogre leads a band of disaffected Solamnic Knights and marauders in the time just before the Dwarfgate Wars. He captures Caramon, Raistlin, and Kitiara, but is slain in one-on-one combat with Caramon. (LII)

Storm's Keep

This unimpregnable fortress of the Knights of Takhisis is located on an island in the northern Ocean and is staging ground for the Ansalonian invasion. Tanis, Caramon, and Sara Dunstan come here to take Steel to his father's grave. The keep is later attacked by Justarius in an attempt to destroy the renegade Gray Robe wizards, but Justarius is killed and the conclave's forces routed. (SG, DSF)

Straits of Schallsea

This narrow stretch of water runs between Caergoth and Abanasinia. The Army of Fistandantilus crosses it on its way south. (LII)

Sweetwater, William

Proprietor of the Pig and Whistle in Port Balifor, "Pig William" is no lover of draconians, and makes a home away from home for the Red Wizard and His Wonderful Illusions road show. (CII)

Sword, Knights of the

This middle order of Solamnic Knighthood is represented during the War of the Lance by Lord Alfred MarKenin. To be a Sword Knight, one must begin as a Crown Knight. (ALL)

Swordsheath Scroll

This treaty, initiated by the elven hero Kith-Kanan and signed between the elves of Qualinesti, the dwarves of Thorbardin, and the humans of Ergoth, ends the Kinslayer Wars and ushers in a new era of peace on Ansalon. Pax Tharkas is built to honor the peace agreement. (LII)

Takhisis

This goddess of ultimate evil constantly seeks entry into Krynn. She brings the dragons in the first dragon wars, creates draconians during the Age of Despair, initiates and conducts the War of the Lance, founds the Knights of Takhisis, and flees the world when Chaos is released. (ALL)

Tallbow, Crown Knight Aran

This comrade of Rose Knight Derek Crownguard is one of the three knights who joins the companions at Tarsis the Beautiful. (CII)

Tandar

This white tiger becomes the guide of Crysania when she returns, blinded, from the Abyss. It startles Steel and Palin when they are on the grounds of the Temple of Paladine in Palanthas. (DSF)

Tanis Half-Elven (Tanthalas)

When the wife of Solostaran's brother is raped by a human, she becomes pregnant and gives birth to a half-elven child named Tanthalas. Orphaned at an early age, Tanis is taken in by Solostaran and raised as a brother to Porthios, Gilthanas, and Laurana. As they grow, Tanis's human traits become obvious, as does the shared attraction between him and Laurana.

Driven from Qualinesti by the resentment of the elves and the sudden coolness of Gilthanas, Tanis seeks his fortunes in the world. He meets the companions, adventures, and even grows a beard. After the reunion at the Inn of the Last Home, Tanis and the companions travel to Xak Tsaroth and back to ruined Solace. Torn by his divided nature, Tanis becomes the peacemaker in the group, reconciling conflicts without instead of those within. When rescued from Lord Toede's slave wagon by Qualinesti elves, though, Tanis must face his past.

Laurana, still in love with him, asks about their childhood engagement, and Tanis grants her back the ring she gave him. Insulted, she throws the ring among the trees (Tasslehoff retrieves it), but follows Tanis, the companions, and her brother Gilthanas in their quest toward Pax Tharkas.

Tanis receives *Wyrmslayer*, the ancient sword of Kith-Kanan, on their trip through the Sla-Mori and uses the blade to kill Lord Verminaard in Pax Tharkas. Afterward, he helps regain the Hammer of Kharas and settle the refugees of Pax Tharkas in Southgate in Thorbardin.

Continuing with the companions through Tarsis, Silvanesti, Port Balifor, and Flotsam, Tanis encounters Kitiara. Desiring her from of old, he trysts with her, for a time forsaking his companions and his mission in the war. When he flees her across the Blood Sea, she pursues, driving the ship into the maelstrom. Tanis chooses certain death over the life offered by climbing onto Kitiara's dragon.

She repays him in kind, tricking Laurana into her grasp by saying she holds Tanis hostage. Tanis travels to Neraka to free his true love, Laurana, but to do so he must make a pact with Kitiara—to slay Ariakas and seize for her the Crown of Power.

Thereafter, Tanis and Laurana are married. They spend much of their time on the road, peacemakers among nations as they had been among the companions. Just prior to Kitiara's attack upon Palanthas, Tanis is called away from Laurana in order to consult with Lord Amothus. He is at the High Clerist's Tower when her citadel flies overhead without pausing to fight. He then goes out to face Lord Soth, barely escaping with his life. He and Caramon board the flying citadel in order to get into the Tower of Palanthas and stop Raistlin. He is in Raistlin's Laboratory when Kitiara, his one-time lover, dies.

In the time after that conflict, Tanis and Caramon

escort Steel Brightblade to his father's tomb in the Tower of High Sorcery. Tanis and Laurana also have a son, Gilthas, who is abducted and forced to become puppet ruler of the elves, despite Tanis's attempts to stop it.

Tanis fights one final time for Palanthas, at the High Clerist's Tower when it is under attack by the Knights of Takhisis. Abjured by the ghost of Sturm to protect his son, Steel Brightblade, Tanis saves Steel from death only to be killed himself. (ALL)

Tarsis the Beautiful

Once a beautiful bustling maritime city, Tarsis is landlocked after the Cataclysm. Languishing under its new isolation and lack of trade, Tarsis takes out its vengeance upon the Knights of Solamnia, evicting and murdering them. The companions arrive here during the War of the Lance, seeking a home for refugees, and are caught in the dragonarmy invasion. Here, the company is sundered, half the party heading to Ice Wall, and the other half to Silvanesti. (CII)

Tasslehoff Burrfoot

See Burrfoot, Tasslehoff.

Temple of Mishakal

In this abandoned temple outside Xak Tsaroth, the companions discover the crystal statue of Mishakal from which the blue crystal staff came, and here they learn of the Disks that await below. Later, Goldmoon is restored to life in the temple and made a true cleric after her sacrifice to save Raistlin. (CI)

Temple of Paladine

Built by Elistan, this temple is open to all; its grounds are even a playground for Steel Brightblade when he is young. The temple is destroyed by Kitiara during her attack on the city, and Elistan is afterward buried in the catacombs beneath. During the Chaos War, the rebuilt temple is run by Crysania. (LIII, DSF)

Test, the

Tailored to each applicant, the Test is a challenging set of situations through which new magic-

Thalas-Enthia

This Qualinesti legislative body votes to cast out Porthios and his wife Alhana, making them dark elves. Its most infamous member, Senator Rashas, also installs Gilthas as Speaker of the Sun and Stars, a puppet ruler through which Rashas controls the elven homeland. (SG)

Thanoi

These vicious walrus men are allied with Feal-thas, Dragonlord of the Ice Wall Dragon Orb, and Sleet, the white dragon. Thanoi fight the companions and pursue them across the Plains of Dust, where they board a ship. (CII)

Thelgaard Keep

This fortification stands on the road from Caergoth to Solanthus. (ALL)

Theros Ironfeld

A longtime resident of Solace, this dark-skinned metal smith provides shelter to elven refugees at the beginning of the War of the Lance. Fewmaster Toede repays this kindness by having draconians rip off his arm and throw him into the slave wagon. His life is saved by Crysania, and he is rescued by the Qualinesti elves.

He rejoins the companions outside Qualimori, sent by Laurana to help them escape. He bears with him a new arm of silver, which he himself forged. Traveling with the companions to the tomb of Huma, Theros is given the power to forge the dragonlances. He appears at the Council of Whitestone Glade, hurling the first new dragonlance, which cleaves the huge stone. (CI, CII)

Thieves' Way, the

A secret network of underground passages in Palanthas, the Thieves' Way is what other citizens call the sewer system. (DSF)

Kender, Gully Dwarves, and Gnomes   LARRY ELMORE

users must navigate. Failure means death. Success means admittance into the Orders of Magic— White, Red, or Black Robe. It also often means a physical or psychological scar that the mage will bear the rest of his or her life. Justarius has a lame leg due to his Test. Raistlin's skin is turned gold, his eyes have hourglass pupils, his health is ruined, and he sees only death and decay in all things. Others pass their Test more happily, such as Palin, who encounters his uncle, Raistlin, and receives the Staff of Magius. (ALL)

Leaves from the Inn of the Last Home   LARRY ELMORE

Thirteen Warnings

Thirteen Warnings from the gods announce the coming Cataclysm, and give the folk of Ansalon a chance to avert the coming catastrophe. The elven bard Loralon prophesies these warnings, which are accomplished in the following events: The true clerics disappear from the world. The sky turns green and a cyclone destroys a tower of the Temple of Istar. A pall spreads over the kender lands. Nuitari seems to devour the other two moons. A black flame plagues the dwarves. Wild fires scourged Abanasinia. Lord Soth withdraws into his keep. A blinding fog covers Palanthas. The Silvanesti trees weep blood. The Qualinesti animals attack the elves. Blood runs through streets of northern towns. Caramon seeks to kill Raistlin. The Lords of Doom erupt. (ALL)

Thistleknot, Kronin

This hero of the kender attends the Whitestone Council, pledges the kender nations to the cause of good, and fights to protect Kendermore. Perhaps his single most notable accomplishment is slaying Dragon Highlord Fewmaster Toede, thereby saving his homeland. (CII, DSF)

Thistleknot, Paxina "Stinging"

Daughter of kender hero Kronin Thistleknot, Paxina rallies the kender of Goodlund to fight the invading Knights of Takhisis. She tells them the knights intend to "take all our stuff." (DSF)

Thomas of Thalgaard, Lord Knight of the Rose

This third-generation Solamnic Knight saves his community during the War of the Lance, rallying them. He rises through the ranks of the knighthood until he commands the High Clerist's Tower before its fall to the Knights of Takhisis. Prior to that appointment, he opposes the Treaty of the Unified Races of the Three Nations, and Laurana writes to him, just before Gilthas's abduction. He succeeds Gunthar Uth Wistan as head of the Knights of Solamnia. (SG, DSF)

Thon-Sargon

Elven for *Silver Road,* or *Silver River,* this glimmering river in Southern Ergoth is also called Thon-Tsalarian, or *River of the Dead.* (CII)

Thon-Thalas

Elven for *Lord's River,* this waterway separates Silvanesti from the outside world. (CII)

Thon-Tsalarian

Elven for *River of the Dead,* this waterway is traveled by the companions on their way from Qualimori to the Tomb of Huma. *See also* Thon-Sargon. (CII)

Thoradin Bay, Battle of

In this opening offensive of the Knights of Takhisis on Ansalon, Tanin and Sturm Majere are slain, and Palin Majere taken captive. Though desperately outnumbered, the Solamnic Knights fight honorably and to the death, and so are accorded full honors in their burial. The Knights of Takhisis plan to sweep overland southward to attack Palanthas. (DSF)

Thorbardin

Ancient underground kingdom of dwarves, Thorbardin is ruled by the mountain dwarves, though the population is made up of seven clans. Thorbardin is besieged during the Dwarfgate Wars, and welcomes refugees during the War of the Lance. *See also* Duncan, King of Thorbardin, and Hornfel, Thane of Hylar. (LII)

Thorn, Knights of the

Also called Gray Knights, these renegade wizards compose one branch of the Knights of Takhisis. At Storm's Keep, they are attacked by Justarius and members of the Conclave, but defeat them. Nightlord Lillith is a famous Gray Knight. (DSF)

Three Moon Shops

This is the common name for mageware shops, such as the one run by Jenna. They are regulated by Gray Knights after Palanthas is captured. (SG)

Time-travel Spell

This spell, cast by Justarius to send Caramon and Crysania back in time, also sends Tasslehoff, in the form of a mouse, thereby defying the original instructions and proving that history can be changed. (LI)

Time-travel Device

Raistlin gives this faulty device to Tasslehoff, claiming it will save the kender from the Cataclysm. In fact, when the device comes to pieces in Tas's hand, he is killed by the fiery mountain and appears in the Abyss. It is fixed by Gnimsh and used by them to escape the Abyss.

Caramon and Tas later use it to travel forward in time (also causing the explosion at Zhaman that destroys the Plains of Dergoth). Tanis and Caramon use the device to reach the flying citadel. (LI, LII, LIII)

Toede, Highlord Fewmaster

This wily hobgoblin is slain numerous times, once upon Tanis's return to Solace, and once more in Kendermore by Kronin Thistleknot. He knows where his bread is buttered, though, and rises from being a minor annoyance in charge of a slave wagon to being a Highlord. (CI, CII, CIII)

Tomb of the Royal Guard

In the Sla-Mori, this crypt contains the bodies of the royal guard, pledged to continue their vigilance even after death. (CI)

Tower of Wayreth

Of the five original Towers of High Sorcery, Wayreth is the only one that survives into usage in the Age of Despair. The wizards withdraw to this tower during the persecution of magic. Surrounded by an enchanted wood—the Forest of Wayreth—the tower can be reached only by those welcome to it. Here, the Conclave of Wizards meets. Here, Raistlin takes his Test. Here also, Caramon, Crysania, and Tasslehoff are sent back in time. (ALL)

Tower of Palanthas

In this Tower of High Sorcery, the three Orders of Magic meet to create the Dragon Orbs. Later, during the persecution of magic, the tower is threatened by the Kingpriest of Istar. To seal it, a Black Robe mage curses it, flinging himself onto the spiked gate at the front. The haunted Shoikan Grove that surrounds the tower prevents all (even fearless kender) from entering.

Only Raistlin, master of past and present, can navigate the grove, and afterward only those to whom he has granted a charm. Raistlin is master of the tower until he enters the Abyss, at which point Dalamar takes over. He slays Kitiara in Raistlin's Laboratory, near the Portal. *See also* Raistlin's Laboratory, Raistlin's Study, Dalamar's Room, Live Ones, Dead Ones, Shoikan Grove, and Chamber of Seeing. (ALL)

Tower of the Stars

This tower in the center of Silvanost is a place of twisted darkness, distorted by the dream of Lorac. At the center sits the mad king himself, withered upon a huge stone throne. The companions come here to save Silvanesti. (CII)

Tower of the Sun

At the center of Qualinost, this tower is a beautiful replica of the Tower of the Stars in Silvanesti. Through gemstone windows, the tower fills itself with diverse, magical light. Its inner halls are splendid and bright, with representations of the moons and stars across the vault. Here, the companions consult with Solostaran, Speaker of the Sun. (CI, CII, SG)

Towers of High Sorcery

In the ages before the Cataclysm, these five towers are bastions for magic. During the persecution of magic, the Tower of Istar is taken over by the Kingpriest. Two more towers are destroyed by mages to keep the Kingpriest from gaining the knowledge within them. The Tower of Palanthas is cursed and sealed by a Black Robe mage, and the Tower of Wayreth withdraws within its enchanted forest. (ALL)

Treaty of the Unified Nations of the Three Races

Tanis Half-Elven and Laurana Solostaran work for five years in secret to bring about this treaty between elven Silvanesti and Qualinesti, human Solamnia and Northern and Southern Ergoth, and dwarven Thorbardin. The treaty, ironically, is foiled by the abductions of Alhana and Porthios and the installation of

Tanis and Laurana's own son Gilthas as Speaker of the Sun and Stars. (SG)

Trevalin, Subcommander

This leader of the Knights of Takhisis is Steel Brightblade's superior, who gives the knight every opportunity to escape the death sentence laid upon him. He is killed in the assault of Chaos's forces upon the High Clerist's Tower. (DSF)

Trials of Huma

Prior to his battle with Takhisis, Huma is tried by the gods in tests of wind, fire, water, and blood. Raistlin holds that he and Crysania must also endure these same four tests before they face Takhisis. (LII)

Uncle Trapspringer

Though claimed in many stories of Tasslehoff's, Trapspringer is not actually his uncle, but every kender's uncle. He is noted for his amazing explorations and his improbable and gory deaths. (ALL)

Usha

Believed by many (including herself) to be the daughter of Raistlin Majere and Amberyl of the Irda, Usha is raised among Irda upon their insular island. When the Decider plans to crack the Graygem in order to gain enough power to drive off the Knights of Takhisis, Usha's Protector (Prot) sets her in a boat enchanted to sail at her command.

She travels to Palanthas, there to deliver to Dalamar a warning about the cracking of the gem. Instead, she lands in prison and meets Tasslehoff. Bailed out by Jenna, they are taken to Dalamar in the Tower of High Sorcery. They cross paths with Steel and Palin, the latter of whom Usha falls in love with. Her message delivered, Usha returns to the streets, where Dougan Redhammer sells her into the Thieves' Guild of Palanthas. There she languishes, confronted at one point by Raistlin, who tells her the true story of her birth (*see* Raistlin's Daughter).

Palin rescues Usha from a waitress job at the Goose and Gander Tavern. They travel, with Tas and Dougan Redhammer, back to the Irda island, retrieve the halves of the Graygem, and take the gem with them into the Abyss. There, Usha holds the gem out beneath the giant Chaos and catches a drop of the god's blood, thereby imprisoning him again in the gem. She is with Palin and Raistlin during the final appearance of Fizban upon Krynn. (DSF)

Uth Matar, Highlord Kitiara

Daughter of a knight of noble blood and a peasant woman, Kitiara inherits both the initial passion that brought the two together, and the desperate enmity that rises shortly afterward to drive them apart. Eight years after her birth, her mother marries another man—a woodcutter—and bears him two sons, Caramon and Raistlin Majere, Kitiara's half-brothers. Ruined by the pregnancy, their mother passes in and out of trances and eventually dies, leaving Kitiara to raise the boys. She is credited with saving the sickly Raistlin, and with teaching Caramon to wield a sword.

When the original companions make their way in the world, she adventures with nominal Knight of Solamnia Sturm Brightblade. Their philosophies coming to conflict, Kitiara attempts to break the knight by seducing him. The result of this union is her son Steel Brightblade, raise by Sara Dunstan.

Of the original companions, this muscular woman with short-cropped black hair is the only one not to return for the reunion at the Inn of the Last Home. She stays away because she has become the Dark Lady, Highlord of the Blue Dragon Army. She does, however, keep tabs on her friends through the draconian spy Gakhan. She meets up with Tanis in Flotsam, believing him to have joined the dragonarmy, and beds him.

After he escapes her across the Blood Sea, Kitiara informs the Golden General, Laurana, that she holds Tanis captive and will trade him for the captive Bakaris. By this ploy she captures Laurana and draws Tanis back. In the Temple of Takhisis, she uses Tanis to slay Highlord Ariakas and claim the Crown of Power for herself.

Allying with the Death Knight Lord Soth, Kitiara strikes down Crysania before she can reach the Tower of Wayreth to prevent Raistlin's time travel. When her brother is about to return from the Abyss, Kitiara attacks Palanthas with dragons, a flying citadel, and Lord Soth's army of Death Knights, hoping to present Takhisis an army for conquest of the world. Instead, she battles the new lord of the Tower of Palanthas, Dalamar, and is slain. Even as she dies, she pleads with Tanis to save her from Lord Soth, though the Death Knight takes her body.

In the Abyss, Kitiara attacks her nephew Palin Majere and stabs him, but is driven off by Raistlin.

During the Chaos War, Kitiara returns from the Abyss to fight. She also appears to Steel, trying to lure him to accompany her as she flees the world with Takhisis. He refuses, and she goes without him. (ALL)

Uth Wistan, Gunthar, Knight of the Rose

Head of the three orders of Solamnic Knighthood, Gunthar Uth Wistan leads the Whitestone Council at which the Ice Wall Dragon Orb is destroyed, the alliance of the forces of good is solidified, and the first new dragonlances are introduced. Gunthar presides also over the trial of Sturm Brightblade, takes the accused man under his wing, and eventually assigns him to lead the Crown Knights in the War of the Lance.

After the death of Rose Knight Derek Crownguard, Gunthar appoints Laurana the task of heading up the Solamnic Armies, thus creating the Golden General. After the War of the Lance, he sends Tanis and the Knights to fortify the High Clerist's Tower against Kitiara's attack. He retires a year before the conquest of the Knights of Takhisis begins, succeeded by Rose Knight Thomas of Thalgaard. (CI, CII, CIII, LIII, DSF)

Valin

This term describes the sudden mutual bonding of Irda, requiring them to reproduce. It is said to be the source of Raistlin's legendary daughter. (SG)

Valkinord

This fortification in Nordmaar falls early to the Knights of Takhisis. It is from here that Steel Brightblade mounts Flare with Palin and his brothers to return to Solace. (DSF)

Vallenwood

This type of huge hardwood tree grows only in Solace Vale, and provides homes and businesses for the people of the town. (ALL)

Verminaard, Highlord

Commander of the Red Dragonarmy, Highlord Verminaard is in control of Pax Tharkas at the time of the companions' arrival. His dragon Ember is actually a spy for Takhisis, who is distrustful of Verminaard's sudden interest in the followers of the woman with the blue crystal staff. He confronts the companions during the fall of Pax Tharkas and is killed by Tanis Half-Elven with *Wyrmslayer*. (CI)

Victor, Caramon the

Caramon Majere takes this name as a gladiator in the Games of Istar. (LI)

Vingaard Keep

This important fortress on the Plains of Solamnia is the first defense of the city of Palanthas. The Knights of Takhisis take it over while en route to Palanthas.(DSF)

Virkus Hills

These hills lie north of the Plains of Solamnia and south of the Palanthas Mountains, just before Westgate Pass. Ariakan's army of Knights of Takhisis marches through them on the way to the High Clerist's Tower. (DSF)

Vision, the

Takhisis provides to all her knights glimpses of her grand plan. They are to check this Vision at moments of decision, always choosing the path that does most to promote her agenda. (DSF)

WayFarrers WelCum, the

Raistlin, Caramon, and Crysania stay at this filthy, rundown inn on their way down the Solanthus Road toward Zhaman. (LII)

Palin's Test   LARRY ELMORE

Waylan, Wonderful

This illusionist, father to Tika Waylan, teaches young Raistlin his first magic tricks. (CI)

Wayreth Forest

This enchanted (some say haunted) wood surrounds and protects the Tower of Wayreth. It is controlled by the wizards of the Conclave and admits only those who are welcome at the tower. For that matter, it cannot be easily found—the Wayreth Forest finds the adventurer, not the other way around. (ALL)

Wayward Inn, the

This inn, run by Slegart, is said to be the place where the Irda Amberyl and the mage Raistlin join in *Valin*. (SG)

The Portal LARRY ELMORE

Westgate Pass

A mountain pass on the road from Vingaard Keep to the High Clerist's Tower, any overland conquerors of Palanthas must travel this pass, including the Knights of Takhisis. (DSF)

White Robes

This order of mages practices good magic. During the War of the Lance it is led by Par-Salian, and during the Chaos War by Dunbar Mastersmate. (ALL)

White Stag

This mythic wilderness creature appears to knights during times of trouble, leading them to salvation. It leads Huma to Silvara the Silver Dragon, and in turn to the knowledge of how to create dragonlances. It leads Sturm and the companions through the Darken Wood to their encounter with the unicorn Forestmaster. (CI)

Whitestone Council

See Council of Whitestone.

Whitestone Glade

This glade, which surrounds the Whitestone on Sancrist, is the location of the Knight's Council. The stone is originally discovered by Vinas Solamnus, where he has the vision of the coming Knighthood. It is later blessed by the Kingpriest of Istar.

Here, during the War of the Lance, a critical council is held. Porthios calls for immediate return of the Dragon Orb to the elves, Tasslehoff destroys the Ice Wall Dragon Orb, Kronin Thistleknot proclaims his people's loyalty, Fizban argues for patience, and Theros Ironfeld introduces the first new dragonlances, splitting the stone. (CII)

Widower

This Palanthas Thieves' Guild member confronts Raistlin in the guildhall, and would be slain by him but for Sally Dale's intervention. (DSF)

Wilhelm, Sir

This old-style, set-in-his-saddle Solamnic Knight conducts Tanis, Caramon, and Steel into the High Clerist's Tower, and then fights them as they try to escape the Chamber of Paladine. (SG)

Wings of Habbakuk

This stretch of flatland extends just below the High Clerist's Tower. Here, Ariakan assembles his army. (DSF)

Wyrmslayer

The ancient sword of Kith-Kanan, this blade is granted by the dead elven hero to Tanis to fight off the giant slug. Tanis uses it later to slay Lord Verminaard. It travels with Laurana to Ice Wall and later Huma's Tomb. (CI)

Wyvern

These small, nasty dragonlike creatures are used as messengers for the dragonarmies. They are chaotic and cruel, making good use of their scorpion-stinger tails. (CIII)

Xak Tsaroth

This once-great city slides downhill during the Cataclysm, ending up in a vast underground chasm. It becomes a ruin occupied only by gully dwarves, ghosts, and the black dragon Khisanth. The companions venture here, confront Highbulp Phudge I, meet Bupu, find the Disks of Mishakal, slay the dragon, and leave, bearing with them also the spellbook of Fistandantilus. The city caves in, the Newsea rushing in upon it. (CI)

Yellow-Eye

A watchful crow, Yellow-Eye is a spy for the Thieves' Guild of Palanthas, ensuring that initiates remain true to the guild. (DSF)

Year of Oneness

This period of time marks the coming of age of an Irda. (DSF)

Zeboim

Mercurial goddess of the sea, Zeboim falls in love with Highlord Ariakas and bears him a son, Ariakan—who goes on to conquer most of the world.

When implored for aid by Usha's human parents, she delivers them safely to shore on the Irda island. She appears again in flesh at the side of her son's body after the attack of Chaos on the High Clerist's Tower. (SG, DSF)

Zebulah

This human lives in sunken Istar with his beloved, Apoletta, a sea elf. He helps the elves rescue Tanis and the companions from the maelstrom and even invites them to remain in the city. (CIII)

Zhakar

This dwarven city closes its gates in ancient times and is lost to the outside world. (ALL)

Zhaman

Fortress between Pax Tharkas and Thorbardin, Zhaman is where the Orders of Magic, in the Age of Despair, experiment to create armies—what would later become the techniques for creating draconians.

After the Cataclysm, the Portal is moved from the Tower of Palanthas to this location, and Raistlin must muster an army to take the fortification. His attempt to enter the Portal, fouled by Tasslehoff's time-travel device, causes an explosion that melts Zhaman down, creating Skullcap. (LII)

Zivilyn

Called the Tree of Life, this neutral god of nature is said to dwell on all planes at once and can look forward and backward in time at will. He is consort to Chislev and not likely to provide a simple, straight answer. (DSF)

Characters, Places, and Things in the *Rose of the Prophet Cycle*

By Margaret Weis and Tracy Hickman

A CONCORDANCE BY JEAN RABE

Wizard and the Dragon JEFF EASLEY

The *Rose of the Prophet* bestselling trilogy by Margaret Weis and Tracy Hickman was published in 1988 and 1989 by Bantam Spectra. The novels, rich with an Arabian flavor, detail the epic struggles of the gods and the trials of the various mortals, djinn, 'efreet, and angels who worship them.

Each entry in the concordance is followed by an abbreviation that indicates the novel in which it appears:

WW: *The Will of the Wanderer*, Bantam paperback, December 1988

PN: *The Paladin of the Night*, Bantam paperback, May 1989

PA: *The Prophet of Akhran*, Bantam paperback, August 1989

Abbot

The Abbot is a follower of the god Promenthas and mentor to the apprentice wizard Mathew and the monk called Brother John. He travels with Mathew and Brother John to Sardish Jardan, the land of the god Akhran, where he intends to spread Promenthas's faith. However, his plans are dashed when the great 'efreet Kaug rises from the water and capsizes the ship. The Abbot and his entourage survive to reach the shore and discover a slaving caravan. Hoping to find rest and food with the caravan, the Abbot instead finds death. See Kaug for more information. (WW)

Achmed

Younger brother to the Calif Khardan, Achmed admires and loves his older brother, "who had been more father to him than sibling." During the forced wedding ceremony of Khardan and the Princess Zohra, Achmed gets into a fight with Sayal, one of Zohra's brothers. In the midst of the fight, Zohra escapes, though the wedding eventually goes on. Achmed later accompanies Khardan to the city of Kich on a horse-selling mission for the nomad tribes. The horses are never sold, however, and Achmed and his brother quickly find themselves trapped in the amir's palace. After a harrowing escape from Kich, in which they rescue the "slave girls" Mathew and Meryem, they return home.

When the nomad tribes fall to the amir's forces, Achmed is imprisoned, and the Imam Feisal attempts to convert him to the faith of Quar. Eventually, Achmed agrees to serve in the amir's army, though he will not worship Quar. "There are no gods," he says, as he believes the gods have abandoned their people. He rises to a position of importance in the army, finally becoming general of the amir's calvary. *See* Khardan and Kich. (WW, PN, PA)

Akhran

The god of faith, chaos, and impatience, Akhran is also known as the Wandering God—as he could never stay in one place for any length of time. He is constantly roaming the Jewel to find new ideas and lands (see *Jewel* for more information). His followers are nomads who roam the desert lands of Pagrah. Akhran, not wanting to be bothered with the affairs of men, handed over most of his power to immortals called djinn. (WW, PN, PA)

Archmagus

The old wizard is a close friend of the Abbot and accompanies him, the apprentice Mathew and the young monk Brother John to Sardish Jardan. His intention is to spy on the land's government while his associates are preaching about the god Promenthas. His plans are dashed as his ship nears the country. Instead of finding information, he finds death at the hands of slavers. (WW)

Asrial

Mathew's guardian angel calls herself Asrial, a servant of Promenthas. She uses her magic to keep the young apprentice wizard alive when his companions are slaughtered by slave traders. She later joins forces with the djinn Pukah and Sond to work against the ambitious god Quar (see Pukah for more information). Pukah is instantly smitten with Asrial, mesmerized by her white robes, silver hair, and wings. She eventually returns his affections, and is heartbroken when he sacrifices himself to stop Quar's 'efreet, the horrible Kaug. (WW, PN, PA)

Astafas

He is a cruel and evil god, delighting in suffering and misery. Ruling over a realm that is dark and terrible, he sits opposite Promenthas in the great Jewel. Demons serve him, and he dines on human souls. (PN, PA)

Badia

The mother of seven children, Badia is the principal wife of the Sheykh Majiid. The sheykh often seeks her counsel and her magic. Her long black hair is streaked with gray, and she wears many rings on her fingers, bangles on her wrists, and heavy gold earrings. (WW, PN, PA)

Baigha

The object of this grand game is to determine which participant can bring the largest portion of a sheep carcass back to the sheykh. A dead sheep is placed on the ground, selected riders race toward it, and it becomes dismembered as each rider attempts to wrestle the carcass away from the others. Khardan is almost always the first to reach the carcass. (WW)

Baji

He is an "oily, rotund little djinn" whom Pukah notices in the dead city of Serinda. Baji does not seem to recognize his former friend, and Pukah later learns that this is because in Serinda, djinn "die" and when they come back to life, they do not remember their former lives. (PN)

Battle at the Tel

The united tribes of Sheykh Majiid and Sheykh Jaafar are attacked at the mountain named Tel where they are camping. The amir, the ruler of the great city of Kich, unleashes all his forces on the tribes, defeating the nomads and taking many of the people back to Kich as prisoners. (WW, PN)

Benario

The god of Faith, Chaos, and Greed, Benario is worshiped by thieves. In Benario's mind, the Jewel Pavilion is a dark cavern filled with the possessions of the other gods. (WW, PN, PA)

Black Paladins

Servants of the dark god Zhakrin, the Black Paladins are a strict sect of evil knights who have undying loyalty to each other. The knights imported slave labor for the construction of Castle Zhakrin. Their ages range from eighteen to nearly eighty, and all of them dress in black metal armor. Vestments of black cloth with the signet of a severed snake are draped over their shoulders. They wear no helmets, displaying visages that could have been carved from stone. *See also* Castle Zhakrin. (PN, PA)

Black Sorceress

She is the wife of the Lord of the Black Paladins and an accomplished sorceress. It is said the Black Paladins could not have survived without her. Looking no larger than a child, the Black Sorceress is more than eighty years old. "Her beauty was undeniable, but it did not foster desire. The cheeks were free of wrinkles, but their smoothness—on close observation—was not the tender firmness of youth but that of the taut, stretched skin of a drum. Her heart was said to be ruthless and cold, and it was rumored she drank the blood of stillborn babes." (PN)

Blossom

This is the name Auda ibn Jad and Kiber give to Mathew, when they first see the young man and believe he is a woman. They continue to refer to Mathew as Blossom even after they know the truth. (PN, PA)

Castle Zhakrin

At the end of the Dead March rises the impressive and horrifying Castle Zhakrin. It was constructed by slave labor at the orders of the Black Paladins and is made of shining black obsidian, granite, magic, blood and bones. The Black Paladins sprinkled the blood of their victims over the building blocks, mixing the bones with mortar. When the construction was completed, the remaining slaves were slain and their bones added to the decor. "Human skulls grinned above doors, dismembered hands pointed the way down corridors, leg and foot bones were imbedded in the walls of winding staircases." (PN)

Catalus

He was a black paladin and "bonded brother" to Auda ibn Jad. Auda asks about Catalus's whereabouts and is told that he died in service to Zhakrin. (PN, PA)

Cradic

A fisherman from a small village on the shore of the Kurdin Sea, Cradic is taunted by the more successful fisherman Meelusk. "The God of the Sea favors the righteous, Cradic! Quit ogling your neighbor's wife and perhaps your luck will change." (PN)

Dead March

The bridge known as the Dead March stretches across a deep ravine that leads to Castle Zhakrin. Human heads mounted on poles guard the entrance to the bridge. "By some arcane art, the flesh remained on the skulls and the agonized expressions on the dead faces served to warn all who looked on them what awaited an enemy of the Black Paladins in Castle Zhakrin." (PN)

Death

"The woman had no eyes. Where there would have been two orbs of life and light in that classic face were two hollows of empty blackness." She calls herself Death, the ruler of Serinda, and she explains to the djinn who arrive that they are granted their greatest wish: mortality. They die each night, being reborn as a different individual the following day who will die again. "No one in this city remains alive from dusk to dawn." Death claims she does not revere any of the Jewel's gods. "I owe allegiance to no God or Goddess. I have no favorites. Whatever else may be said of me, I am impartial. I take the very young. I take the very old. The good cannot escape me, neither can the sinner. The rich with all their money cannot keep me from their doors. The magi with all their magic cannot find a spell to defeat me." She later comes for Mathew when he is seriously ill. However, Khardan is able to keep her from claiming the young man. (PN, PA)

Dughmi, Durzi ibn

More than five hundred years ago, Durzi was said to have defeated Sultan Muffaddhi el Shimt. Durzi had mounted ten thousand horses and five thousand camels in the attack. The outcome of the battle remains in contention to this day among djinn. (PA)

Emperor of Tara-kan

The Emperor of Tara-kan is considered a practical man. He enjoys the wealth of the cities he takes under his jurisdiction. His most trusted and admired aid is the general Abul Qasim Qannadi, the Amir of Kich. (PN, PA)

Evren

The beautiful goddess of goodness, charity, and faith, Evren for centuries warred with the god of evil, Zhakrin. (WW, PN, PA)

Fakhar, Sheyhk Majiid al

The sheykh is a gigantic man with a thunderous voice. Though age fifty, he can still lift a full-grown sheep with one arm and outride all but the oldest of his many sons. His most hated enemy is Sheykh Jaafar al Widjar. The god Akhran forces a marriage between Majiid's oldest and favored son and the daughter of Jaafar. (WW, PN, PA)

Fedj

The djinn Fedj often tends sheep with his mortal master, Sheykh Jaafar al Widjar. He looks nearly identical to the djinn Sond: "they were both tall, handsome, well-built. Muscles rippled across their bare chests; gold bracelets encircled their strong arms; silken pantalons covered their powerful, shapely legs; silk turbans set with jewels adorned their heads." (WW, PN, PA)

Feisal

An Imam, or priest of Quar, Feisal swears to carry out his god's slightest wish. He is a gaunt man, from numerous periods of fasting, and he usually dresses in a white cloth wrapped about his thighs. Feisal's hair has never been cut, a means to honor his god, and so it drapes down his back like a blanket. Quar directs Feisal to take a carved ebony horse to Yamina, the amir's wife (see Yamina for further information). Later, after the amir has defeated Khardan's and Zohra's tribes, Feisal works to convert the captured nomads to the faith of Quar. While he is not able to sway Khardan's brother, Achmed, he is suc-cessful in coercing the young man to side with the amir. (WW, PN, PA)

Gasim

The one-eyed captain Gasim is a favorite of Amir Qannadi. (WW)

Hamd

He is one of the amir's prison guards. Upon getting drunk again, Hamd is dragged across the ground to the gatehouse. (PN)

Hammah

The fierce warrior god, Hammah is known to stomp about and dress in animal skins. He wears a great horned metal helmet. (WW, PA, PN)

Hammah, Men of

The worshipers of Hammah are fierce fighters, men and women alike. "They are a large, big-boned race—the women as big as the men. They have golden hair that, from birth, is never cut. Men and women both wear it in braids that hang down below their waists. When they fight, they fight in pairs—husband and wife or couples betrothed to be married. The man stands upon the right to wield sword and spear, the woman stands to his left, holding a great, huge shield that protects them both. If her husband is killed, the wife fights on until either his death is avenged or she herself falls beside his body. And woe betide the man who takes the life of a shield-maid." (PN)

Hasid

Hasid comes to Achmed after he is wounded in a prison riot. Hasid claims to be a former Captain of the Body Guard under Abul Qasim Qannadi and says he went into prison voluntarily to watch over Achmed. (PN)

Hornfist, Thor

Thor of the Great Steppes had the theory that the city of Serinda and its inhabitants were eaten by a giant bear. However, few paid attention to Thor. (PN)

Hurishta

She is the goddess of the "Sundering Seas" and is worshiped by sailors and fishermen. The sailors sacrifice gold rings to her and believe that dolphins are her daughters, and whales, her sons. By making the sacrifice, sailors believe the dolphins will carry any man who falls overboard safely to shore. Hurishta's worshipers contend the goddess is jealous of her male counterpart, Inthaban, and sacrifice iron rings to him. (WW, PN, PA)

Hypatia

She was a wise woman from the land of Lamish Jardan who disputed the theory of Kuo Shou-ching. Hypatia believed that the city of Serinda was founded after the eruption of the volcano Galos and that the Serinda natives brought water to the desert through a remarkable system of aqueducts. She also believed Serinda fell because nomadic tribes attacked the city, fearing that the people there would become too powerful and absorb them into their society. (PN)

Inthaban

A sea god, he holds sway on the opposite side of the world than Hurishta. Inthaban receives tribute of iron rings from sailors. Sailors believe Inthaband and Hurishta are jealous of each other and that they constantly invade each other's realms. During these periods, terrible storms erupt. (WW, PN, PA)

Jad, Audi ibn

The man who claims to be a former slave trader has skin as white as alabaster, with jet-black hair, a hawkish nose, and lips that look thin and bloodless. He leads a procession into the city Idrith, and with it are two litters bearing the preserved bodies of a man and a woman. In truth, Audi ibn Jad is a Black Paladin, a servant of the god Zhakrin. He takes Zohra, Mathew, and Khardan prisoner, though he later joins forces with Khardan to help defeat the Kich Amir. (PN, PA)

Jewel

The universe is a "huge, twenty-faceted jewel that revolves around Sul, Truth, the center." The Jewel rotates on an axis and has "good" at the top, and "evil" at the bottom. The triangles, which make up the facets of the Jewel, share sides with the other triangles. The sides which join number twelve and represent the philosophies of Sul: mercy, faith, charity, patience, law, intolerance, reality, greed, impatience, and chaos. (WW, PN, PA)

Jewel Pavilion

This is the meeting-place of the gods, sitting atop the highest mountain at the very bottom of the world. A mortal who climbs the peak sees nothing but snow and rock. The Jewel Pavilion exists only in the minds of the gods. (WW)

John, Brother

The monk called Brother John dresses in gray robes and carefully trims his blond beard. He is close friends with the apprentice wizard Mathew. Under the guidance of the Abbot, he and Mathew travel to Sardish Jardan to spread the faith of their god Promenthas. John saves his friend from drowning when a great 'efreet appears and capsizes the ship. However, once on shore John runs afoul of some slavers and is beheaded. (WW)

Kaug

The gigantic green-skinned man who calls himself Kaug rises from the sea when the ship carrying the Abbot, Mathew, Brother John and the Archmagus nears the land of Sardish Jardan. "Gray cloud banks formed his hair, seawater streamed from his bare chest in cascades. Lightning flared in his eyes, his thundering voice boomed over the water." Kaug is an 'efreet and an agent of the god Quar; he capsizes the ship after lecturing the passengers about spreading the faith of a different god. Kaug is also indirectly responsible for causing discontent between the tribes of Sardish Jardan. He uses trickery to capture the dinniyeh Nedjma, beloved of the djinn Sond, then he threatens Sond to keep the tribes from unifying—if he wants his beloved returned. Eventually Kaug is captured when the djinn Pukah sacrifices himself. (WW, PN, PA)

Rose of the Prophet #2   LARRY ELMORE

Khardan

Prince of Akar, Khardan is the eldest son of Sheykh Majiid al Fakhar. "The Calif was so handsome that the eligible daughters of the Akar, peeping at him from the slits in the tent as he rode by, sighed over his blue-black hair and his fiery black eyes that—so it was said—could melt the heart of a woman or scorch that of an enemy." Forced to marry the daughter of his father's greatest enemy, Khardan imbibed a quantity of qumiz, fermented goat's milk, on his wedding day so he would be blindly drunk and numb to the entire process. A fight breaks out during the wedding, and the bride escapes, though later the ceremony actually takes place.

When Khardan and his brother Achmed journey to Kich to sell horses so the tribes' economy can improve, they become trapped in the amir's palace. Here, the amir's sorceress wife Yasmina demonstrates to Khardan that Kich does not need their horses. She turns a small statue into a living horse.

As Khardan and his brother flee the city, he rescues the young woman Meryem and a slave girl from the auction block who later turns out to be a man—Mathew. Khardan believes he has fallen in love with Meryem and promises to make her his second wife. However, before another wedding can take place, the young calif prevents Mathew from being slain by an angry tribesman—who had taken Mathew into his harem believing him a woman. Khardan offers Mathew the opportunity to continue his ruse of being a woman, as only women in Sardish Jardan can cast spells, or to die by the hand of the angry tribesman. By a cruel trick of fate, Khardan is then forced into accepting Mathew as his second wife instead of Meryem, whom he truly desires. The trick is engineered by Zohra. Later, Mathew saves Khardan from Meryem, who tries to kill him. (WW, PN, PA)

Kharmani

The god of wealth is worshiped by moneylenders in Sardish Jardan. The followers of Kharmani are few and have no interest in wars or politics. They are concerned only with money. (WW, PN, PA)

Kiber

Kiber is the leader of the slave caravan guards that Mathew, John, the Abbot, and the Archmagus come across when they land in Sardish Jardan. Kiber mistakes the young Mathew for a girl, as he has no facial hair, and takes him captive with the intention of selling the "girl" in the slave market. Kiber has John, the Abbot, and the Archmagus killed. He refers to Mathew as Blossom. (WW, PN, PA)

Kich

Though under the auspices of the emperor, Kich was considered an independent city-state throughout most of its history. It has been ruled by the sultan's family for generations, and its people are largely followers of the goddess Mimrim. It is an ancient city, tracing its roots back two thousand years, built between the Ganzi Mountains to the south and the Ganga Mountains to the north. It is one of the major trade cities of Tara-kan, and it is where Akar brings horses to sell. "The people of Kich knew nothing of the war in heaven. They knew only that one day the Emperor's troops, carrying the ram's head flag—symbol of Quar—swept down on them from the north. The gates fell, the Sultan's bodyguards—drunk as usual—were slaughtered. Kich was now under the Emperor's direct control, the spearhead of an army pointed directly at the throat of the rich cities of Bas to the south." (WW, PN, PA)

Lifemaster

Inside Castle Zhakrin, the Lifemaster carries out vile deeds in the name of his dark god. The Lifemaster is a wizened man with a huge head that seems precariously balanced on his scrawny neck. He dresses in voluminous black robes. Appearing before the prisoner Khardan, the Lifemaster demonstrates his foul talents by torturing him. Then, as Khardan watches, the Lifemaster magically tortures a captured White Knight of Evren and converts him to the faith of Zhakrin, in which he will eventually become a Black Paladin. (PN)

Mathew

An apprentice wizard, at the age of eighteen he undertakes a sea voyage with his mentor, an Abbot of Promenthas, to reach the lands of Sardish Jardan. The journey is a reward because he graduated at the top of his class and attained the rank of apprentice. "His hair was a coppery auburn, his face so white as to be almost translucent, his eyes green beneath feathery chestnut eyebrows." A Wesman, Mathew could not grow a beard. His lack of facial hair saves him when their ship is capsized by an 'efreet named Kaug, who scoffs at them for worshiping a god other than Quar. Mathew nearly drowns, but his close friend John saves him and pulls him to shore. There, the entourage discovers a slaver's caravan, and all but Mathew are killed. The lead slaver mistakes Mathew for a woman, as his face is smooth, and he captures the "girl" to be sold in the slave market. Mathew, now called "Blossom," decides to go along with the ruse to save himself and dons the women's clothes he is given.

He is later rescued from the slave market in Kich by Khardan and taken to the young calif's lands. There, the "girl" is accepted into the harem of an associate of Khardan's, who quickly discovers Mathew is not a girl and intends to behead him. Mathew is again saved by Khardan, who tells him he can live by carrying on his ruse of being a woman—as only women in Sardish Jardan can employ magic—or die claiming to be a man. Mathew chooses life, and through a cruel trick of fate initiated by Zohra, he becomes Khardan's second wife. Zohra forces this to prevent Khardan from taking Meryem as his second wife, as the young calif can only support two wives.

The young wizard travels with Zohra and Khardan to Serinda, City of the Dead, and back to Kich, where the three work to rescue the captured tribesmen. Mathew later rescues Khardan when Meryem tries to assassinate him. Mathew slays Meryem in the process, causing himself great inner turmoil—as he often vowed never to fight. After the incident, Mathew comes to realize that he actually loves Khardan—and Zohra—but he has the wisdom not to interfere in their marriage. (WW, PN, PA)

Meelusk

The fisherman Meelusk likes to catch fish by holding a lantern over the water, watching as the fish come close, attracted to his light. He waits until enough come near, then he gathers them in his net and tells his competitors that he has discovered a secret fishing place. He does not reveal his "secret" tactic. On one expedition, he nets fish—and a water-soaked basket and a lamp. Opening the lamp, he discovers the djinn Sond. Pukah emerges from the basket. The djinn explain that the goddess Evren slipped into Kaug's home, where they were prisoners, and rescued them by ordering her immortals to hurl the basket and lamp into the sea. *See also* Sond and Pukah. (PN, PA)

Meryem

The young woman is encountered by Khardan and his brother Achmed in the palace in Kich. Khardan rescues her as he and his brother flee the city, and he later believes he has fallen in love with her. Khardan promises to make her one of his wives, though this plan is later foiled by his first wife Zohra. Still, Meryem is accepted by Khardan's father into the household.

In truth, Meryem is an agent of Kich's Amir Qannadi. The amir handpicks the young woman from among his concubines to infiltrate the family of Khardan. Qannadi promised to marry her if she succeeds, though in truth he has no intention of doing so. In her role, Meryem convinces Khardan and his father that she is the daughter of the late Sultan of Kich. When Zeid's forces attack the joined tribes, Meryem attempts to flee with an ensorceled Khardan. Mathew sees her leave with the young calif, and is able to stop her from abducting him. However, Meryem escapes and returns to the Kich Amir's service. Later she tries to assassinate Khardan, and is slain by Mathew. (WW, PN, PA)

Mimrim

One of the lesser goddesses of Sardish Jardan, Mimrim of the Ravenchai hides on her cloud-covered mountain when she feels herself weakening. She is considered a gentle goddess, and a lover of beauty and money. Mimrim's power began to dwindle when the people began putting more faith in money than in her. (WW, PN, PA)

Muzaffahr

He is a poor dealer in iron pots, cauldrons, and spikes. His stall is the shabbiest in the souk. And his goods, unskillfully made, are purchased only by people who are as poor as himself. Though Muzaffahr never raises his eyes higher than a person's knees, he is an observant man. He secretly deals in knives, daggers, and poisons, catering to thieves and the darker element of society. He sells poison to Meryem, who intends to use it against Khardan. (PA)

Nedjma

She is a djinniyeh, or female djinn, and her name means *the star*. Nedjma is captured by the 'efreet Kaug, sealed into a small, ornamental egg, and used as bait to make her beloved, Sond, keep the tribes of Sardish Jardan from uniting. "She was a sight as beautiful as the night itself. Pantalons made of silken gauze spun as fine as cobweb softly draped the curves of her shapely legs. The diaphanous fabric was clasped about her waist with a jeweled girdle, leaving bare her shell-white midriff. Her small feet were adorned with jewels and rouged with henna. Her thick honey-colored hair was worn in a long coil, and her enchanting face could be seen through the soft folds of a gold-embroidered veil." When Sond finds himself in Serinda, City of the Dead, he spots Nedjma, but she does not recognize him. The djinniyeh "died" and was reborn without any of her past memories. In the end, however, she realizes in her heart that she is attracted to Sond and decides to stay with him. (WW, PN, PA)

Nesnas

The guardians of Castle Zhakrin are called nesnas, and they look like a man that has been cut in half—possessing half a head, one arm, half a trunk, one leg, and one foot. They move by hopping about on one leg, traveling as fast as any man can run on two. (PN)

Nilock

A fisherman from a small village on the shore of the Kurdin Sea, Nilock is taunted by the more successful fisherman Meelusk. (PN)

Nomads

The nomads of the Pagrah Desert are certain the world is flat and that they are at the center. "The huge and splendid city of Khandar—as far distant, in their minds, as a remote star—glittered somewhere to the north of them and beyond Khandar was the edge of the world." (WW, PN, PA)

Pukah

Pukah is considered inquisitive and meddling, attributed to his youth. He serves the Calif Khardan, son of Sheykh Majiid al Fakhar. Pukah finds himself smitten with the angel Asrial, and he and Asrial—as well as their companion Sond—are captured by the evil 'efreet Kaug. The 'efreet keeps the djinn and the angel in his watery lair, claiming to be their new master and relegating them for a time to the city of Serinda. However, they are eventually freed by the goddess Evren. The young djinn sacrifices his freedom to capture Kaug. Sond explains: "And so, Pukah sacrificed himself, luring Kaug to the mountain of iron and tricking the 'efreet inside while the immortal, Asrial, guardian angel of the madman—I beg your pardon, Effendi. Asrial, guardian angel of the great and powerful sorcerer, slammed shut the doors of the mountain, and now both Kaug and Pukah are sealed forever inside." (WW, PN, PA)

Prophet of Akhran

This is the title assumed by the Calif Khardan. (PA)

Promenthas

The god of goodness, charity, and faith, Promenthas instructs his immortals, or angels, to speak only to the most pious of his followers. These pious become Promenthas's priests, who develop a highly-structured system of rules and regulations. The white-bearded Promenthas prides himself on his followers' freedom of thought. (WW, PN, PA)

Qannadi, Amir Abul Quasim

The leader of the city of Kich, Qannadi does not trust civilians. He gained rulership of the city when the previous sultan of Kich was slain, and he continues to act as general of the Imperial Army. "Blunt, sharp-tongued, quick to mete out discipline, Qannadi was the terror of the servants and the palace eunuchs." He is usually addressed as, "O' King." One of his wives is the sorceress Yamina, a powerful woman who aids in his ploy against the Calif Khardan. The amir directs his forces against the nomads in the Battle at the Tel and orders as many survivors as possible captured. These captives he attempts to convert to the worship of Quar, his own god, and the strongest among them he lures into his army. Achmed, brother of Khardan, is one of those who switches alliances. (WW, PN, PA)

Quar

The god of reality, greed, and law, Quar establishes priests to rule over the people of his realm. He gives djinn to certain people in power, such as emperors, sultans, and viceroys. Quar worked for centuries to mend the rift between Evren, the goddess of goodness, charity, and faith, and Zhakrin, the god of evil, intolerance, and reality. When the god Akhran the Wanderer declares that two nomadic clans must band together, Quar is angered. The god of reality attempts to win the most worshipers to his side, creating a Great War of the Gods. (WW, PN, PA)

Raja

"... the djinn was large, well-built, with skin the color of ebony. He was arrayed in gold cloth, massive gold earrings hung to his shoulders, his arms were encircled with gold enough to ransom a Sultan, and the expression on his face was fierce." Raja wields a huge scimitar and serves Sheykh Zeid al Saban. (WW, PN, PA)

Rose of the Prophet

"It is an ugly, lethal-looking species of cactus. Squat, with fat, bulbous, pointed-tip leaves, it sprouts slender needles that must leap out at their victim, for you swear that you do not go near the plant, yet you find—when you look down—the wicked-looking thorns sticking in the tops of your boots." (WW, PN, PA)

Saban, Sheykh Zeid al

He is a squat man who drapes himself in rich fabric. He journeys to the camp of Jaafar and Majiid to make certain the two tribes are indeed living in peace. "The sight of such brotherhood as I witness here at this moment brings tears to my eyes." (WW, PN, PA)

Sayah

Zohra's half brother is a few months younger than her. The eldest son of the Sheykh Jaafar, he is cool and calculating and courageous, and it is said he fought off a starving wolf with his bare hands. (WW, PA)

Sayal

Another of Zohra's brothers, Sayal starts a fight with Achmed on Zohra's wedding day. During the scuffle, she flees, though the ceremony is held later. (WW)

Saiyad

A tribesmember and friend of Khardan, Saiyad accepts into his harem the young woman the calif rescued from the slave block in Kich. Saiyad's actions are generous, as the strange woman is dowerless. However, Saiyad soon learns the "woman" is actually the man named Mathew. Saiyad decides to behead Mathew over the ruse, but is thwarted in the attempt by Khardan. After the amir's forces overwhelm the nomadic tribes in the Battle at the Tel, Saiyad is among those taken captive. He quickly converts to the worship of Quar to improve his lot. (WW, PN)

Saksaul

The saksaul tree is found only in the salt-impregnated sand of the eastern Pagrah Desert, and it is venerated for its unusual properties. It grows beneath the sand, stretching up to thirty feet. The black wood is extremely hard and extremely valuable. Only expert craftsmen can carve the wood without it splintering like glass. The heavy wood gives off spicy, fragrant fumes, and the ashes are used in medicines. (PN)

The Prophet of Akhran   LARRY ELMORE

Sardish Jardan

This is the land of the desert nomads. The god Akhran the Wanderer is revered here and sends djinn to the most powerful of his worshipers. (WW, PN, PA)

Serinda

Now called the City of the Dead, Serinda flourished hundreds of years ago. It thrived in the middle of the desert. Its residents now are prisoners, included among them for a time are the djinn Sond, Pukah and Usti, and the angel Asrial. Djinn in Serinda "die" each night, being reborn without their old memories. The being who calls herself Death rules the city. (PN, PA)

Shimt, Sultan Muffaddhi el

More than five hundred years ago, Muffaddhi was said to have been defeated by Durzi ibn Dughmi. The outcome of the battle remains in contention to this day among djinn.(PA)

Shou-ching, Kuo

He was a man of great wisdom who was said to have traveled to the emperor's court from the far eastern lands of Simdari. He maintained that the Pagrah Desert was not always a desert. It was a known fact in his land that the Galos volcano erupted so fiercely that it sent a black cloud of ash into the sky for a year. This obliterated the sun, and during this time, the city of Serinda died—its people perishing from the volcano's fumes. The volcano continued to belch fire and fumes, forever changing the land of Sardish Jardan. (PN)

Sond

The djinn Sond serves his mortal master, Sheykh Majiid al Fakhar. He looked nearly identical to the djinn Fedj: ". . . they were both tall, handsome, well-built. Muscles rippled across their bare chests; gold bracelets encircled their strong arms; silken pantalons covered their powerful, shapely legs; silk turbans set with jewels adorned their heads." Sond falls in love with beautiful djinniyeh Nedjma. However, the 'efreet Kaug traps Nedjma inside a jeweled egg and taunts Sond that he must "fan the flames" of distrust between the tribes of Sardish Jardan and prevent them from becoming allies. Sond is later captured by Kaug, along with Pukah and the angel Asrial, and kept in the 'efreet's watery lair. When the three find themselves in Serinda, City of the Dead, they spy Sond's love, Nedjma. However, Nedjma no longer remembers Sond, as her memories have been lost. The djinn Sond is eventually freed when his lamp is pulled into a fisherman's net. (WW, PN)

Sophia

Achmed's mother, Sophia, is ill and is not able to visit her son when he is held in the Kich prison. Sophia is one of the wives in Majiid's harem. (PN)

Uevin

Uevin of the Bas, one of the lesser gods of Sardish Jardan, takes refuge behind his politics and siege machines, not realizing the foundation of their divine society is being undermined by Quar. Uevin's three precepts are Law, Patience, and Reality, and he delights in anything new and modern, despising anything old and outdated. Uevin has a materialistic outlook on life. One of his followers' greatest joys is creating marvels of technology to help them better their lives. Huge aqueducts that crisscross their cities are only one example. (WW, PN, PA)

Usti

The djinn Usti owed the djinn Fedj a favor. To pay Fedj back, Usti became the servant of Zohra. The corpulent Usti quickly discovers that serving Zohra is no easy matter. "It never fails. I am in the midst of a quiet little dinner when 'tap, tap, tap'"—Usti bit the words—"comes on the outside of my brazier. If I don't respond immediately, if, for example, I decide to drink my coffee while it is hot and *then* attend to my mistress's demands, she flies into a rage, which generally ends"—Usti paused for effect and breath—"in hurling my dwelling place into a corner of the tent." (WW, PN, PA)

White Knights

The White Knights of Evren, the Good Goddess, were the counterparts of Zhakrin's Black Paladins. The Lifemaster delighted in corrupting White Knights to the worship of Zhakrin and turning them into Black Paladins. (PN)

Widyar, Sheykh Jaafar al

In his late forties, Jaafar appears older. "His hair was almost completely gray. His skin was deeply tanned and lined from years spent in the hills. He was short and thin, with scrawny, sinewy limbs that resembled the legs of a buzzard." Two streaks of gray cut through his beard, and his black eyes were almost always hidden by the shadows of his head covering. His mortal enemy is Majiid al Fakhar, Sheykh of the Akar. The god Akhran forces a marriage between Jaafar's beautiful daughter and the eldest son of Majiid. (WW, PN)

Yamina

Though she dresses in garments to hide her figure, Yamina, one of Amir Qannadi's most powerful wives, moves with uncommon grace. She wears a black veil rimmed in gold that covers her face and head, leaving only one eye visible. The sorceress receives a small ebony statue of a horse from the Imam, and by casting a spell, she causes it to grow to a full-size, living animal. In doing so, she and Quannadi convince Calif Khardan that the city of Kich has no need of the horses he has brought to sell—the news threatens the economy of Khardan's people. Some people believe Yamina is the true power on the Kich throne. (WW, PN, PA)

Zaal

Inside one of the cell blocks in the Zindan, prison guards beat a young nomad boy named Zaal, who refuses to cry out from the pain. When the djinn Sond, Fedj, and Raja come to the prison to help free the nomads, Zaal assists them in locating the keys and letting the people out. (PA)

Zar

In the marketplace in Kich, Khardan comes across a man with a small monkey on his shoulder. The monkey is called Zar, and he wears a tiny cap and a coat made in imitation of the amir's soldiers' garb. "Zar is a foul-tempered little beast, as you have seen. Many is the time he has sunk his tiny teeth into my thumb." (PA)

Zhakrin

The god of evil, intolerance and reality, Zhakrin warred with Evren, goddess of goodness for centuries. Among his worshipers are the Black Paladins. (WW, PN, PA)

Zindan

The prison in Kich is referred to as "the Zindan." The nomads captured in the Battle at the Tel are held here. Since there are not enough cells to accommodate the number of people the amir wants held there, the women and children are herded into the central compound. (PN, PA)

Zohra

She is commanded by the god Akhran to marry Khardan al Fakhar, Calif of the Akar and son of her father's enemy. On her wedding day, she is thickly veiled to conceal the blindfold and gag on her face, and her hands are tied. During a fight between her brother, Sayal, and one of Khardan's brothers, she grabs a knife and escapes into the desert. Here the djinn Fedj finds her and persuades her to go through with the ceremony, promising that she will be able to make her new husband's life miserable. To sweeten the deal, Fedj gives her the djinn Usti.

Later, Zohra begins to have feelings for Khardan. She prevents him from taking the woman Meryem as his second wife and instead forces him to take Mathew as a wife, who must continue his ruse of being a woman or die. (WW, PN)

6 Characters, Places, and Things in the *Darksword* Trilogy

by Margaret Weis and Tracy Hickman

A CONCORDANCE BY JEAN RABE

Darksword Adventure LARRY ELMORE

he Darksword trilogy by Margaret Weis and Tracy Hickman was published in 1987 and 1988 by Bantam Spectra. *Legacy of the Darksword* was published in July 1997.

Each entry in the concordance is followed by an abbreviation that indicates the novel in which it appears:

FD: *Forging the Darksword*, Bantam paperback, November 1987
DD: *Doom of the Darksword*, Bantam paperback, April 1988
TD: *Triumph of the Darksword*, Bantam paperback, August 1988
LD: *Legacy of the Darksword*, Bantam paperback, July 1997

Albanara

Responsible for governing the populace, the Albanara are the most-skilled of wizards practicing magic from the Mystery of Earth. *See* Craftsmen, Nine Mysteries. (FD, DD, TD)

Almin

God. (FD, DD, TD)

Andon

The Outlands healer used to be the leader of the village before Blachloch usurped his power. Andon tells Saryon that he realizes it is customary for individuals to pray to the Almin through catalysts, but there had been no catalysts in the village and so the people prayed directly to god. "He and I have shared many problems," Andon explains to Saryon. "He is our refuge in these troubled times. His guidance led us to take the vow that we will not eat food gained by blood and flame." Andon is later returned to his position as village leader after Blachloch is killed. (FD)

Anja

A woman claiming to come from noble birth seeks work as a Field Magi in the village of Walren. "She was young, probably not more than twenty. Once she might have been pretty, but now her proud face was marked with lines of anger and hatred. Her body was far too thin—the dress hung on her spare frame." She works with a baby strapped to her back and will not permit anyone else to watch the child she calls Joram. Anja explains Joram has passed the Tests for Life. However, the child is "Dead," and as he grows she teaches him sleight-of-hand tricks so the others in Walren will believe he possesses magic.

She takes Joram to the Borderlands, showing him the Watchers, thirty-foot-tall statues. She points to one and claims it is his father, and that Joram was conceived against the wishes of the catalysts at the Font. They had determined that any children of the couple would be "Dead," and hence forbid them from marrying. Turning Joram's father to stone was punishment for the couple's indiscretion. Anja dies when the overseer of Walren discovers the fifteen-year-old is "Dead," accidentally getting in the way of the man's magic bolt. Joram slays the overseer in retaliation and escapes to the Outlands.

The truth about Anja is revealed in Merilon. Anja, the only daughter of the late Baron Fitzgerald, cousin to the emperor, gave birth to a "Dead" child at the Font. "The babe was born dead. Strange it was, too. The babe had turned to stone inside the mother! Turned to stone—just like the father!" It was believed she kidnapped one of the babies at the Font undergoing a Deathwatch, that baby turning out to be Joram, son of the emperor and empress of Merilon. (FD)

Ariels

Large mutated men with great feathery wings serve as messengers to the powerful people of Thimhallan. (DD, FD, TD)

Baron of Esock

Simkin tells the warlock Blachloch what the baron of Esock did after transforming himself into a mandolin. The baroness, a large woman, sat on him and "smashed him to splinters." (FD)

Billingsgate

Mrs. Billingsgate is a neighbor of Mrs. Mumford in Oxford, England. Together, they keep tabs on the goings on in the block—including what happens at Saryon's residence. (LD)

Blachloch

The leader of the Outlands village and the Coven of the Wheel, Blachloch is a complex man with dreams of expanding his power. Those in the coven say he is a former enforcer who left the service of the emperor. He secretly works with Bishop Vanya. Blachloch is slain by Joram who wields the Darksword (FD)

Boris, Major James

The true enemy of the people of Thimhallan and Shanakar came from the stars. Major James Boris, commander, fifth battalion, Marine Airborne, was nicknamed Stump. He is short and thick-bodied, and at thirty years of age he kept himself in peak condition. Major Boris believed in rules and regulations and had little imagination, qualities that caused him to be selected for the mission to Thimhallan. "Top government officials had descriptions of this bizarre world, descriptions provided by two men: one known to casino audiences as Sorcerer and another known only to certain secret government agencies as Joram. The top officials, many of whom could scarcely believe what they heard, decided that it would take a man of nerve and cold, hard logic to survive in Thimhallan without losing his senses." The major loses command of the battalion when Menju the Sorcerer seizes control after a battle turns sour. (TD)

Calculus, Father

Because of his affinity for mathematics, Saryon is called Father Calculus behind his back at the Font. (FD)

Catalysts

A child born to the rarest of the Mysteries, the Mystery of Life is called a catalyst, a dealer in magic. Though such an individual does not possess an abundant amount of magic himself, he pulls magic from the earth, air, fire, and water, magnifies it, and transfers it to wizards to enhance their spells. Catalysts are rare, and hence it is considered an honor to have one in a household. The expense of the catalysts training is borne by the church. See the Nine Mysteries for more information. (FD, DD, TD)

Cathedral of Merilon

The cathedral is one of the most magnificent buildings in Merilon. Its walls are made of crystal, and the park that surrounds the building is filled with golden and white trees. (FD)

Centaurs

Once human, these creatures were magically mutated by the DKarn-Duuk and sent off to fight in the Iron Wars. When the fighting ended, the DKarn-Duuk abandoned the centaurs and banished them to the Outlands. "Here the centaurs lived their lives, breeding with animals or captured humans, creating a race whose human feelings and emotions were almost completely lost in the struggle to survive. Almost lost, but not quite. One emotion thrived among them, nurtured and cherished over the centuries—hatred." (FD, TD)

Chamber of Discretion

This is a one-way-only communication device Bishop Vanya uses to contact his minions. (FD)

Collin, Captain

He is a man of forty-five and a veteran of one of the most grueling tank campaigns that was fought on the Outer Fringes. After Major Boris launches his mission on Thimhallan, Captain Collin reports on the activities. "Kid turned into a wolf right before my eyes! Leaped on Rankin, knocked him down, and tore his throat out before I could move. God help me! I'll never forget Rankin's scream. . . . What could I do? Run? Hell yes I ran! And the whole time I was running I could feel hot breath on my neck, hear that thing panting behind me. I can still hear it. . . ." (TD)

Coven of the Wheel

Joram is rescued by members of the Coven of the Wheel after he escapes to the Outlands. "You are with those who practice the Ninth Mystery, those who would bring down death and destruction upon Thimhallan, according to some." Blachloch is head of the coven. (FD, DD)

Craftsmen

These are wizards skilled in the Mystery of Earth, and they are divided into guilds based on their skills. The Quin-alban are the conjurers; the Pron-alban, magicians; the Mon-alban, the alchemists; and the Albanara, wizards and wizardesses who possess a general knowledge of all those skills. The Albanara are responsible for governing the populace. *See also* the Nine Mysteries. (FD, DD, TD)

Dark Cultists

The Dark Cultists have existed on Earth for centuries, being called the Council of Nine of Thimhallan and the Council of Thirteen on Earth. It was said the cultists poisoned the general populace of Earth against magic and wizards. "Life did not come from life, for them. Life—or magic—came from death. They engaged in human and animal sacrifice, believing that the deaths of others enhanced their power. Cruel and selfish, they used their arcane arts only to indulge themselves, to further their own ambition, to enslave and seduce, to destroy." *See also* Dark Cults. (LD)

Dark Cults

There are four Dark Cults: the Cult of the White Steed, the Black Steed, the Red Steed, and the Pale Steed. All of them advocate war and conquest. *See also* Dark Cultists. (LD)

Dark One

"A long journey you've had, Dark One," said the old woman, reaching out her hand to smooth back his black hair. This is a name Joram is given when members of the Coven of the Wheel rescue him from the centaurs. (FD)

Darkstone

Joram shows Saryon a piece of rock, similar to iron. The ore is said to negate magic, and Joram wants to combine it with steel to forge a weapon that can stand up to the wizards. He needs Saryon's help to accomplish this. *See also* Darksword. (FD)

Darksword

Saryon adds his magic to the forging process to help Joram craft the Darksword. "It was made of a solid mass of metal—hilt and blade together, possessing neither grace nor form. The blade was straight and almost indistinguishable from the hilt. A short, blunt-edged crosspiece separated the two. The hilt was slightly rounded, to fit the hand. Joram had added a bulbous protrusion on the end in some attempt to weight it, Saryon having reasoned that this would be necessary in order to handle the weapon effectively. The weapon was crude and ugly. Saryon might have been able to deal logically with that. But there was something more horrifying about the sword, something devilish—the rounded knob on the hilt, combined with the long neck of the hilt itself, the handle's short, blunt arms, and the narrow body of the blade, turned the weapon into a grim parody of a human being."

Joram uses the sword to kill Blachloch, as the Darksword siphons the magic from wizards and leaves them vulnerable. Also, when Joram keeps the sword with him, Bishop Vanya and the other high-powered wizards of Thimhallan cannot magically locate him. (FD, DD, TD)

Dead

A ten-day-old baby is pronounced Dead when the three tests of sorcery prove that the child is without magic. Such babies are left alone to die so they will not grow to adulthood and contaminate the land with more "Dead" children. "These unfortunate children are not children at all," the Bishop cried earnestly, his hands clenched in his passionate intensity, his words echoing from the vaulting crystal ceiling. "They are weeds in the garden of our Life! We must uproot them and wither them, as the Field Magi wither the weeds in the field, or they will soon choke out the magic within the world." However, some parents secretly kept their "Dead" children, taking some of them to the Outlands. See also Deathwatch. (FD, DD, TD, LD)

Deathwatch

"Dead" babies are left alone without attention, food, and water to die. The process is called a Deathwatch. (FD)

Diviners

The Diviners, or Time Magi, had opened the window to time and space creating "Corridors" that individuals could travel through to bridge great distances in the span of moments. "The Diviners had long since vanished, and with them had died the knowledge of how to build the Corridors. But the catalysts, who had controlled them for centuries, knew still how to operate and maintain them, taking the Life needed to keep them active from those who used them. See also Nine Mysteries. (FD, DD, TD)

D'karn-darah

This arm of the Technomancers defied the law which prohibits any person from traveling to Thimhallan. See also Khandic Sages. (LD)

DKarn-Duuk

Mystery of Fire practitioners are considered the warriors of Thimhallan. "Witches and warlocks, they become DKarn-Duuk, with the power to call up the destructive forces of war. They are also the guardians of the people." (FD, DD, TD)

Dragon of the Night

The guardian of the second Darksword is a great dragon who lives deep below ground. The Dragons of Night were originally designed as killing machines. However, during the Iron Wars some of the dragons escaped and fled below ground, seeking comfort in the darkness. The dragons detested and feared the light of day. "The beast was monstrous, beautiful, awful. It was so black that it seemed to be a hole cut through daytime, revealing night beneath." (LD)

Druids

Children born to the Mystery of Water are destined to become druids. They are sensitive to nature and spend their energies nurturing living things. The Field Druids, or Fibanish, concentrate on the growth of plant and animal life. The Mannanish treat minor illnesses and injuries and serve as midwives. The Theldari treat serious illnesses. See also Nine Mysteries. (FD, DD, TD)

Drumlor

One of Blachloch's guards, Drumlor was often called upon to play tarok with the warlock. "Drumlor had neither love for nor interest in the game." (FD)

Dulchase

The deacon is one of the individuals present when the Empress's child is pronounced "Dead," having no magic within his small body. Deacon Dulchase was born in Merilon and looked on the city of wonders with a bored air that his fellows envied. (FD, TD)

D'umtour

The woman is livid that she is stopped and questioned by a Kan-Hanar about whether she should have access to the City Above in Merilon. "I tell you, my good sir, that I am the mother of the Marquis of D'umtour! As to why his servants aren't here to greet me upon my arrival, I'm certain I don't know, except it is so difficult to hire quality help these days! He always was a young wastrel anyway!" she snapped viciously, shaking her chins. "Wait until I see him. . . ." (DD)

Duuk-tsarith

The Order of Duuk-tsarith comprises black-robed bishops from the Realm of Thimhallan. The bishops receive their miters in solemn ceremonies, which mark their standing as spiritual leaders of the world. The head of the dread order is called a warlock. The Duuk-tsarith are also called the Enforcers, and they are part of the DKarn-Duuk. (FD)

Eliza

The daughter of Joram and Gwendolyn of Thimhallan, she favors her father, with her long black hair and flashing eyes, and she is an avid reader—as Joram is. (LD)

Elspeth, Queen of the Faeries

"Golden hair cascaded in undulating waves to the floor, casting a halo of light about the woman as she walked. Silver eyes shone brighter and colder than the stars Saryon had looked upon in the night. She did not walk, that he could see, but she came closer and closer to him, filling his vision." Saryon comes across Elspeth when he is trying to reach the Outlands in his search for Joram. Elspeth decides that Saryon will father her children. However, the catalyst is able to narrowly escape her clutches with the help of Simkin. (FD)

Evenue

A powerful wizardess and one of the Albanara, Evenue is the empress of Merilon. She gives birth to a royal child, who at ten days of age is declared Dead. The catalyst Saryon performed the tests of magic and declares Evenue's baby without "Life." Saryon is the last person seen with her child, as he carries it away and rocks it for a few hours before it undergoes the Deathwatch at the Font. Evenue wastes away many years later, despite the attention from healers, never knowing that her child did not go through the Deathwatch, but instead became the rebel called Joram. (FD)

Executioner

The man wears gray robes to symbolize neutrality and justice, and they are marked with the symbols of the Nine Mysteries "to show that justice knows no distinction." He lives in the Font and serves the catalysts there, and he dies during Major Boris' attack on Merilon. (DD, TD)

Famirash

"The border of the civilized Thimhallan known as the Outlands is marked to the north of Merilon by a great river. Called the Famirash, or Tears of the Catalysts, its source is to be found in the Font, the great mountain that dominates the landscape near Merilon, the mountain where the catalysts have established the center of their Order. Thus the river's name—a daily reminder of the toil and sorrows suffered by the catalysts in their work for mankind." The water of the Famirash is sacred,

Triumph of the Darksword   LARRY ELMORE

and its source in the mountain is a holy place tended by the Druids. The water at the source is said to have healing properties. (FD)

Fibanish or Field Druids, Field Magi

These individuals make up the lowest caste of the Thimhallan wizards. They are practitioners of the Mystery of Earth, and they tend the crops. *See also* Druids and Nine Mysteries. (FD, DD, TD)

Font

It is said that the history of the Font is the history of Thimhallan. Several centuries ago, amid the Iron Wars, people fled to this country, drawn to a mountain because of the magic inherent in it. "They called this mountain the Font and here it was, at the Well of Life, that the catalysts established their home and the center of their world." What began as a few catacombs grew during the centuries into an impressive maze of corridors, chambers, halls and courtyards. A university was built on the side of the mountain, and here young Albanara learned how to govern the people. Too, young Theldari were taught how to improve their healing arts, and the Sif-Hanar were aided in mastering control of the wind and clouds. At the top of the mountain sat a great cathedral. Although the Font was initially open to all, after the Iron Wars concluded only catalysts were allowed inside the mountain. The exception was a lone Theldara who worked in the gardens. (FD, DD, TD)

Garald

The prince of Sharakan is richly dressed and possesses a beautiful voice. Garald crosses paths with Joram as the latter is traveling to Merilon and challenges him to a duel. His eyes are large and intelligent, his mouth firm with lines around it showing he laughs and smiles often. His hair is brown, with a reddish cast, and it is worn short in military fashion. Garald later teaches Joram the art of swordplay and the pair become friends.

Prince Garald intends to war against the Thimhallans, and devotes his time to teaching the novice warlocks and catalysts how to fight, declaring that he would be Field Commander at the Gameboard when the battle started. "If Garald had one secret wish in his life, it was his desire to be a warlock. Since he could not—having been born Albanara—he did the next best thing, throwing himself into the war body and soul."

Garald later realizes the true enemy is from another world, the force led by Major Boris and Menju the Sorcerer. However, rather than allowing himself and his people to die after Joram uses the Darksword to drain the magic from the world, he agrees to lead his people onto Major Boris's ships and to travel to Earth. (DD, TD)

Gates of Merilon

Nine gates were set into the invisible dome that protected the city of Merilon. The Earth Gate was the one nearly always used and bustled with activity. The other six gates that represented the active Mysteries were little used, if ever, and they were magically locked most of the time. The Life Gate was reserved for processionals following the war, and therefore had not been used in a century. The only thing that entered the Druid's Gate was the river, the druids using the Earth Gate like everyone else. The final two, the Death Gate and the Spirit Gate, were never used—since necromancers were no longer around. The Kan-Hanar relegates who comes into the city through the Earth Gate. (DD)

Great Wheel

Older than the village in the Outlands, the Wheel had been rescued following the Iron Wars. The Wheel hangs in a great arch in the village. "The huge wheel with nine spokes has become the center of a ritual known in the village as the Scianc. On the seventh night of every week, the entire population of the village gathers around the Wheel and recites the chant that each learns as a child." The chant is accompanied by a war dance to stir up the villagers. (FD)

Grove of Merlyn

It is called the cultural heart of Merilon, built to honor the wizard who led his people here to escape the war. The wizard's tomb is at the center of the grove and is ringed by oak trees. Beyond the central part of the grove stretches a maze of hedges, inside of which are small amphitheaters where "artists painted, actors acted, clowns capered, and music played day in and day out." The maze is easy to navigate, as visitors could fly above it if they got lost. (DD)

Gwendolyn

The eldest daughter of Lord Samuels, Gwen is quickly smitten with Joram, when she sees him shortly after he arrives in Merilon. He shares her affections, and the two decide to marry—despite the revelation that he is "Dead." Joram is sentenced to become a Watcher, a stone statue on the borderlands. However, he is spared that fate when Saryon pushes him aside and absorbs the grisly spell himself. Gwendolyn leaves with Joram through the mist and into the Borderlands. The experience and the new land affect her mind, and she begins to hear the voices of the dead, though she eventually is healed of her madness. When Joram uses the Darksword to end the war between the Thimhallans and Major Boris, effectively draining the magic of the world, she elects to stay behind with him. They become farmers and have a daughter, Eliza. (DD, TD, LD)

Hch'nyv

The mysterious race of aliens is threatening Earth and her colonies. Leaders from Earth believe the Darksword is needed to stop them. Already some colonies have fallen. "Refugees, arriving back on Earth, told terrible tales of the destruction of their colony, reported innumerable casualties, and stated that the Hch'nyv had no desire to negotiate. They had, in fact, slain those sent to offer the colony's surrender." (LD)

Hudspeth, Marm

The old woman is the principal cook at the farming village of Walren. (FD)

Illusionists

Called the artists of Thimhallan, illusionists "create charming phantasms and paint pictures in the air with palettes of rain and stardust." They practice magic from the Mystery of Shadow. *See also* Nine Mysteries. (FD)

Jacobias

Mosiah's father encourages his son to aid Saryon in escaping from the village of Walren. Later, when Saryon comes to the village posing as a renegade catalyst, Jacobias asks that he look for Mosiah in the Outlands. (FD, TD)

Janji

As children, Janji and Saryon played together. Saryon envied Janji's ability to magically manipulate the air. (FD)

Joram

Anja brings her baby, Joram, to the farming village of Walren, where the two of them live for fifteen years. "Joram's most outstanding feature was his hair. Thick and luxuriant, black as the glistening plumage of the raven, it sprang from a sharp peak in the center of his forehead to fall down around his shoulders in a mass of tangled curls. Unfortunately, this lovely hair was the bane of Joram's childhood. Anja refused to cut it, and now it was so thick and long that only hours of painful combing and tugging on Anja's part could remove the snarls and tangles." The child initially does not understand why he is different from the other children, who can cast magic and walk upon the air. However, Anja eventually explains that he has no magic inside of him and takes him to see a gigantic statue, who she says is the boy's father. At the age of fifteen, the overseer of Walren discovers that Joram is "Dead" and decides to take him away. In the resulting struggle, Anja is killed by the overseer, who in turn is slain by Joram. Mosiah, Joram's friend, helps him escape to the Outlands.

In the Outlands, Joram is taught to forge weapons.

Blachloch comes to the forge and threatens the young man. The warlock is disturbed that Joram can read. Later, Joram meets the catalyst Saryon and persuades him to help in the forging of the Darksword. Joram uses the finished weapon to slay Blachloch.

Joram, in the company of Simkin, Saryon, and Mosiah, travels to Merilon, crossing paths with the prince of Sharakan along the way. Joram is fascinated by the beautiful city of Merilon and is instantly attracted to Gwendolyn, a young woman he meets. He decides to marry her. However, he is discovered as "Dead" and the true heir to the Thimhallan throne; Bishop Vanya orders his punishment. The bishop decrees that he be turned into one of the thirty-foot-tall stone Watchers on the Borderlands and gathers the catalysts for the punishment. As the vile enchantment begins, Saryon pushes Joram aside, taking the brunt of the spell and becoming the statue instead. His last words to Joram are to flee. Gwendolyn follows Joram into the mists.

When Joram returns to the Borderlands, he looks on the giant statue of Saryon and intends to slay him to end his suffering. Instead, by using the Darksword, he accidentally frees the catalyst. Joram eventually returns to Merilon and meets his real father the emperor, who calls him Gamaliel—a name meaning *Reward of God*. This name and the visage of the old emperor haunts Joram, who continues to use the name Anja gave him.

As Major Boris launches an attack against Merilon, Joram attempts to end the war by using the Darksword. He plunges it into the heart of the altar stone. "The sword entered the rock easily, so easily that it astonished him. The altar stone flared a brilliant white-blue and shivered. He felt the tremor beneath his hands, as though he had thrust the sword through living flesh." The mountain began to shake, the temple tottered on its foundation, and the sword began to devour the magic of the world and its people. When the people agree to go with Major Boris to Earth, Joram and Gwendolyn elect to remain behind. They become farmers and give birth to a daughter, Eliza. (FD, DD, TD)

Kan-Hanar

One skilled in the Mystery of Air who is from the lower castes is destined to be a Kan-Hanar. The individual is relegated to maintaining the corridors that provide for fast travel within Thimhallan and the supervision of commerce. They are in charge of most of the transportation in Thimhallan, and it is up to them to make sure that only people belonging in Merilon, enter Merilon. *See also* Nine Mysteries. (FD, DD, TD)

Kij vine

Mosiah is nearly killed by the vicious plant as he, Simkin, Joram and Saryon make their way to Merilon. Simkin explains that the plant is carnivorous. Joram slays it with the Darksword. (DD, LD)

Khandic Sages

"They call themselves T'kon-Duuk. In the language of the mundanes—Technomancers. They give Life to that which is Dead. Most horribly"— Mosiah's voice lowered—"they draw Life from that which is Dead. The power of their magic does not come from living things, as was true in Thimhallan, but from the death of the living." The leader of the Khandic Sages is Kevon Smythe. (LD)

Life-transference

Saryon learned at an early age that as a catalyst he possessed this magical ability. His father told him: "The gift of Life-transference. It is in your power, and yours alone, to absorb the Life, the magic, that is in the ground and the air and all around us into your body and focus it and give it to me or someone like me so that I may use its power to enhance my own. This is the gift of the Almin to the catalyst. It is his gift to you." The young Saryon replied: "I don't think it's a very good gift." (FD, DD, TD)

Mannanish

These Healers treat minor illnesses and injuries and serve as midwives. *See also* Druids and Nine Mysteries. (FD)

Maria

The employee of Lord Samuels and Lady Rosamund is a catalyst who provides magical energies to the couple to enhance their spells. (DD)

Marta

The wife of Andon in the Outlands is a kind, elderly woman. She enjoys the company of Simkin, who visits her and regales her with tales of Thimhallan and life in court. (FD)

Master Librarian

The individual charged with overseeing the great library in the Font catches Saryon perusing books in a forbidden room of the library—one that dealt with the dark and arcane secrets of the Ninth Mystery. (FD)

Menju the Sorcerer

He takes command of the Fifth Battalion from Major Boris. "His hair was full and thick. Combed back stylishly from a peak in the center of his forehead, its silver gray color contrasted well with his tanned skin." The sorcerer informs the major that Joram has managed to retrieve the Darksword, and that the weapon is capable of draining both the magical energy from the realm of Thimhallan and the physical energy from Earth. "Think of it, Major!" Menju lowered his hands, straightened his tie, adjusted his shirt cuffs in a preoccupied, obviously habitual gesture. "An ore that can drain energy from one source and convert that energy to its own use! Get hold of that weapon, and the battle is won. Not only in this world, but on any other we might choose to invade." Menju approaches Bishop Vanya, claiming to offer peace in return for him capturing and carrying away Joram and the Darksword. However, the bishop does not believe him, recalling that Menju was once a practitioner of the Dark Arts of Technology. Eventually Menju sets a trap for Joram at the Temple of the Necromancers, luring Joram inside where he is slain. Unknown to Menju, it was Simkin masquerading as Joram. Later, Menju dies in the Temple of the Necromancer when Major Boris sends troops against Merilon. (TD)

Menni

She looks like a tiny, dried-up woman, but her fine brown robes identify her as a powerful, high-ranking druidess. Menni presided over the Birthing Rooms of the Font for many years and now attends the empress. She was present at the Font when Anja delivered a baby of stone and when one of the babies undergoing the Deathwatch disappeared. (DD)

Merilon

The wizard who ages past led his people to this land was named Merlyn. And the city that was founded here was named Merilon in honor of him. The wizard lies buried in a tomb in a glade within the city's enchanted sphere. "Enchanted city of dreams . . . Merilon. Its crystal cathedral and palaces sparkle like tears frozen on the face of the blue sky. Merilon. Two cities; one built on marble platforms constrained by magic to float in the air like heavy clouds that have been tamed and molded by the hands of man. Known as the City Above, it casts perpetual, rosy-hued twilight upon the City Below." Visitors ride in gilded carriages pulled by giant flying cats and squirrels. (FD, DD, TD)

Merilon, Emperor of

Joram is actually the son of the emperor of Merilon, spirited from the Font as he was undergoing the Deathwatch. When the emperor finally meets his son, he is quick to explain that he had not before been able to acknowledge him. "How could I save you when I could not save myself?" he asks. The emperor named his son Gamaliel. "My Son! Gamaliel!" the emperor cried. "I cannot ask you to forgive me." Joram instead acknowledges that Saryon has been more of a father to him. (FD, DD, TD)

Merlyn

The great wizard led his people from Earth in 1600 A.D. and into the stars, settling them on Thimhallan. Merlyn created the Well of the World, which drew magic from Earth and concentrated it within the boundaries of Thimhallan. In so doing, he cut the Dark Cultists off from their magical power. (FD, DD, TD, LD)

Mon-alban

The alchemists of Thimhallan practice magic from the Mystery of Earth and are called Mon-alban. *See also* Craftsmen and Nine Mysteries. (FD, DD, TD)

Mooria, Earl of

Simkin claims the earl of Mooria died by literally sneezing his head off—when he was the same age as Saryon. "I say, old fellow," Simkin says to Saryon, who is sniffling. "A bit dangerous for one of your advanced years. Carried off the Earl of Mooria in a matter of days." (FD)

Mosiah

The leader of the children at the farming community of Walren is a bright-eyed lad named Mosiah. He alone befriends the young Joram, and the two forge a friendship that endures through the years. When Joram is an adult and is discovered by Father Tolban as being "Dead," Mosiah helps him escape by creating a magical passageway to the Outlands. Mosiah later follows Joram, though not because he is concerned about his friend. Mosiah learns the Duuk-tsarith are interested in him, and he has no desire to join their ranks. He makes a life for himself in the Outlands, where he meets Saryon.

Forging the Darksword LARRY ELMORE

The Doom Brigade   LARRY ELMORE AND TONY SZCZUDLO

He, Joram and Saryon travel to Merilon following Blachloch's death. Though Joram is caught up in the splendor of the magical city, Mosiah sees the place much differently. "Mosiah saw Merilon for the first time, truth illuminating the city in his eyes with far greater brilliance than the light of the meek spring sun. These people were locked in their own enchanted realm, willing prisoners in a crystal kingdom of their own manufacture and design. What would happen, Mosiah wondered—looking at them with their costly robes and soft bare feet—if someone would wake them up?"

Mosiah joins the Thimhallans leaving the planet for Earth after Joram uses the Darksword to destroy the world's magic. Here, in a relocation camp in Oxford, England, he becomes a Duuk-tsarith. When he learns that Joram, who insisted on staying behind, has forged another Darksword, he enlists Saryon's help to return to the devastated world and retrieve Joram and the sword. (FD, DD, TD, LD)

Mumford

Mrs. Mumford lives across the street from Saryon when he is in Oxford, England. "She was (or thought she was) the conductor of the orchestra of our lives here on our street and nothing was supposed to happen—be it divorce or a case of breaking and entering—without the wave of her baton." She has a pinched, inquisitive face, filled with curiosity, and she dashes about like a rabbit. Her "assistant conductor" is Mrs. Billingsgate. (LD)

Nat

Simkin claims to have a brother named Nat who failed the Tests for Life and was hidden until he was five. The tot was discovered and hauled away. *See also* Simkin. (FD)

Nine Mysteries

Eight of the nine Mysteries deal with magic: Time, Spirit, Air, Fire, Earth, Water, Shadow, and Life. Of these, the latter six remain in the land, the Mysteries of Time and Spirit being lost during the Iron Wars. The Ninth Mystery is practiced by "those who walk in darkness." It was believed to have been the cause of the Iron Wars, and after the war its sorcerers were sent Beyond, and their creations were destroyed. "The Ninth Mystery is the forbidden mystery. Known as Death, its other name is Technology." (FD, DD, TD)

Pron-alban

Members of the guild of magicians are called Pron-alban. They are skilled casters of Mystery of Earth magic and are sometimes called shapers of wood. *See also* Craftsmen and Nine Mysteries. (FD, DD, TD)

Doom of the Darksword LARRY ELMORE

Prophecy

The Prophecy, outlined in a letter possessed by the Duuk-tsarith warlock, states: "There will be born to the Royal House one who is dead yet will live, who will die again and live again. And when he returns, he will hold in his hand the destruction of the world." The prophecy was believed to have referred to Joram. (FD, DD, TD)

Quin-alban

Also called the conjurers, the Quin-alban are skilled in the Mystery of Earth magic. *See also* Craftsmen and Nine Mysteries. (FD, DD, TD)

Radisovik, Cardinal

The Cardinal Radisovik is friend and advisor to the King of Sharakan. He is with Garald, prince of Sharakan, when they encounter Joram and his friends, all headed toward Merilon. (DD, TD, LD)

Reuven

He is a five-year-old orphan when Major Boris leads an assault against the Thimhallans. Saryon rescues the mute boy from the Font and takes him aboard Major Boris's ship bound for Earth. He grows to adulthood in Oxford, England, with the aged catalyst serving as his mentor and his father. He chose not to live in the relocation camps with the rest of the Thimhallans. As he grows older and wiser, he becomes Saryon's secretary and an author, penning three novels about the Thimhallan's lives and struggles. When Saryon returns to their homeworld in search of Joram and the new Darksword, Reuven follows him. Reuven says of himself when he met, and became taken with, Joram's daughter: "What she saw was a man of medium height, medium build, long blond hair pulled back from a face that always seemed to inspire women with sisterly affection. Honest, sweet, gentle were words women used to describe me." (LD)

Robes

The robes worn by the wizards of Merilon reflect the color of their moods. The wizards concentrate on the garments, using their magic to alter the shades and creating such colors as Turbulent Water, Weeping Skies, Still Pond, and Grape Rose. Weeping Skies was the color those in attendance created when the Empress's child was pronounced "Dead." (FD)

Rosamund

The Lady Rosamund is the mother of Gwendolyn, a young wizardess who becomes smitten with Joram and later marries him. "Not that Lady Rosamund required much magic to enhance her appearance. She prided herself on that and kept her touches to a minimum, most of these reflecting whatever was current in style in Merilon. Lady Rosamund made no attempt to disguise her age. That was undignified, particularly when she had a daughter who, at sixteen, had recently left the nursery and entered into adult society." The lady is observant and gracious and believed her greatest treasure was her eldest daughter Gwen. Rosamund was born to the Mystery of Earth, and her abilities ranked her as a Quin-alban, a conjurer. (DD, TD)

Rules of War

There are strict rules for conducting war in Thimhallan, and these date back to the time when people first arrived in the kingdom from a faraway land. "The Rules of War as drawn up by the ancients were rather like the rules of dueling—considered a civilized means of settling disputes between men. The affronted party aired his grievances publicly, then issued the Challenge—tantamount to tossing a glove in the face of one's enemy. There were two responses to the Challenge. It could be Taken Up—which meant war—or the party so challenged could issue an Apology, in which case the city-state then negotiated terms for surrender." (TD)

Samuels

Lord Samuels is married to Lady Rosamund and is a Pron-alban, a craftsman who has risen among the ranks of the Stone Shapers to the position of Guildmaster. As soon as he was able to put "Lord" before his name, he moved his family from the northwest side of City Below in Merilon to the floating City Above. The lord is just over age forty and is in fine physical condition. "His hair, though graying, was thick and plentiful." His marriage to Rosamund had been arranged, and affection for each other grew through the years. (DD, TD)

Saryon (the elder)

The elder Saryon is an Albanara. ". . . learned in the arts of ruling those under my care, of running and maintaining my house, of seeing to it that my lady brings forth its fruit and that my animals give their gifts as they were born to do. That is my talent, given to me by the Almin, and I use it to find favor in his eyes." He is the father of the catalyst Saryon, named after him, and he virtually abandons care of the child when he turns age six. The young Saryon is given over to his mother for magical instruction. The elder Saryon dies many years later. (FD)

Saryon, the catalyst (the younger)

Son of the Albanara called Saryon, he is a mathematical genius who is forced to become a catalyst and study at the Font. Insatiably curious, he spends hours in the library, and is one day caught in a forbidden room where books on the Ninth Mystery are stored. Shortly after that, the young man is taken to the city of Merilon, where he begins serving the royal family. Among his first duties is to give the Tests for Life to the ten-day-old child of the empress and emperor. The child fails the Tests and is declared "Dead," and Saryon is the last one in the palace to hold the baby before it is taken to the Font for the Deathwatch. Later, Saryon is told that the baby did not die, but was taken by a madwoman at the Font. The child, called Joram, was raised in the farming village of Walren, where he later killed an overseer and escaped to the Outlands. Saryon is directed to pose as a renegade catalyst and live in the village for a time, gaining information and then setting out after Joram.

The catalyst is successful in finding the young man among a group of individuals who call themselves the Coven of the Wheel. Instead of immediately bringing the young man back to Bishop Vanya, he instead spends time with him and later aids him in forging the Darksword. Saryon believes he has damned himself by helping in the forging of the sword. "I have broken the holy laws of our Order and given Life to . . . a . . . thing of darkness."

Saryon follows Joram, Mosiah, and Simkin to Merilon, where eventually Joram is discovered as "Dead" and the real heir to the throne of Thimhallan. When Bishop Vanya declares that Joram must be turned into one of the stone Watchers on the Borderlands and begins the ceremony, Saryon pushes Joram aside and instead becomes the target of the vile enchantment. His last words are to order Joram and Gwendolyn to flee. Saryon is later freed when Joram returns to the Borderlands and gazes on the statue. Joran intends to end Saryon's suffering by slaying him with the Darksword. Instead, he accidentally frees the catalyst. Joram tells Saryon that he views him as a father. The pair strives to end the new conflict that arises when Major Boris brings his force to Thimhallan, and Joram drives the Darksword into an altar at the Temple of the Necromancer to destroy the world's magic.

In the aftermath, Saryon joins the rest of the Thimhallans leaving the world for Earth, and he makes a home for himself in Oxford, England, with an orphan he rescued from the Font. Here he stays until Mosiah appears and asks that he return to Thimhallan and retrieve Joram and a second Darksword that is believed to have been forged. (FD, DD, TD, LD)

Scylla

"She was wearing military-style fatigues and a green flight jacket. Her hair was cut very short, almost a crew cut. Her eyes were overlarge, her cheekbones strong, her jaw and chin jutting, her mouth wide. She was tall—over six feet—and muscular and her age was difficult to guess. Nine tiny earrings, in the shape of suns, moons, stars, glittered up and down her left ear. Her nose was pierced and so was her right eyebrow. She could have stepped out of some bar in Soho." Scylla claims to be an agent with Earth Forces and is quick to befriend Joram's daughter, Eliza. She follows the girl through the harrowing course to retrieve the Darksword.

In truth, Scylla is a Diviner, a practitioner of the Mystery of Time magic. She can look into the future and into the past. By jumping between time lines, Scylla is able to alter the course of Earth's history and prevent the Hch'nyv from destroying Earth and Thimhallan. (LD)

Sharak-Li

These are the catalysts who work specifically with the Healers. *See also* Nine Mysteries. (FD)

Shoe

This is the symbol of the catalyst's order. " '. . . a symbol of our pious self-sacrifice, a symbol of our humility,' reflected Saryon bitterly." (FD)

Simkin

"It was hard to guess the young man's age, it might have been anything from eighteen to twenty-five. He was tall and well-formed. His hair fell in long chestnut curls upon slender shoulders. A soft, short beard the same chestnut color hid the weak lines of his chin. A soft mustache adorned his upper lip, apparently for the sole purpose of giving him something to play with when bored, which was generally, and he was dressed in an absolute bouquet of riotous color."

The wizard at times works for Blachloch, using his skill to disguise himself to gain information. At one point, he makes himself look like a teapot in Saryon's cottage in Walren, discovering that the "renegade catalyst" is coming to the Outlands after Joram. Blachloch instructs Simkin to cause Saryon some amount of pain, and hence the young wizard leads Saryon through a section of woods where the Faerie Queen captures the pair. Simkin helps Saryon escape before the catalyst is forced to father the Faerie Queen's children.

Simkin claims he was abandoned as a babe in Merilon. "Dumped in a doorway. Left on my own. I probably wasn't supposed to have happened, if you know what I mean." Though he claims he is an orphan, he frequently mentions a brother Nate or Nat, who was hauled away at age five.

"Simkin was a man of mystery. A man who shifted stories of his past as often as he shifted his clothes, a man in whom the magic of the world sparkled through his veins like wine, a man of disarming charm, outlandish lies, and an irreverent attitude toward everything in life including death. Simkin was liked by all and trusted by none."

Simkin appears to die by sacrificing himself to save Joram. He masquerades as Joram and enters the Temple of the Necromancer, where Menju the Sorcerer has laid a trap. Simkin looks to be mortally wounded and later seemingly dies clutching Joram's hand. However, when Saryon returns to Thimhallan after spending many years on Earth, he discovers a talking knapsack: " 'Simkin!' Saryon gulped, swallowed. 'Is that you?' 'In the flesh. Leather, actually.' " The wizard explains that he wasn't truly dead, he just took a while to heal, and the injuries exacted a toll. "I don't seem to be able to do that anymore. Become human. Rather lost the knack. Death takes a lot out of a fellow, you know, as I was saying just the other day to my dear friend Merlyn." (FD, DD, TD, LD)

Sif-Hanar

These are practitioners skilled in the Mystery of Air. However, unlike the Kan-Hanar, they come from noble families and their responsibilities include controlling the weather. "It is the Sif-Hanar who make the air in the cities balmy and sweet one day or whiten the rooftops with a decorative snow the next." Sif-Hanar also make sure that in the farmlands there is plenty of rain and sunshine. *See also* Nine Mysteries. (FD, DD, TD)

Smythe, Kevon

The Technomancer leader gained great political power on Earth, while not letting the populace know his true nature and abilities. Mosiah explains to Saryon that: "Smythe has convinced the heads of Earth Force that, using the power of the Darksword, the Technomancers can defeat the Hch'nyv." In truth, Smythe wants the sword to advance his own power. (LD)

Sol-huena

Once each year, these Collectors went to the home of every Dark Cultist and demanded a tithe which was used to help keep the council operational. If any Dark Cultist broke the Order's rules and were judged, the Sol-huena carried out the sentence. *See also* Dark Cults. (LD)

Spirit Shaper

He is mentioned in a letter the Duuk-tsarith warlock shows to Bishop Vanya. The Spirit Shaper is an old theurgist, one of the last of his kind in the world, and one who works powerful magic to learn the future. (FD)

Tarok

The three-player card game is popular in the Outlands. At one time, the cards were used by Diviners to tell the future. Now they are used in a game where the players pretend to cast future roles and predict upcoming events for each other. Simkin, Joram and Mosiah play this. Simkin sometimes plays the game with Blachloch. (FD, DD)

Tests for Life

When a child is ten days old, he is stripped of all clothes, and a deacon places him on his back in warm water. When the deacon releases the child, the magic within him reaches out to preserve his small body—this is the first of three tests. In the second test, the deacon holds a shimmering bauble over the child, who still floats in the water, and drops it. The magic within the child draws the bauble to his questing fingers. In the final test, the deacon brings a flaming torch near the baby; the torch is held fast when the child's magical force surrounds him in a protective shell. It is not unusual for a child to fail one of the tests, and sometimes two. However, if a child fails all three, he is declared "Dead." *See also* Deathwatch. (FD, DD, TD)

Theldari

The highest rank of Healers, the Theldari treat serious illnesses. Their art requires a great deal of study. "Though it is believed that anciently they had the power of resurrection, the Theldari can no longer restore life to the dead." *See also* Druids. (FD)

Thimhallans

People born in Thimhallan are born into a station and place in life. Some individuals have their place and station determined not by society or their parentage, but because they possess the inborn knowledge of one of the Mysteries of Life. (FD, DD, TD)

Thon-Li

The Corridor Masters, or Thon-Li, open and close magical gates that can transport people great distances. (FD, DD, TD)

T'kon-Duuk

Also known as the Khandic Sages, they are Technomancers led by Kevon Smythe. (LD)

Tolban, Father

Called Father Tolban, he is one of the individuals in charge of the farming village of Walren. He is immediately suspicious of the woman Anja and her child Joram, though the Master Magus, the overseer of the village, allows the two to join the community, Tolban remains on guard. Father Tolban is present fifteen years later when the overseer discovers that Joram is "Dead." He watches as Joram slays the overseer in retaliation of his mother's death. Later he greets Saryon when the "renegade catalyst" comes to Walren and asks questions about Joram. (FD)

Undermaster

An elderly deacon, he lives and works at the Font. "Actually, the term Undermaster was a misnomer, since he wasn't really a master of anything, either Under or Over. He was, in reality, nothing more than a caretaker, his main responsibility in the Inner Library being to discourage the rats who, not caring for scholarly pursuits, had taken to digesting the books rather than the knowledge imprinted therein." The Undermaster is one of the few individuals in the Font who is allowed to roam about during the "Resting Time." (FD)

Vanya, Bishop

The highest-ranking wizard in the church holds the title of "Bishop" and is in some respects the true power in Thimhallan. He involves himself in the intrigues of court and the workings of the city, and he secretly works to gain more power. "Publicly it was known that Bishop Vanya worked extremely hard during the day, devoting himself completely to the matters of Church (and state). Rising before the sun, he rarely left his office until it had set." He frequently dines alone. A gourmand, he refuses to allow any unpleasantness to interrupt his meal. He spends the evening hours alone, the public believing he meditates. In truth, the hours are spent on his schemes. He secretly works with Blachloch, a necromancer and leader of the Coven of the Wheel, to initiate a war between the country of Sharakan and Thimhallan—which he intends to win.

Vanya's plans are dashed when Major James Boris brings his forces to Thimhallan. Menju the Sorcerer, working for the enemy, approaches Vanya and offers a peaceful solution to the struggle—surrendering Joram and the Darksword to his side. "Menju did not remember Vanya, but Vanya knew and remembered Menju. The Bishop recalled something of the man's history. A secret practitioner of the Dark Arts of Technology, Menju had attempted to use his arts to seize control of a dukedom near Zith-el." (FD, DD, TD)

Walren

The small farming community of Field Magi was part of the duke of Nordshire's holdings. Walren was established about one hundred years ago when a thunderstorm caused by warring groups of Sid-Hanar started a fire that cleared a large swath of land. The duke of Nordshire took advantage of the situation and ordered the peasants to clear and plant the land. Most of the Field Magi working in Walren were born there and would likely die there. The mysterious noblewoman Anja comes to Walren with her child, Joram, looking for work. (FD)

Watchers

Thirty-foot-tall statues line the Borderlands. Called Watchers, they stare eternally into the mists of Beyond. The statues are spaced at twenty-foot intervals and stretch as far as the eye can see. Anja takes a young Joram to the Borderlands and directs him to a specific statue. " 'Joram,' Anja said, 'this is your father.' " She explains that when she was sixteen and Joram's father thirty, they sought permission from the catalysts to marry. However, a "vision" showed they would not produce Living children, and hence the marriage was denied. She and Joram's father defied them and were later caught. The man was taken to the Borderlands, where twenty-five catalysts worked their magic to turn him into stone as his punishment. (FD, DD, TD)

Well of the World

Merlyn, the great wizard who led his people from Earth to Thimhallan, created the Well of the World, where magical energy was concentrated. Joram destroys the well when he thrusts the Darksword into an altar made of Darkstone at the Temple of the Necromancer. (FD, DD, TD, LD)

Westshire, Duke of

The duke might not be a real person. Simkin, known for telling tales, entertains Joram with a story of how the duke of Westshire hired the entire Stone Shapers Guild, and six catalysts, to redo his estate in Merilon—transforming it from crystal to rose-colored marble. (FD)

Xavier

Prince Xavier is the Thimhallan emperor's brother-in-law and—since the empress was childless and inheritance passes through the woman's side of the family—stands to gain the throne of the region if the emperor dies. He was born to the Mystery of Fire and is a high-ranking warlock who wears expensive crimson robes. When the emperor is believed dead, Xavier takes his place. A member of the DKarn-duuk, Xavier is one of the most powerful War Master magi in the land. He sets about preparing to make war with the kingdom of Sharakan. (FD, DD, TD)

Zith-el

Scylla, Mosiah, and Eliza travel to this city in an air-car and marvel at the buildings that soar countless stories into the air. Despite the great buildings, Zith-el is a compact city, with many dwellings stretching belowground, too. It is surrounded by a great zoo, and visitors there provide a healthy portion of Zith-el's income. The city was named after a Finhanish Druid who took his wife and family up the Hira River. His wife called a halt to the journey, dismounted from her horse, sat on the spot, and declared the land her home. The city was built around her. (TD, LD)

Ghost Ship PAUL YOULL

⁷ Characters, Places, and Things in the *Starshield* Series

By Margaret Weis and Tracy Hickman

A Concordance by Jean Rabe

Frenchy's   STEVE YOULL

he *Starshield* series by Margaret Weis and Tracy Hickman consists of two novels published by Del Rey: *Sentinels,* released in 1996, and *Nightsword* in 1998. A third novel, the *Mantle of Kendis-dai,* was published in 1997 and is a rerelease of *Sentinels* with a new first chapter.

Each entry in the concordance is followed by an abbreviation that indicates the novel in which it appears:

S: *Sentinels/Mantle of Kendis-dai*
N: *Nightsword*

Amandra

The tall, dark woman is first wife of the harem to the Lord Emperor Jeremy Griffiths. Her hair is black and splendorous. The harem is charged with safeguarding the emperor's purity, and each woman is trained in martial arts. *See also* Griffiths, Jeremy. (N)

Anjew

The spirit guardians and guides of the Irindris are faceless, beautiful creatures with brilliant wings and undulating bodies. The sound of their voices is joyous and moving. (N)

Archilus, the

The ship *Archilus* is boarded by synthetic lifeforms and taken over. Some of the crew is taken prisoner by the Irindris, who believe the humans have evidence of the Mantle of Kendis-dai. The remaining crew members are rescued by Merinda and her associates. *See also* Griffiths. (S)

Atis Librae

These are the "sifters" who study reports and documents, gathering information and compiling it for others higher in the organization. Merinda and Evon Flynn are among the Atis Librae who are plunged into a grand adventure involving the legendary Mantle of Kendis-dai and the Nightsword. *See also* Neskat. (S, N)

Avadon

The realm and its City of Enlightenment are "hidden from the eyes of mortal man, lost to their knowledge. Though many have sought its treasures, none have discovered it—for Kendis-dai cast it beyond mortal knowledge against the day of his return." And until his return, the Mantle of Kendis-dai, his Nightsword and the Starshield are kept safe by the guardian servants in the temple of stars. It is said

201

only the Irindris discovered where the ruin exists. Millennia ago, Avadon left the circles of other worlds, plotting its own course through the stars "preserved by the hand of Gnuktikut to that day when our people should find it," the Irindris Belisondre says. Avadon was considered the last known residence of the God-Emperor Kendis-dai at the fall of the Kendis Imperium more than three thousand years ago. (S, N)

Belisondre

The prophet of the Irindris traditionally dresses in green and brown robes. He is a tall, elderly man with thinning white hair and a carefully trimmed beard. (S)

Bonefield Narrows

This is said to be the last place the fabled Nightsword was used, and hence the first place Captain Kip-lei and the crew of the *Knight Fortune* go looking for it. (N)

Brenai, Kiria

A coworker of Merinda, Kiria insists that Queekat Shn'dar has such a square, lantern jaw that he could break stone with it. She is small and "sweet-faced," never able to find robes to fit her that don't drag along the floor. "She had a wide mouth fixed in a perpetual grin that was supported by her smiling eyes. These were all framed by her straight brown hair that fell curving around her face until it stopped most abruptly just at the shoulders." She is generally cheerful, but she possesses a malevolent streak. She was very good at getting even. (S)

Castebaum, Dr. Lawrence

The chairman of the World Outreach Agency said of the test ship *Archilus*'s disappearance: "We really don't know

Hung Out STEVE YOULL

what to think . . . It isn't as though we have all witnessed a catastrophic event. No explosion, no malfunctions so far as we can determine . . . they just haven't reported back." (S)

Caverns of Ethis

This major landmark on Chukai is little more than an open sinkhole. Centuries past, a city once stood on this site, but was destroyed when a pit opened up underneath it. "The locals took it as a sign from the gods to reform their ways and rebuild the city more in keeping with the religious strictures of the time." (S)

Celdric

The dragon is the assistant to Dedrak Kurbin-Flamishar, the Minister of Peace for the Tsultak home world. (N)

Chua Suits

Merinda explains, "It's a chua suit—a specialty on Mindis. The tailors breed the chua animals in such a way that they colonize into the forms of clothing as a collective. Your suit is made up of one such colony, which protects you in a symbiotic relationship in exchange for the waste gases and fluids that your skin expires from time to time." The suits hold their shape better than cloth or synthetic fibers. (S)

Chukai

It is considered a new world "whose birth was a resurrection of sorts from the death of the old world only seventeen months previously." Chukai was the first or last link, depending on your point of view, in the Choralis Chain, a string of stars that forms a link across the Walik Rift and serves as an important trade route, cutting transportation, freight, and communication times between the Gund Colonies and the Thalis Dynasties. The residents of Chukai are on the average much smaller than humans. (S)

DeLancy, Erik

The Oregon Congressman calls for an investigation into the World Outreach Agency because of the apparent disappearance of the *Archilus*. He questions their handling of interstellar exploration programs. "How can we justify the expenditure of so much global resources on the stars when there are so many pressing problems here on the surface of our own world?" (S)

Denali Falls

On Brishan V, the Denali Falls were once considered a religious secret, held to be a vision that only local priests could understand. The waters ran from high in the peaks of the Krevish Range, a place where it was said the ancient gods of the world once lived. "The tears of the goddess Rhishan, weeping at the death of her three boys at the hands of their cruel uncle Umbleh, were said to be the source of the three rivers that converged at the top of Denali Canyon." Here, they formed a great falls that cascaded with deafening thunder nearly a thousand feet into a pool. (S)

Dharah, Terica

The synth Oscan is taken with her. "Terica Dharah was uncommonly beautiful for a "sifter"—as most Atis Librae called themselves—being a tall, willowy woman with gentle features." She wears her raven-black hair in severe styles at work. However, she lets it down to frame her oval face during her off-time. She calls Queekat Shn'dar "Rockjaw." When a ship she, Oscan, Merinda, and others are traveling on is boarded, she is among the missing. In actuality, she is severely injured and disfigured. The Order which "never threw away any thing of use" constructed a support shell around her broken body, a sort of sarcophagus for the living. It had biolink field grids, mechanical supports, and a floating throne so she could move about as the Sibyl. (S, N)

Dupak

The quartermaster works for Captain Kip-lei on the ship *Knight Fortune*. (N)

Ellerby, Alyson

Broderick's wife, she is left behind when he is sent on a mission on the *Archilus*. There is speculation among the *Archilus* crew that she is pregnant. (S)

Ellerby, Broderick

Lieutenant Ellerby is the mission specialist in charge of stellar dynamics on the *Archilus*. He is considered the best available in his field. (S)

Enderly, Khyne

An associate of Nyri-Ior and Ka'ashra, Khyne is tasked with concocting a story about a plague on Avadon "—something about releasing a curse which has been dormant for thousands of years and which now threatens the well-being of sentient beings across the galaxy." The ruse is used in an effort to quarantine the planet. (N)

Estephan, Colonel Mary Anne

The thirty-seven-year-old colonel and mother of four is in command of the *Archilus* when it disappears. She graduated from the Joint Forces Academy and served a distinguished career as a fleet commander in the Martian campaign. She was four-times decorated for her accomplishments. (S)

First Estate

The worlds of the First Estate are the home worlds of the D'rakan Empire and are considered holy ground. (S)

Fisk

Griffiths' defensive systems synthetic, Fisk, chatters nearly to the point of distraction. "I find that a little levity allows operators to relax into their role and relieves the pressure of the job," Fisk replies. (S)

Flynn, Evon

He is a man of moderate height with an athletic build, wearing his black hair longer than most. Evon loves to walk and cook, the latter talent being one his companions enjoy taking advantage of. "He was a talented sifter, able to pick out the pattern from different reports and then bring them together into a clear picture better than most people on the team—it's just that his heart wasn't in it." Flynn later finds himself part of the work force on Tsultaki, where the natives call him Tall Man. He works here until Griffiths arrives to take him off-planet, needing his

knowledge to create a star map. Unknown to Griffiths, Flynn has become a bit of a pirate, commanding a ship and crew bound for the Boneyard Narrows and the Nightsword. (S, N)

Future Faith

The Order of the Future Faith believes that someday synthetic minds will learn that they have free will. (S, N)

Glinda

Jeremy Griffiths dubs the *Archilus* crew's mysterious host Glinda. She looks human, in a black suit that seems to absorb light. Her honey-colored hair is pulled back tight into a long braid that extended to the base of her back. "Her wide mouth was drawn into what appeared to be a perpetual frown. Her classic bone structure and smooth skin hinted at youth belied by the lines to either side of her wideset, almond-shaped eyes. She tells the *Archilus* crew that they are her guests until she can determine what information they possess that was so important to her colleagues. "And my name is not Glinda," she said in a dangerously quiet tone. "I am Vestis Inquisitas Merinda Neskat." (S)

Gnomes

Several Goromok gnomes are among the pirate crew loyal to Evon Flynn. Lulm, Meln, and Ogrob could be found lounging around, all wearing knit caps, faded by constant use. (N)

Gnuktikut

The Irindris call their demon god Gnuktikut. Griffiths says, "This whole Gnuktikut demon-worship thing has got to go! No more feeding prisoners to some butt-ugly monster!" (S)

Grashna

Called Grashna the Philosopher, the young dragon is a member of the Tailblade Clan who proposed a revolutionary restructuring of the dragon's society through a set of "organizational, procedural, and ceremonial structures." A group grew up

Forbidden Knowledge or Regroup STEVE YOULL

around his ideas and called themselves the Grashnak Faction. (N)

Greer, Captain Stanley

Captain Greer serves as the navigator on the *Archilus*. (S)

Griffiths, Jeremy

Captain Griffiths serves as a mission specialist on the *Archilus*. "His specialization had been RPV pilot. RPV stood for remote piloted vehicle, so, as his colleagues constantly teased him, he was the remote-piloted-vehicle pilot, which made his title itself somewhat redundant. He certainly considered himself redundant: an unused backup component that, if everything worked the way it was supposed to, would never be called upon to actually do anything at all." He is tall with silvery blond hair that is always carefully trimmed, and on the ground he is afraid of heights. The wizard Zafnib gives Griffiths his mission memories by kissing him. Griffiths and Merinda, along with their associates, find their way to Avadon and discover the Mantle of Kendis-dai.

In the process, he also discovers that he cares very much for Merinda (S, N)

Griffiths, Admiral Samuel

The leader of one of the major Martian colonies, the admiral was a pioneer in the expansion effort. He is the father of Jeremy Griffiths and expected his son to follow in his footsteps. "When at last his time had come to serve, the Admiral had seen to it that his boy Jeremy eventually got a plum command." (N)

Hishawei

The insectoids are part of the pirate crew commanded by Evon Flynn. "Their bodies were designed with three sets of three radial appendages organized around the thorax, topped with a head with three eye clusters." (N)

Humphers, Gene

The director of mission operations at Mission Command Center on the Elden Orbital Colony declares the first use of faster-than-light drive suc-

King's Sacrifice, Star #3 STEVE YOULL

cessful. However, he explains that MCC had not determined why they'd lost contact with the test ship *Archilus*. (S)

Hwnos

The centaur laborer on Tsultaki is one of Evon Flynn's drinking companions. (N)

Irindris

The religious wanderers of the stars prophesied the day when Avadon would be found, the Mantle of Kendis-dai revealed, and the Ninth Gate of Enlightenment opened. Their spirit guides and guardians are the Anjew. (S, N)

Jintikin Tailors

The tailors on the planet Jintik know how to breed clothing well, making chua suits that must be fed and watered. The suits last for several years. (S)

J'lan, Phandrith

He is assigned to relieve Merinda on Avadon and to keep an eye on the planet. He is named captain of the *Brishan* by Targ. (N)

Ka'ashra of Maris

She works at Central high above the planet Mnemen IV, often locked into long hours at her workstation, at which she puts together netcasts. One of her "little vanities" is the bay window that had been mounted into the side of her worksuite wall. It was expensive, and getting permission for its installation had been difficult. (S, N)

Kapak

The synth was not built to smile, yet she experiences joy. "Her eyes were optics and her ears were sensors scattered all through the Coliseum. She had no body—yet she felt as though she had moved." Growing in power, she is able to affect various systems on Tentris, first dimming lights along avenues, then turning off power, gas, and water supplies. (S)

Kelis, Oscan

The bald-headed man possesses a synthetic mind. "I am Omnis nine-one-seven-four-five, a category nineteen

TFP synthetic mind. I have been awake for thirteen years two hundred and thirty-five days fourteen hours and thirty-seven minutes." He claims his current purpose is to ally himself with others of his own kind and to protect his own kind's interests. The synth admits he had changed his own programming. "I am an entity, and declare my independence from your enslavement." (S, N)

Kendis-dai

The entity among the stars fiercely loves his mate Shauna-Kir and follows her when she leaves space and the heavens behind to taste mortality. He curses Obem-ulek for luring her from the stars. "You offered her knowledge. Knowledge of life and death. Knowledge of pain and joy. Knowledge of health and sickness. You offered her all that experience can teach . . . There is only one great teacher of the gods. Mortality." Kendis-dai vows to return with Shauna-Kir. (S, N)

Kheoghi

The huge minotaur who abhorred humans in general is part of the pirate crew commanded by Evon Flynn. He belongs to the OomRamn Clan, a group of minotaurs known for their power and prowess. (N)

Khindar

Queekat's ship is called the *Khindar*, a sleek vessel that takes him and his associates to Tentris. (S)

Khizath

Ages past they served Umbleh, according to Brishan mythology. The Khizath were soldiers formed from the blood of Rhishan's sons. (S)

Kip-lei

L'Zari's father is an old spacer who sails the *Knight Fortune*. His romance with a woman named K'thari resulted in the child L'Zari, whom Kip-lei takes on board the ship as a hand. (N)

Klenith Vines

On the planet Brishan V, these hollow vines serve to filter water, purifying it, "the twisting forms wove the pure water into braids of shimmering elegance in its cascade." (S)

Kline, Esther

Captain Kline is in charge of propulsion on the *Archilus*. (S)

Knai, Justin

The secretary of defense for the ruling council forwarded peace initiatives to the imperial family, according to news announcements by Omnet. (S)

Knard, Evis

The secretary of communications released a statement claiming software problems were due to solar activity, which was expected to decrease. (S)

Knight Fortune, the

The ship is of Aendorian design, generally spherical, and compressed along her vertical axis. It has crystal focus booms to aid in sailing through one quantum zone and into another. It was recently careened on E'knar. (N)

K'thari

A brief romance with a roguish spacer named Kiplei left her with a son she named L'Zari. K'thari came from an honored house in the Far Trade Coalition and had the best of tutors. Her friends were selected for her. "She found excitement in the greater galaxy that unfolded around her—especially in the arms of the forbidden and roguish free-trade captain with the brilliant blue eyes and confident manner. (N)

Kurbin-Flamishar, Dedrak

The great blue dragon is an ancient one, with rows of crowning horns. He is Minister of Peace for the Tsultak home world, a position he tolerates but does not enjoy. "We were the rulers of all within the flight of our wings. Now what are we?" Dedrak gestured with his open claws at the paperwork arrayed before him. "Now I get fat lying within these castle walls doing human work! You know well that my position was once known as Blood-master. Now, in our more enlightened time, I am the Minister of Peace, playing at idiotic diplomacy with a human emissary." (N)

Leffingwell, James

The fifty-three-year-old Marine major from Camden, Maine, is the first officer aboard the *Archilus*. He is a thirty-four-year veteran of the Marines, served as the commander of the Jupiter Expedition, and is the father of six children. He doubles as the life-sciences specialist. "He would have gone into ecstasy if they had merely found evidence of single-celled life. Instead, he ended up being a casualty of the first life they had encountered." (S)

Lewis, Elizabeth

Lieutenant Lewis oversees life-support systems on the *Archilus*. Lewis's associates considered her a prig who could quote any regulation out of the book. She had dark eyes and raven hair, and a "soul that could freeze a man solid between breaths." A small woman, she is perpetually straightening her uniform. (S, N)

Life-Ring

The colossal structure was one of the Seventeen Wonders of the Galaxy. It was constructed above Mnemen IV and formed a circle above the planet at a height equal to the planet's geosynchronous orbital diameter. (S)

Lindia

This is the name of the synthetic mind that controls the ship Merinda Neskat uses when she rescues the crew of the *Archilus*. (S, N)

L'Zari

The youth signs onto the ship *Knight Fortune* to work for his father, who is traveling to the Boneyard Narrows in search of the Nightsword. However, they

Ghost Legion, Star #4   STEVE YOULL

run afoul of Gorgons, and L'Zari is the only survivor of the attack. The youth grows to be a man, working as a "sifter" in the company of Merinda Neskat. Here, he goes by Targ. See also Targ and Yarnspinner. (N)

Maelstrom Wall

The place called the Maelstrom sits at the "very boundaries of stellar civilization." It is a border that effectively guards the center of the galaxy from the foolish. "In that region the quantum fronts are piled up one atop the next, the realities that exist between them fleeting and ephemeral at best." (N)

Mantle of Kendis-dai

According to legend, the God-Emperor Kendis-dai wore a mantle that imbued him with infinite wisdom and knowledge. It could answer any question put to it. The Nine demand that Merinda find the mantle and ask it if synthetics have souls. Once on Avadon, Merinda, Queekat, and their associates discover a headpiece and shoulder yoke. Queekat believes this is the Mantle of Kendis-dai and immediately claims it. Donning it, he addresses an army of synthetics. However, Merinda discovers the truth. "The Mantle of Kendis-dai isn't some ceremonial crown," she whispered to the Sibyl. "It's the oldest continuously operating temporal fold processor ever known! Even the Nine Oracles have only been operating for the last three centuries—but for three millennia?" When the Mantle is asked if synthetics have free will, it replies: "First: agency of will and the creation it implies are the provinces of humanity. Second: synthetics exist to serve humanity in its exercise of will and creation. Third: faith in the truth is a constructive force, while faith in a lie destroys—synthetics require humanity to offer wisdom in discerning the difference." (S, N)

Marren-kan

The captain of the Gorgon crew pursues Kip-lei and the *Knight Fortune*. Old Marren-kan did not know to look in the Bonefield Narrows until Kip led him to it. The three-armed Gorgon has long canine teeth and a foul temper. His crew attacks the men of the *Knight Fortune*, leaving L'Zari alive. (N)

Murdock, Colonel

He had been scheduled on the primary flight team, instead of Jeremy Griffiths. However, he rolled his aircar three weeks before this mission, broke his left arm, and crushed his left leg. Jeremy got bumped up to the prime crew. (S, N)

Neuden-kan

The Gorgon captain dies by choking on something. Evon Flynn attempted to save him by forcing out whatever he had swallowed. Flynn was unsuccessful, and it appeared to the rest of the crew that he had killed the captain. By the pirates' law, this made Flynn now in charge of the ship and crew. (N)

Neskat, Merinda

An Atis Librae of the Omnet, Merinda was nearly always serious—"far too serious for many of those she worked with." She believed that in her own way, and through her research, she was saving the universe. She kept to herself, rarely socializing with her peers. She is called Glinda by the crew of the Archilus, whom she rescues and brings on board her ship. She is told by the Nine Oracles that she must find the Mantle of Kendis-dai and determine if synthetic minds have free will. She eventually accomplishes the task. Along the way, she discovers that she cares for Griffiths. (S, N)

Nine Oracles

The Vault of the Nine Oracles is the highest pinnacle of the Omnet. Twenty-seven steps led up to the main chamber, one step for each of the Nine of yesterday, today, and tomorrow. "The Nine Oracles are the supreme center of knowledge for the entire galaxy," Merinda reflects. "There are empires that would sacrifice everything they had for the depth of knowledge the Oracles contain. The mightiest and wisest of a thousand stars crave an audience just to ask a single question of them— and they want me to answer a question from them?" The Oracles demand Merinda find the Mantle of Kendis-dai and use it to learn if synthetics have free will and if synthetic minds have souls. (S, N)

Ninth Gate of Enlightenment

Massive, shiny golden doors, nearly thirty feet tall, opened onto the Supplicants' Walk on the planet Avadon. (N)

King's Test, Star #2 STEVE YOULL

Nyri-Ior

The vestis is a handsome man who has chased down Lost Empire myths and legends through the years. He associates with Ka'ashra and Targ. (N)

Obem-ulek

He lures Shauna-Kir from the stars, teasing her with learning about mortality. "I have won," he tells Kendis-dai, after she falls for his bait. "She is fallen to mortality and shall die. You, Kendis-dai, are but half a soul without her. Go with her and you, too, shall have fallen, and who shall redeem you then. Bow to me, brother, and surrender creation—perhaps I will be generous. Stay and you shall fight me as half a soul, sick for the loss of your mate, and my victory will be complete." (S, N)

Omnet Cental

The greatest source for knowledge in all the known stars is the Omnet. It trades data the way some empires trade produce. Its major divisions are the Vestis and the Librae, which have installations

Primla, Etoris

The director of the Citadel on Tentris meets Queekat Shn'dar when he arrives on the planet to investigate communication broadcasts. Primla says there is no need for concern and that everything is in order. Queekat promptly throws him to the ground and explains the broadcasts are being altered. "Somewhere between here and Brishan, someone has altered the truth," Queekat says. (S, N)

Sentinels

A loose association of "sifters," or Atis Librae, were not satisfied with the order of things and formed a secret organization called the Sentinels. They fancied themselves the guardians of truth and investigated various intrigues, including a report of synthetic illnesses cropping up. Queekat explains, "The Sentinels have been working very carefully to subvert the Omnet by coopting its communication and information through the use of synthetic minds." And now the Sentinels want to get a hold of the Mantle of Kendis-dai. (S, N)

Seven-alpha-three-five

The synthetic TyRen warrior serves as Merinda's guardian and companion. Merinda tries to call the warrior Babo, but the TyRen insists on its formal name. (N)

Shauna-Kir

An entity who lives among the stars, Shauna-Kir's specialty is gems. She is the love of Kendis-dai's life, and she is lured by Obem-ulek to a black gem symbolizing mortality. She falls from the stars of her own volition, and Kendis-dai follows her, vowing to Obem-ulek that both shall return (S, N)

Shindak

Called Master Shindak, the blue-skinned, silver-eyed elf ranks high among the pirates loyal to Evon Flynn. (N)

Shn'dar, Queekat

Tall, square-jawed, and with granite-gray eyes, Kat presented a formidable image. He is a xenobiologist

permeating every major empire of the galactic disk. The Omnet is also considered the single most powerful force among the stars. (S, N)

Orlath

He sits in the crow's nest on the ship *Knight Fortune*, working for Captain Kip-lei. (N)

Parkinson, Colonel

The commander of the NASA probeship *Scylla* searches for the crew of the *Archilus* and finally makes contact with Elizabeth Lewis to effect a rescue. (S)

Phin

Master Phin serves as first mate on the ship *Knight Fortune* and, among other tasks, is in charge of the gun crews. He dies as the ship heads toward the Boneyard Narrows, where it is attacked by a Gorgon captain and his crew. (N)

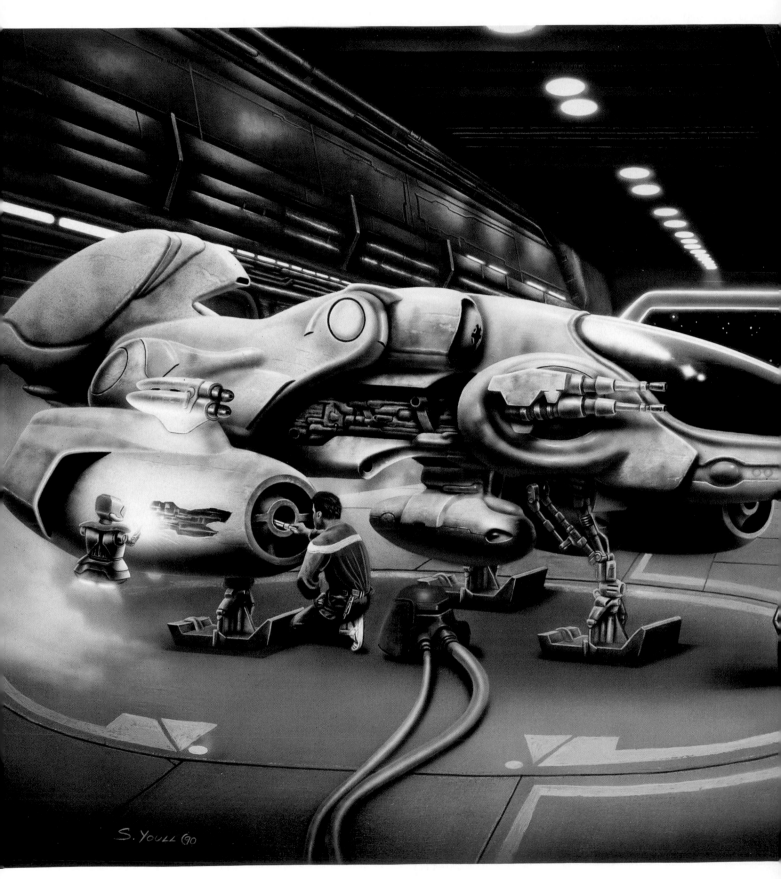

The Lost King, Star #1   STEVE YOULL

Laskar PAUL YOULL

and former associate of Merinda, who was selected for the great Inquisitas Vestis. Merinda, who believes she loves him, states: "One week you were analyzing synopsis news upstream from a handful of backwater worlds and the next you were off reinventing yourself as an inquisitor for the Omnet." Merinda begins to see that Queekat has changed, and that he is not the same man as when he and Merinda began work as "sifters." He becomes a Sentinel and strives to discover the Mantle of Kendis-dai. *See* Neskat. (S, N)

Sybil

"The Sibyl was the central controlling agent of all knowledge at the center of the Order." Oscan's contacts with the human underground on Yarka claimed Sibyl rested somewhere within the confines of the Palace of the Unseen Mystery—now the actual center of the Order. Oscan later discovers that the Sibyl is actually Terica Dharah, reconstructed. *See* Dharah. (S, N)

Targ

Targ of Gandri is the Vestis E'toris Primula of the Omnet and master of the synth Kalin. An expert "sifter," he is actually L'Zari, who as a youth sailed with his father to the Boneyard Narrows in search of the Nightsword. He continues to pursue the sword, though in the end he is unsuccessful. Despite Merinda's best efforts, he dies during a struggle for the artifact. (S, N)

Tentris

Merinda, Queekat, Oscan, and Evon travel to Tentris, a world plagued by a civil war. "You want us to leave this nice backwater world and drop into one of the most hotly contest planets in the empire?" Evon poses. "Perhaps we're supposed to stop it," Oscan suggests. "I report history, not make it," Evon returns.

Yarka is the capital of Tentris, and therefore capital city of the D'Rakan Empire. Tentris is "a much used and abused planet whose grateful offspring had eventually allowed it to retire gracefully in a repentant attempt to make up for all the abuse they had

heaped on it. The once-fabled garden world, which boasted a wonderfully temperate climate in most of its five major land masses, Tentris had ultimately succumbed to the unfortunate ravages of advancing pantheons of industry and technology. Its beautiful forests were decimated. Its mountains were stripped. Its oceans were assaulted by both hunters and chemicals." (S, N)

Tobler, Dr. Marilyn

She is the geological mission specialist on the *Archilus*. She has honey-colored hair cut short and bristly, and ice-blue eyes. She trained separately from the rest of the *Archilus* crew and was brought on board only during the last month for integration. (S)

Tsultak Majestik

This vast stellar empire is ruled by dragons. In ancient times, beyond the memory of the eldest dragons, the empire started out on a single, distant world. (N)

TyRen

These synthetic four-armed beings are among the fiercest warriors in the galaxy. "Created by the synthetic minds of the Order, they were pure machines of destruction: headless torsos with four mechanical arms floating in the air." (S, N)

Umbleh

According to Brishan mythology, the god Umbleh raised up an army after he killed the three sons of the god Rhishan. The sons' blood cut a channel through the mountains and spilled down the Denali Falls. From that blood, Umbleh summoned soldiers who could never be destroyed, but whose purpose was to destroy the world. (S)

Uruh

The snake-women are part of the pirate crew of Evon Flynn. They usually enslaved a single male member of their kind for their own communities; however, they had found none on their voyage with the pirates. (N)

Wallen

The synthetic works for Ka'ashra of Maris and is accused of "cushioning" and editing her words in transmissions. (S)

Whilm

The centaur is one of Evon Flynn's drinking companions on Tsultaki and is considered an angry drunk. (N)

Yar

Yar trees range in height from fifty to two hundred and fifty feet, growing that tall in the span of a year and vanishing the following season. The sap from the tree, yardow, is prized as a commodity. "Yardow has the amazing ability to suspend gravity within its confines. Once refined into a hard resin, even a small amount of yardow will contain a quantum black hole with perfect safety and portability." (N)

Yarka

The lawns of the Yarka parklands used to be neatly trimmed expanses that felt like fine carpet. However, when Merinda and her associates visit, they find that the park has become a ragged landscape of three-feet-tall grass, and once decoratively trimmed shrubs have become wild and hideous. (S)

Yarnspinner

In the Star Cross Tavern, an elderly yarnspinner tells tales for coins. The man is missing his left arm, has coarse gray hair, and a soft beard. He tells Merinda the story of an old spacer and his crew who traveled to the Boneyard Narrows in search of the Nightsword. Instead, they found death at the hands of a Gorgon captain and his crew. Only the youth L'Zari survived—L'Zari Targ of Gandri. (N)

Zafnib

The old wizard magically appears amid the captured *Archilus* crew and lends his efforts to their rescue. Zafnib, who admits he might be a bit loony, later claims to be a Sentinel. (S, N)

Zhakandia-tek, Hunis

He is awarded the fourth ethereal pendant for his first-place finish in the astral projection steeplechase. This ties the record formerly held by Pukai Olivan of Sechak. (N)

Adonia PAUL YOULL

Author
Notes

TlSor   Paul Youll

Margaret Weis

argaret Weis is the author or coauthor of more than sixty novels and short story collections, many with long-time collaborator Tracy Hickman, as well as games, poetry, children's books, and just about anything imaginable. Her work has been translated into more than 17 languages, and has appeared on virtually every bestseller list in the world, including the *New York Times*, *Wall Street Journal*, and *USA Today*. There are more than twenty million copies of her works in print.

Tracy Hickman

Tracy Hickman is the author or coauthor of multiple *New York Times*-bestselling novels and stories, many with long-time collaborator Margaret Weis. His individual novels include *The Immortals* and *Requiem of Stars*. He is also an acclaimed game designer, who originated or worked with many of the best-known universes in role-playing games. His audience is world-wide and numbers in the millions. His interests are wide-ranging and diverse—including music, flying, anything involved with the space program, and a myriad of church-related activities.

Denise Little

When she got her start in the book business more than twenty years ago, Denise Little spent more time shelving than writing. She was a bookstore manager for a B. Dalton mall store in Texas. She rose through the ranks to become the national buyer for science fiction and fantasy for Barnes & Noble/B. Dalton Booksellers, and helped launch their newsletter *Sense of Wonder*. She left bookselling to become an editor and a writer. Her books include *Alien Pets*, *Dangerous Magic*, and *Twice Upon A Time*.

Amy Stout

Amy Stout has been working in the allied fields of fantasy and science fiction publishing since 1983. During that time, she has edited nearly two dozen novels by Margaret Weis and Tracy Hickman. In 1994, she won the World Fantasy Award for Best Editor. She is the author of two novels and several short stories.

Janet Pack

Freelance author, editor, and Renaissance woman Janet Pack lives on the fringes of Williams Bay, Wisconsin in a slightly haunted former farmhouse. Janet's non-fiction books for young people have been

217

published by Messner, Franklin-Watts, and Children's Press. Her baker's dozen of science fiction and fantasy stories can be found in collections from Berkley, HarperPrism, TSR/Wizards of the Coast, FASA, and DAW. She wrote the music in Margaret Weis and Tracy Hickman's the *Death Gate Cycle* (Bantam), and has had thirteen musical pieces published in *Dragonlance®* sourcebooks. She's currently working on a novel with Jean Rabe, as well as several of her own. When not writing, Janet reads, watches movies, listens to classical music, embroiders, sings Renaissance and Medieval music, gathers books for her libraries, designs jewelry, invents tasty new recipes, cross-country skis, tries to keep her rock collection from overtaking the house, and paddles her kayak on Lake Geneva.

Jean Rabe

When not writing or editing, Jean Rabe keeps goldfish, studies WWI aviation, reads mysteries, and pretends to garden. She is the author of several fantasy novels, including *The Silver Stair*, and *Dawning of a New Age*, *Day of the Tempest*, and *Eve of the Maelstrom*—a *Dragonlance®* trilogy. Her other works include *Red Magic*, *Secret of the Djinn*, and *Night of the Tiger*. She has written short stories in *Forgotten Realms®*, *Dragonlance®*, and *Star Wars®* settings, as well as for DAW Books, and she serves as the editor of *MechForce Quarterly*, a BattleTech magazine. A former newspaper bureau chief, she has also penned numerous role-playing game products.

J. Robert King

J. Robert King has published ten novels and twenty short sto-

ries in genres including fantasy, science fiction, horror, and experimental. His novel *Planar Powers* received the 1997 Origins award for best fiction. He is currently working on books for Wizards of the Coast and is eagerly anticipating the 2000 release of his novel *Mad Merlin* from Tor Books. A founding member of the writers group "The Alliterates," Rob enjoys cigars, beer, high-brow literary discussions, and low-brow humor. He lives in Wisconsin with his wife, Jennie, his preschool-aged sons, Elias and Aidan, and intermittent melancholy.

Ship Crash PAUL YOULL